BOARD OF EDITORS

RICHARD J. CONVISER
Professor of Law, IIT/Kent
MICHAEL R. ASIMOW
Professor of Law, U.C.L.A.
JOHN A. BAUMAN
Professor of Law, U.C.L.A.
PAUL D. CARRINGTON
Professor of Law, Duke University
JESSE H. CHOPER
Professor of Law, U.C. Berkeley
GEORGE E. DIX
Professor of Law, University of Texas
JESSE DUKEMINIER
Professor of Law, U.C.L.A.
MELVIN A. EISENBERG
Professor of Law, U.C. Berkeley
WILLIAM A. FLETCHER
Professor of Law, U.C. Berkeley
MARC A. FRANKLIN
Professor of Law, Stanford University
EDWARD C. HALBACH, JR.
Professor of Law, U.C. Berkeley
GEOFFREY C. HAZARD, JR.
Professor of Law, University of Pennsylvania
STANLEY M. JOHANSON
Professor of Law, University of Texas
THOMAS M. JORDE
Professor of Law, U.C. Berkeley
HERMA HILL KAY
Dean and Professor of Law, U.C. Berkeley
JOHN H. McCORD
Professor of Law, University of Illinois
PAUL MARCUS
Professor of Law, College of William and Mary
RICHARD L. MARCUS
Professor of Law, U.C. Hastings
ROBERT H. MNOOKIN
Professor of Law, Harvard University
THOMAS D. MORGAN
Professor of Law, George Washington University
JARRET C. OELTJEN
Professor of Law, Florida State University
JAMES C. OLDHAM
Professor of Law, Georgetown University
ROGER C. PARK
Professor of Law, U.C. Hastings
WILLIAM A. REPPY, JR.
Professor of Law, Duke University
THOMAS D. ROWE, JR.
Professor of Law, Duke University
JON R. WALTZ
Professor of Law, Northwestern University
DOUGLAS J. WHALEY
Professor of Law, Ohio State University
CHARLES H. WHITEBREAD
Professor of Law, U.S.C.
KENNETH H. YORK
Professor of Law, Pepperdine University

gilbert
LAW SUMMARIES

COMMUNITY PROPERTY

Seventeenth Edition

William A. Reppy, Jr.
Professor of Law
Duke University

THE **barbri** GROUP

HARCOURT BRACE LEGAL AND PROFESSIONAL PUBLICATIONS, INC.
EDITORIAL OFFICES: 111 W. Jackson Blvd., 7th Floor, Chicago, IL 60604

gilbert
LAW SUMMARIES

REGIONAL OFFICES: Chicago, Dallas, Los Angeles, New York, Washington, D.C
Distributed by: **Harcourt Brace & Company** 6277 Sea Harbor Drive, Orlando, FL 32887 (800)787-8717

SERIES EDITOR
Elizabeth L. Snyder, B.A., J.D.
Attorney At Law

QUALITY CONTROL EDITOR
Blythe C. Smith, B.A.

Copyright © 1998 by Harcourt Brace Legal and Professional Publications, Inc. All rights reserved. No part of this publication may be reproduced or transmitted in any form or by any means, electronic or mechanical, including photocopy, recording, or any information storage and retrieval system, without permission in writing from the publisher. Printed in the United States of America.

gilbert
LAW SUMMARIES

Titles Available

Administrative Law
Agency & Partnership
Antitrust
Bankruptcy
Basic Accounting for Lawyers
Business Law
California Bar Performance
Test Skills
Civil Procedure
Commercial Paper & Payment Law
Community Property
Conflict of Laws
Constitutional Law
Contracts
Corporations
Criminal Law
Criminal Procedure
Dictionary of Legal Terms
Estate & Gift Tax
Evidence

Family Law
Federal Courts
First Year Questions & Answers
Future Interests
Income Tax I (Individual)
Income Tax II (Partnership Corporate)
Labor Law
Legal Ethics (Prof. Responsibility)
Legal Research, Writing,
   & Analysis
Multistate Bar Exam
Personal Property
Property
Remedies
Sale & Lease of Goods
Secured Transactions
Securities Regulation
Torts
Trusts
Wills

Also Available:
First Year Program
Pocket Size Law Dictionary
The Eight Secrets of Top Exam Performance In Law School

*All Titles Available at Your Law School Bookstore,
or Call to Order: 1-800-787-8717*

Harcourt Brace Legal and Professional Publications, Inc.
111 W. Jackson Boulevard, 7th Floor
Chicago, IL 60604

There are two things BAR/BRI will do for you:

1 Get you through LAW SCHOOL

2 Get you through the BAR EXAM

[O.K. we'll throw in a highlighter*]

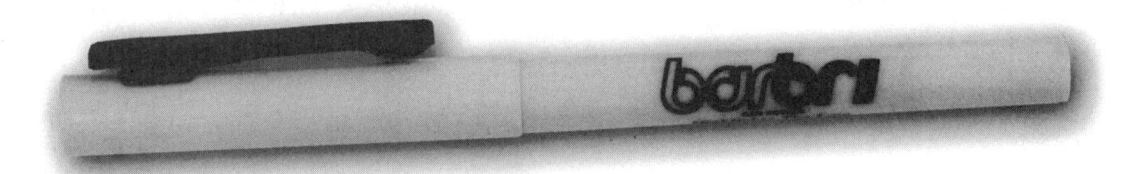

*Available at your local BAR/BRI office.

gilbert LAW SUMMARIES

Over 4 Million Copies Sold!

- Gilbert Law Summaries
- Legalines
- Law School Legends Audio Tapes
- Employment Guides
- Casebriefs Interactive Software

barbri BAR REVIEW

Relied On By Over 600,000 Students!

- Lectures, Outlines & Mini Review
- Innovative Computer Software
- Multistate, Essay & Performance Workshops
- Complete MPRE Preparation
- First Year Review Program

THE barbri GROUP

Our Only Mission Is Test Preparation

BAR/BRI Bar Review 1-888-3BARBRI
GILBERT LAW SUMMARIES 1-800-787-8717

SUMMARY OF CONTENTS

Page

COMMUNITY PROPERTY TEXT CORRELATION CHART i

COMMUNITY PROPERTY CAPSULE SUMMARY I

APPROACH TO EXAMS .... (i)

INTRODUCTION 1

I. CLASSIFYING PROPERTY AS COMMUNITY OR SEPARATE 3
Chapter Approach 3
CHART: Characterization of Property as Separate or Community 4
   A. Basic Statutory Framework 5
   B. Presumptions Respecting Ownership 5
   C. Special Presumptions 8
   D. Overcoming Pro-Community Presumption by Proof of Separate Ownership 10
   E. Altering Statutory and Case Authority by Husband-Wife Agreement 40
   F. Exceptions to Normal Classification Rules 47
CHART: Characterization of Property That Is Difficult to Classify 51

II. MANAGEMENT AND CONTROL OF PROPERTY 52
Chapter Approach 52
   A. Separate Property 52
   B. Community Personal Property 52
   C. Community Real Property 55
   D. Restrictions on Management Powers—Gifts of Property 58
   E. Restrictions on Management Powers—Fiduciary Duty of a Spouse 60
   F. Restrictions on Management Powers—Incompetency of One or Both Spouses ... 62

III. LIABILITY FOR DEBTS 63
Chapter Approach 63
   A. General Rule 63
   B. Exceptions to General Rule 63
   C. Special Rules for Tort Liability 64
   D. Effect of Separation or Divorce on Liability for Debts 66
   E. Alimony Pendente Lite and Lump Sum Alimony 68

IV. DISSOLUTION OF THE COMMUNITY 69
Chapter Approach 69
   A. Division of Property at Divorce 69
   B. Devolution of Property at Death 78
   C. Administration of Property and Creditors' Claim at Death 83

V. RELATIONSHIPS SHORT OF VALID MARRIAGE 87
Chapter Approach 87
   A. Putative Marriages 87
   B. Coexisting Bigamous Marriages 92
   C. No Putative Marriage ("*Marvin*" Relationships) 94

VI.	**CONFLICT OF LAWS PROBLEMS**	98
	Chapter Approach	98
	A. Selection of Applicable Law	98
	B. Statutory Changes—Quasi-Community Property	100
VII.	**CONSTITUTIONAL LAW ISSUES**	103
	Chapter Approach	103
	A. Scope of "Separate Property" Under California Constitution	103
	B. Equal Protection Standards Under California Constitution	103
	C. Due Process Issues Under California Constitution—Retroactivity of Changes in Community Property Law	104
	D. Federal Preemption Under United States Constitution (Supremacy Clause)	106
	CHART: Characterization of Property with Federal Aspects	112

REVIEW QUESTIONS AND ANSWERS	115
SAMPLE EXAM QUESTIONS AND ANSWERS	131
TABLE OF CITATIONS TO CALIFORNIA FAMILY CODE	149
TABLE OF CASES	151
INDEX	155

TEXT CORRELATION CHART

Gilbert Law Summary Community Property	Bird **California Community Property** 1994 (6th ed.)	Blumberg **Community Property in California** 1993 (2nd ed.)	Reppy, Samuel **Community Property in the United States** 1997 (5th ed.)
I. CLASSIFYING PROPERTY AS COMMUNITY OR SEPARATE			
A. **Basic Statutory Framework**	10-12	145-161	1-1 - 1-10
B. **Presumptions Respecting Ownership**	60-86	165-182	4-1 - 4-5, 10-14, 12-17
C. **Special Presumptions**			
1. Transfers to Married Women	86-98	184-191	3-14 - 3-22, 3-27, 10-2 - 10-3, 22-7
2. Special Presumption Against Joint Tenancy and Tenancy in Common at Divorce	98-116	192-228	3-14 - 3-22, 3-24 - 3-28
D. **Overcoming Pro-Community Presumption by Proof of Separate Ownership**			
1. Proof of Acquisition by Inheritance, Devise, or Bequest	70, 74-78	145-152	5-1 - 5-5, 11-30 - 11-36
2. Proof of Acquisition by Gift to One Spouse Alone	78-81, 394-395	145-148, 156-161	5-5 - 5-6, 5-11, 7-3, 11-30 - 11-36
3. Acquisition by Gift to Both Spouses as Co-Equal Donees			5-5, 5-6 - 5-10
4. Proof of Acquisition While Spouses Are Living Apart	81-86	156-161, 569-573	6-19 - 6-28
5. Establishing Separate Ownership by Tracing to Pre-Marriage Source	10-14, 70-74	161-163	10-1
6. Commingling and Uncommingling of Assets	265-279	239-261	10-1 - 10-17
7. Rents or Profits from Separate Capital	273-296	261-278	11-1 - 11-36
8. Establishing Separate Property Share in Mixed Consideration Cases	160-177, 296-301, 313-319, 340	293-305, 316-323, 324-342, 390-397, 418-424	6-1 - 6-19
9. Establishing Separate Interest in Credit Acquisitions	301-320	278-293	8-1 - 8-7
10. Calculating Separate Interest in "Improvement" Cases	313-331	228-235	9-1 - 9-13
11. Determining Separate Interest in Tort Recoveries	331-340, 380-388, 464	306-316, 405-414	12-1 - 12-23
E. **Altering Statutory and Case Authority by Husband-Wife Agreement**			
1. In General	21-27		3-1 - 3-2
2. Antenuptial Agreements	27-42	101-121	3-1 - 3-6
3. Postnuptial "Transmutations"	42-58	121-143	3-1 - 3-3, 3-6 - 3-11
4. Situations in Which Transmutations May Be Inferred or Presumed	42-58, 74-75, 94-109, 320-323, 452, 461, 478-482	192-228	3-11 - 3-28
5. Effect of Husband-Wife Agreement on Third Parties			3-28 - 3-31, 17-25 - 17-26
F. **Exceptions to Normal Classification Rules**	133-169, 255-263, 340-380	53-83, 324-435	7-1 - 7-14, 13-1 - 13-15, 17-25 - 17-26, 18-7 - 18-11
II. MANAGEMENT AND CONTROL OF PROPERTY			
A. **Separate Property**	396	437-445	14-1 - 14-4
B. **Community Personal Property**	396-400, 402-407, 430-437	459-466	14-1 - 14-10
C. **Community Real Property**			
1. General Rule—Equal Management	396-399, 401-402	446	14-1 - 14-6
2. Dual Management for Alienation	397, 401-402, 407-410, 437-451	446-459	15-1 - 15-22
D. **Restrictions on Management Powers— Gifts of Property**	396-402, 416-420, 422-430, 437-461	466-484	15-22 - 15-30
E. **Restrictions on Management Powers— Fiduciary Duty of a Spouse**	397, 399-400, 412-423	484-497	16-1 - 16-10

Community Property—i

TEXT CORRELATION CHART—continued

Gilbert Law Summary Community Property	Bird California Community Property 1994 (6th ed.)	Blumberg Community Property in California 1993 (2nd ed.)	Reppy, Samuel Community Property in the United States 1997 (5th ed.)
F. Restrictions on Management Powers—Incompetency of One or Both Spouses	402, 463	477-480	16-8
III. LIABILITY FOR DEBTS			
A. General Rule	408-409, 462-469	497-506	17-1 - 17-4
B. Exceptions to General Rule	464-465	502-514	17-4 - 17-8, 17-18 - 17-20
C. Special Rules for Tort Liability	409-412, 464, 468-478	497-501, 507	17-5 - 17-6, 17-8 - 17-20
D. Effect of Separation or Divorce on Liability for Debts	74-75, 478-483, 484	569-573, 600-603	17-20 - 17-25
E. Alimony Pendente Lite and Lump Sum Alimony			
IV. DISSOLUTION OF THE COMMUNITY			
A. Division of Property at Divorce	101, 109, 484-587	575-647	18-1 - 18-6
B. Devolution of Property at Death	430-437, 588-605	649-676	19-1 - 19-23
C. Administration of Property and Creditors' Claims at Death	589-590, 593-602	670-671, 681-682	19-18 - 19-21
V. RELATIONSHIPS SHORT OF VALID MARRIAGE			
A. Putative Marriages	177-179, 180-192	515-534	20-1 - 20-5
B. Coexisting Bigamous Marriages	179-181, 192-207	515-534	20-5 - 20-16
C. No Putative Marriage ("*Marvin*" Relationships)	207-226	535-569	20-16 - 20-25
VI. CONFLICT OF LAWS PROBLEMS			
A. Selection of Applicable Law	226-232	677-685	21-1 - 21-5, 21-23 - 21-26
B. Statutory Changes—Quasi-Community Property	232-249	685-722	21-6 - 21-26
VII. CONSTITUTIONAL LAW ISSUES			
A. Scope of "Separate Property" Under California Constitution	7, 11-14	86-99	11-2
B. Equal Protection Standards Under California Constitution		98-99	22-6 - 22-7
C. Due Process Issues Under California Constitution—Retroactivity of Changes in Community Property Law	14-18, 117-124, 130-132, 133-141, 232-255	214-228, 693-701	22-8 - 22-14
D. Federal Preemption Under United States Constitution (Supremacy Clause)	255-263	731-747	22-14 - 22-32

gilbert
capsule summary
community property

Text Section

I. CLASSIFYING PROPERTY AS COMMUNITY OR SEPARATE

A. BASIC STATUTORY FRAMEWORK

1. **Statutory Definition of Community Property:** Community property consists of all real and personal property acquired by a married person while domiciled in California, except for statutorily defined separate property . . . . [1]

2. **Statutory Definition of Separate Property:** All property owned by the husband (H) or wife (W) *before marriage* and property *acquired while living separate and apart* from the spouse is separate property. Separate property also includes *that acquired by gift, bequest, devise, or descent, with the rents, issues, and profits thereof* (and items taken in exchange for) . . . . [2]

B. PRESUMPTIONS RESPECTING OWNERSHIP

1. **Types of Presumptions:** There is a broad general presumption in favor of community ownership applicable in most cases. There are also two special statutory presumptions applicable in narrower fact situations . . . . [4]

2. **Requirements for General Pro-Community Presumption:** Courts have differed as to what proof suffices to raise the presumption. Three tests have been used in assessing the requisite proof . . . . [5]

   a. **Acquisition during marriage test:** Most courts apply the "*during marriage*" test and hold that the general presumption does not arise until there is proof that the asset was acquired during marriage. A change of form of the asset supplies a new acquisition date . . . . [6]

   b. **"Possession" test:** Other courts have required proof only that an asset was possessed by H or W during marriage in order to raise the general presumption . . . . [9]

   c. **"Possession plus long marriage" test:** Some courts apply the presumption (despite failure to show acquisition during marriage) if the evidence shows possession by H or W at the end of a long marriage . . . . [10]

3. **Possible "Unlimited" Presumption:** Some community property states permit the *mere assertion* of community ownership to raise the general presumption . . . . [11]

4. **Acquisition While Living Separate and Apart:** Where H or W acquires property after separation but before the divorce, it could be either separate property or community property if pre-separation funds were used. There is no definitive holding, but cases imply the pro-community presumption applies where the source of consideration is unknown, though the spouses were separated . . . . [12]

5. **Acquisition After Dissolution:** For the general presumption to apply, a party must show that the consideration for a post-dissolution acquisition was itself acquired or possessed during marriage or possessed at the end of a long marriage . . . . [14]

6. **Effect of Contrary Evidence on General Presumption:** Contrary evidence of separate ownership, if unopposed, will require a directed verdict despite the presumption. If there is conflicting evidence, the presumption places the burden of proof on the party alleging separate ownership . . . . [15]

Community Property—I

7. **Exception to Pro-Community Presumption:** Under California Family Code section 802, the presumption does *not* apply to property possessed by a former spouse at death when the marriage was dissolved by divorce more than four years before death .... [19]

C. **SPECIAL PRESUMPTIONS**
1. **Transfers to Married Women:** An asset transferred to W in her name by written instrument **prior to 1975** is presumed to be W's separate property. The **date of acquisition** is usually the date of delivery of the instrument .... [22]
    a. **Where W is not the only transferee:** Where a pre-1975 instrument names W and other(s) as transferees (owners), there is a **presumption** that W's share is her separate property absent a contrary intent expressed in the instrument .... [25]
        (1) **Transfer to W and H:** If the pre-1975 instrument **describes the transferees as husband and wife**, there is a pro-community presumption as to the entire property. Otherwise, W's interest is presumed to be her separate property while the other half interest is community property .... [26]
    b. **Exception to "pro-wife" presumption:** The pro-community presumption applies where a pro-wife presumption plus W's management powers could convert community assets into W's separate property .... [27]
    c. **Overcoming pro-wife presumption:** The pro-wife presumption is generally rebuttable by proof that community funds were used to pay for the acquisition. If the evidence conflicts, the burden of proof is still on the party alleging community ownership .... [28]
        (1) **Bona fide purchaser:** The special pro-wife presumption is conclusive in favor of a bona fide purchaser or encumbrancer .... [30]
        (2) **Constitutionality:** Due to discrimination by sex (anti-male), the pro-wife presumption may be unconstitutional in all but bona fide purchaser situations .... [31]
2. **Special Presumption Against Joint Tenancy and Tenancy in Common at Divorce:** This is discussed *infra*, §193.

D. **OVERCOMING PRO-COMMUNITY PRESUMPTION BY PROOF OF SEPARATE OWNERSHIP**
1. **Proof of Acquisition by Inheritance, Devise, or Bequest:** Such methods of acquisition will rebut the general presumption of community ownership. However, such property may still be shown to be community if traceable to community consideration .... [33]
    a. **Bequest to both spouses:** A bequest or devise to spouses as co-owners and receipt during marriage makes an asset community property .... [34]
    b. **Effect of tracing:** Even though acquired during marriage, an item will be separate property if the consideration given can be traced back to a bequest, inheritance, or other source of separate property .... [35]
2. **Proof of Acquisition by Gift to One Spouse Alone:** Such gifts during marriage and before separation will rebut the presumption. However, donative intent must be proved .... [36]
    a. **Partial donative intent:** If some community consideration is paid but the value of the acquired asset is much greater, it is likely that the transferor had some donative intent and the asset is partly separate and partly community .... [37]
    b. **Remunerative gifts:** When H or W receives a gift in appreciation for services rendered, the asset is community property on the theory that it is really the fruit of a spouse's labor .... [38]
    c. **Unclear donative intent:** If the donative intent is unclear, the pro-community presumption should apply .... [39]

			Text Section
3.	**Acquisition by Gift to Both Spouses as Co-Equal Donees:** Such gifts during marriage will **not** rebut the pro-community presumption unless it is shown that the donor intended H and W to hold title to the asset as tenants in common or joint tenants		[40]
	a.	**Wedding gifts:** A gift to both H and W delivered prior to marriage is tenancy in common unless the donor intended that title not pass until the marriage occurred	[41]
4.	**Proof of Acquisition While Spouses Are Living Apart:** Acquisition by the labor of one spouse while living apart will establish separate ownership. But a post-separation acquisition traceable to pre-separation labor or community funds is community owned		[43]
	a.	**Intent of spouses governs:** Intent governs whether a physical separation constitutes "living separate and apart." If both spouses feel the marriage is dead and they physically separate, subsequent earnings are separate property	[45]
		(1) **Unilateral intent:** If *either* spouse during a trial separation comes to believe the marriage is dead, the parties are probably "living separate and apart"	[47]
	b.	**Effect of reconciliation:** Reconciliation of the spouses would not in itself convert separate property to community	[49]
5.	**Establishing Separate Ownership by Tracing to Pre-Marriage Source:** Tracing to a pre-marriage source through changes in form of an asset may establish separate ownership		[50]
6.	**Commingling and Uncommingling of Assets:** Commingling of separate and community property will not change the character of the separate property per se. However, the pro-community presumption usually makes the commingled mass community property until "uncommingling" identifies the separate and community shares		[51]
	a.	**"Drawer's intent" test:** Uncommingling after unearmarked withdrawals and deposits is accomplished by applying the *drawer's intent* test. Self-serving, after-the-fact testimony can prove such intent	[53]
	b.	**"Family expense" doctrine:** Absent direct evidence of the drawer's intent, funds withdrawn from a commingled account to pay for household expenses are *presumed to be community funds*. A "family expense" is determined by a family's relative wealth and customary standard of living	[55]
		(1) **Reimbursement:** Under the *See* case, when family expenses were paid from a commingled account with insufficient community funds, withdrawal of separate funds by their owner is presumed a *gift* to the community; thus, there is no reimbursement. Reimbursement is *allowed*, however, where post-separation separate property earnings are used to pay family expenses	[57]
	c.	**Result where intent cannot be proved or inferred:** In cases of uncommingling where the drawer's intent is not known, California seems to treat separate ownership as forfeited. Elsewhere, the courts:	[62]
		(i) Treat each withdrawal as a *pro rata portion of community and separate*;	
		(ii) Assume that the *community property is withdrawn first*;	
		(iii) Assume that *withdrawals favorably invested were community funds*, to the extent possible; or	
		(iv) Give all investments *to the community* but *reimburse* the separate estate.	
7.	**Rents or Profits from Separate Capital:** Rents or profits from separately owned capital, generated without applying community labor, are separate property. Earnings from separate capital during marriage must be **apportioned** between community and separate estates where one or both spouses contributed labor to make the capital productive. The *Pereira* or *Van Camp* formula is used to apportion the earnings		[63]

				Text Section

    a. ***Pereira* formula:** Under this approach, separate capital is valued and an annual return at a particular interest is calculated for the period in question. That portion of gain is separate and the remainder is community ... [64]

        (1) **Appropriate interest rate:** The rate used is the legal rate of interest unless a party proves that a higher or lower rate is more appropriate. It appears that a court may **compound interest** if it will do substantial justice for the separate estate .... [65]

        (2) **Varying profits:** If profits are uneven over time, courts might make a year-by-year calculation of the community gain. However, if a separate business goes **bankrupt**, its separate status is terminated .... [67]

        (3) **Distributions from business:** Withdrawals earmarked as **salary** should be community property even if the apportionment formula would make them partly separate .... [69]

    b. ***Van Camp* formula:** Under this formula, the community labor applied to the separate capital is valued. This amount is community and the remainder of the gain is separate .... [70]

        (1) **Withdrawals:** **Salary** payments or other withdrawals used for family expenses will reduce the community share retained in the business. The receipt of a reasonable salary by a laboring spouse will not bar use of an apportionment formula to obtain a larger community share of gain .... [71]

        (2) **Retention of community earnings in business:** Arguably, retained community earnings should be viewed as invested in the business and treated as new additions to capital, whereby future capital will not be solely separate property. The return on capital would be apportioned into community and separate shares .... [72]

    c. **"Compromise" formula:** An apportionment formula combining *Pereira* and *Van Camp* is seldom used today .... [73]

    d. **Which test should be applied?** The court determines whether separate capital or community labor is the chief contributing factor and then selects the formula most favorable to that estate .... [74]

    e. **"Reverse apportionment":** Reverse apportionment with either formula is necessary for earnings from **community capital** while the parties are living separate and apart and the **labor is separate** .... [75]

8. **Establishing Separate-Property Share in Mixed-Consideration Cases:** Each estate contributing consideration for an asset before or at the time title is acquired is credited with a pro rata share, and the asset is owned by the acquiring estates as tenants in common .... [77]

    a. **Purchases by installment contract:** For installment contract purchases, the principal (as opposed to the interest) component of each installment payment is treated as purchasing a share of the title. Under this rule, the dollar paid years ago purchases the **same pro rata ownership share** as the dollar recently paid, thus ignoring inflation and opportunity costs .... [78]

        (1) **Contract ownership:** When the marriage is dissolved **before title passes**, ownership of the installment contract presumably should be divided pro rata based on the monies paid in by the time of dissolution .. [79]

        (2) **Inception of title doctrine:** This doctrine permanently fixes ownership of an installment contract on the basis of the acquiring spouse's marital status **at the time the contract was entered into**. The nonacquiring estate is reimbursed without interest for any subsequent contributions .... [81]

            (a) **Generally rejected in California:** California has generally rejected the doctrine in favor of a pro rata shared ownership approach .... [82]

            (b) **Applies where land acquired by labor:** The inception of title doctrine has been applied in California where acquisition of property is by labor over a period of time (*e.g.*, adverse possession) ..... [83]

IV—Community Property

b. **Apportionment of pension benefits:** Pension benefits earned by work while single and while married and cohabiting are usually *apportioned* on the basis of time on the job while single or separated vs. time while married . . . . [85]
   (1) **Defined benefit plans:** These plans require no periodic contributions by employers or participants and keep no account of funds in the participant's name; thus "time" apportionment is proper. An *exception* occurs where the defined benefit plans use a different measure than time on the job to qualify the spouse for benefits . . . . [86]
   (2) **Defined contribution plans:** Such plans involve periodic contributions and an account for each participant. Apportionment based on money is possible; however, time apportionments continue to be made (achieving rough justice) . . . . [88]
   (3) **Incentive stock options:** "Time" apportionments are made to determine community and separate interests in stock options awarded to an employee spouse based on labor over time that include community labor and separate labor . . . . [91]
c. **Apportionment of life insurance:** Pro rata money apportionment is applied to the cash surrender value of a policy when premiums have been paid with separate and community funds. Older cases applying pro rata apportionment to characterize *death benefits*, based on the total of separate and community funds used to pay premiums, are no longer followed. Recently, it has been held that a *term policy* is a series of separate contracts; the sole value lies in the coverage in effect at the time the asset is classified, and it is separate or community depending on the funds used to pay the last premium. Another case adds that the court should also value the right to continued insurance even though the insured becomes uninsurable. All premiums paid are viewed as buying this right, so it is classified under the pro rata approach . . . . [92]

9. **Establishing Separate Interest in Credit Acquisitions:** Borrowed money or items purchased therewith (plus items bought on credit) are characterized depending on whether the vendor or lender relied *primarily* on separate or community property in extending credit . . . . [96]
   a. **Contrary authority:** One case rejects the *primary* reliance test and holds that the pro-community presumption can be overcome only by proof that the lender relied *solely* on separate assets of a spouse for repayment . . . [97]
   b. **Effect of security:** The use of separate property as security will rebut the pro-community presumption but is not conclusive regarding a creditor's intent. Where the *security is the item acquired on credit*, the entire asset could be characterized according to the nature of the down payment or, alternatively, by the character of the property that a lender would likely seize if such security was inadequate . . . . [98]
   c. **Effect of other spouse's signature:** A creditor's insistence that both spouses sign a note may indicate reliance on the separate property of the spouse not seeking the loan . . . . [100]
   d. **Effect of repayment:** The manner in which the loan is repaid is irrelevant in characterizing assets . . . . [101]
   e. **Criticism:** When a lender relies on both community and separate estates for repayment, ownership logically should be apportioned, but California has yet to do so . . . . [102]

10. **Calculating Separate Interest in "Improvement" Cases:** When funds from one estate are expended to improve property owned by the other, the former estate is likely to be entitled to reimbursement from the improved estate, absent a finding of a gift . . . . [103]
    a. **Fixtures doctrine:** The improvement rule is based on the fixtures doctrine, under which an accession to real property takes on the same ownership character as the realty improved . . . . [104]

		Text Section

- b. **Scope of improvement doctrine:** The rule applies to tangible assets affixed to realty, payment of taxes levied on the property, sums expended for major rehabilitation and upkeep, and probably to community labor applied to increase the value of separate property .... [108]
- c. **Effect of reimbursement on creditors:** A creditor of the improving estate who cannot reach the improved estate can perhaps seize the former's right of reimbursement; it can force an immediate sale of the improved estate where the improvement expenditure is *fraud on the creditors* ..... [109]
- d. **Mortgage payments:** Older cases treated mortgage payments as improvements. More recently, at least purchase money mortgage payments are treated as buying a share of ownership to the extent equity is increased. This latter approach results in a shift of fractional ownership each time a mortgage payment is made .... [111]
- e. **Amount of reimbursement:** The amount of reimbursement under the improvement doctrine is unclear. Some cases state that the amount is value added (determined at dissolution) not to exceed the amount spent; however, this does not give sufficient protection to the community paying for separate improvements .... [116]
  - (1) **Constructive fraud:** Where a spouse uses community property to improve his own separate estate without agreement for reimbursement (*i.e.,* constructive fraud), reimbursement is the greater of the value added or the amount spent (without interest) .... [120]
- f. **Gift situation:** Before W attained management powers over community property, the law presumed a gift when H used separate or community funds to improve W's separate property or used his separate funds to improve community property. This presumption is now gender neutral. There are, however, special rules pertaining to presumption of gift with respect to: mortgage payments on realty titled in the names of both spouses; divorce; and joint tenancy deeds .... [122]
- g. **Liens:** In California, the right to reimbursement probably is not secured by an automatic lien on improved property, contrary to the rule in most other community property states .... [127]
- h. **Unknown source of funds:** In California, there is no presumption as to the character of the funds used to make an improvement where the source is unknown. Most of the other community property states presume that the funds used were of the same character as the improved estate .... [128]

11. **Determining Separate Interest in Tort Recoveries**
    - a. **Property damage:** Recovery for damage to property takes on the same character as the property damaged .... [129]
      - (1) **Business property:** Recovery for lost business profits should have the same character that would have attached under a *Pereira-Van Camp* apportionment, with a downward adjustment for the estate that would have provided labor .... [130]
      - (2) **Insured property:** Money recovered from an insurer should be classified by tracing to the property insured. However, one case has traced it to the insurance contract and funds used to pay premiums . [131]
    - b. **Personal injury damages:** Such damages received by H or W are classified according to the time when the tort occurred (*i.e.,* when the cause of action arises) .... [133]
      - (1) **Tort occurring before marriage:** Recovery on a premarriage cause of action rebuts the pro-community general presumption and is separate property of the victim even if received after marriage. However, an argument can be made that marriage changes the recovery for postmarriage lost earnings to community property .... [134]
      - (2) **Tort occurring during separation:** Recovery for a tort occurring while the spouses are living apart is the separate property of the victim. If

community funds or the other spouse's separate property was used to pay medical or other expenses generated by the tort, a right to reimbursement exists .... [136]

    (3) **Tort occurring during marriage and cohabitation:** Personal injury damages received during marriage and cohabitation are presumptively community. California, contrary to other states, *will not trace recovery* for pain, suffering, and disfigurement to a *right of personal security* owned by the victim before marriage .... [140]

        (a) **Treatment at divorce:** Community personal injury damages are not divided 50-50 at divorce, but go to the victim spouse unless justice otherwise requires. The victim spouse must be awarded at least half of the funds on hand that had been paid as tort damages. Reimbursement claims will arise if community money was used to pay medical bills before the recovery was treated as if separate .... [144]

        (b) **Dissolution by death:** Death of the nonvictim spouse converts a cause of action from community to the victim's separate property. The victim's own death does not change the character of a cause of action that does not abate at death .... [149]

    (4) **Interspousal recovery:** Recovery by one spouse from the other for personal injuries is separate property. This also applies to insurance proceeds on a policy paid for with community funds .... [151]

    (5) **Imputed negligence:** The contributory negligence of the noninjured spouse will not, under comparative negligence law, reduce the damages recoverable by the victim even though such damages are community .... [154]

  c. **Loss of consortium:** Recovery for loss of consortium is community property .... [155]

  d. **Workers' compensation awards:** Such statutory recovery is not treated as a personal injury tort recovery; rather, "in lieu" tracing is used—the benefits are in lieu of post-injury lost wages. There is no tracing to sums contributed to a general compensation fund by the victim or community. Individual contracts may be treated differently .... [156]

  e. **Private disability benefits:** Benefits paid to a spouse who retired due to a disability are treated like tort recoveries with one important exception: When the injured spouse reaches the normal retirement age (had no disability occurred), all returns on the disability insurance contract may be ordinary community; under a pension plan the community share is the sum that would have been paid on retirement without the disability .... [158]

  f. **Wrongful death:** Recovery for wrongful death has been held community if the action arises during marriage and before separation (though recovery in lieu of gifts by decedent logically may be separate property) ...... [162]

    (1) **Effect of separation or divorce:** If the cause of action arises after separation, each spouse's recovery is separate property .... [163]

    (2) **Imputed negligence:** Where recovery is community, the negligence of H or W will probably reduce that recovery. *Transmutation* to the nonnegligent spouse's separate property will not avoid reduction; however, a written agreement before death that the action would be one spouse's separate property would be effective .... [164]

E. **ALTERING STATUTORY AND CASE AUTHORITY BY HUSBAND-WIFE AGREEMENT**

  1. **In General:** Rules for classifying property may be altered by agreement between spouses or may be unilaterally waived by a spouse upon whom the benefits are conferred .... [166]

  2. **Antenuptial Agreements:** Under the Uniform Premarital Agreement Act, antenuptial agreements affecting marital rights in property must be in writing and

can be amended or revoked only by a writing. In the past, courts always avoided this Statute of Frauds issue, generally by finding post-marriage affirmance. It remains to be seen whether they will do so to avoid the Uniform Act .... [167]
    a. **Public policy:** An antenuptial agreement is void as against public policy if it promotes divorce .... [169]
  3. **Postnuptial "Transmutations":** Post-marriage transmutations can alter the character of property. Neither consideration nor delivery is required .... [171]
    a. **Older rule—no formalities:** No formalities were required for effective postnuptial transmutation. A transmutation could be implied from the conduct and comments of the parties. Even where land was involved, no writing was required *except* that an agreement to hold property in *joint tenancy* was required to be in writing .... [172]
      (1) **"Treatment" of property:** Pre-1985 treatment of property could imply a transmutation agreement which *supersedes* a prior formal contract .... [173]
    b. **Post-1984 transmutations writing required:** Today, Family Code section 852 requires, with limited exceptions, that for a transmutation to be valid there must be a *written* express declaration. This requirement applies to both real and personal property. An exception applies to gifts between the spouses of clothing, jewelry, and other personal items. A will is not a sufficient writing .... [174]
      (1) **Writing must be unambiguous:** To be sufficiently express, generally the writing must indicate that the transmuter knows that she has or may have a property interest affected by the writing .... [175]
  4. **Situations Where Transmutation May Be Inferred or Presumed**
    a. **Traditional gifts:** Traditional gifts purchased with community funds do not per se prove transmutation to a donee spouse's separate property, but merely offer an *inference* of donative intent which the trier of fact may or may not accept .... [179]
      (1) **Improvements to property:** Donative intent has sometimes been *presumed* when separate funds were used to improve community property .... [180]
    b. **Effect of recitals in pre-1985 deeds:** Recitals of separate ownership by H or W do *not* establish transmutation unless a deed is signed or accepted by the party alleged to have given up ownership rights under normal classification rules. Under post-1984 law, the writing must also indicate the grantor's awareness of her interest in the consideration paid .... [181]
      (1) **Recital of joint tenancy:** Here, it is *presumed* that H and W agreed to transmute property to joint tenancy, even though neither signs the instrument. Proof that neither H nor W understood the difference between community property and joint tenancy *will* rebut the presumption; proof that one spouse, aware of the deed, did not intend a transmutation will *not*. The joint tenancy presumption does not apply at divorce, and creditors may overcome the presumption by proving no transmutation occurred .... [185]
        (a) **Bank accounts:** At divorce, a pro-community presumption can be overcome by tracing to separate funds deposited in a joint tenancy bank account held in names of both spouses .... [192]
      (2) **Tenants in common:** It is unsettled whether a recital of tenancy in common raises a presumption of transmutation .... [193]
  5. **Effect of Husband-Wife Agreement on Third Parties:** A transmutation of property is binding on third parties who become creditors *after* the transmutation occurs. However, an *existing creditor* is not bound by a transmutation that renders the debtor spouse insolvent .... [194]

F. EXCEPTIONS TO NORMAL CLASSIFICATION RULES

1. **"Terminable Interest" Doctrine:** The "terminable interest doctrine," formerly followed by California, provided that a community pension earned by H and awarded to W would terminate at W's death even though retired ex-H was still alive, thus depriving ex-W of testamentary power over her share. Family Code section 2610 generally abrogates this rule. However, the Supreme Court has interpreted a federal statute that governs most pensions (E.R.I.S.A.) as forcing California to employ the discarded terminable interest doctrine .... [198]
2. **Educational Degrees and Licenses to Practice:** College degrees and governmentally issued licenses to practice a profession are considered to be the *separate property* of the acquiring spouse even though earned by labor during marriage. However, at divorce the community is entitled to *reimbursement* for funds used to educate or train the spouse .... [200]
    a. **Distinguish business goodwill:** Goodwill can be owned as community property and is awarded at divorce to the professional spouse. The other spouse receives an offsetting award of property .... [204]
        (1) **Incorporated professional:** Where a professional business is incorporated, the goodwill should appear in the value of the community-owned stock .... [205]
        (2) **Partnership:** If a spouse is a member of a business partnership, the community may own the right to enforce the partnership contract, but specific assets acquired by the partners are not community property. The community will at least indirectly benefit from the partnership goodwill .... [206]
3. **Pensions with "Vesting" Requirements:** Prior to 1976, future pension rights not "vested" at divorce (subject to a condition precedent) were not community property. However, 1976 case law changed this rule, so that contract rights earned by labor during marriage are community even if subject to conditions yet to occur .... [208]
4. **Earned Expectancies:** Certain *future employee benefits* may be community-owned even though there is no contract right to receive them .... [209]
    a. **Tips and bonuses:** Tips are community property to the extent based on labor during marriage and cohabitation; as to employee bonuses, there is a split of authority .... [210]

II. MANAGEMENT AND CONTROL OF PROPERTY

A. SEPARATE PROPERTY
1. **In General:** Each spouse has *exclusive management* of his or her separate property. The other spouse can manage only as the owner's *agent* .... [215]
2. **Concurrent Ownership:** Each spouse *can* use all co-owned tenancy in common and joint tenancy property, but can *sell* only his or her own interest ..... [216]

B. COMMUNITY PERSONAL PROPERTY
1. **Equal Management:** Equal management is the general rule; this means that one spouse alone can deal with or sell the full community interest .... [217]
2. **Exceptions**
    a. **One-spouse business:** A statute empowers one spouse to *exclude* the other spouse from a community-owned business. An attempt by the other spouse to sell a business asset would not pass title .... [218]
    b. **Bank accounts:** A spouse has *exclusive management* of community funds in a bank account in her name .... [223]
    c. **Right to "seize control":** Some types of community property (*e.g.,* causes of action) do not lend themselves to equal management and thus are subject to one spouse's seizing control, thereby denying equal management power to the other spouse .... [224]
    d. **Transactions requiring consent of both spouses:** The nonacting spouse must consent in writing to the sale or encumbrance of community household items and clothes of children or of the other spouse .... [225]

				Text Section
		(1)	**Oral consent:** If *both* spouses deal with the buyer or lender, oral consent may be sufficient	[227]

C. **COMMUNITY REAL PROPERTY**
   1. **General Rule—Equal Management:** The equal management rule applies to the ordinary day-to-day management of community realty . . . . [228]
   2. **Dual Management for Alienations:** *Both* spouses must join in an instrument conveying, encumbering, or leasing for more than one year community realty . [229]
      a. **Leasehold as realty:** A leasehold is realty for purposes of the joinder rule . [230]
      b. **Presumption of validity:** If title is in *one spouse* and only that spouse signs the instrument, there is a presumption that it was his separate property. This presumption can be rebutted by proof that community funds were used in the acquisition . . . . [231]
      c. **Scope of joinder rule:** Joinder is not required where community realty is transferred or encumbered without a written instrument . . . . [234]
      d. **Oral consent may be sufficient:** Oral consent may bar a spouse from invoking the joinder statute if a third party acts in reasonable reliance on such consent . . . . [236]
      e. **Commercial dealings:** The joinder rule also applies to commercial real property dealings in a single-spouse business . . . . [237]
      f. **Purchase money mortgage:** The joinder requirement does *not* apply to a purchase money security interest in favor of a party selling to the community; thus, one spouse alone can encumber the property with a purchase money mortgage . . . . [238]
      g. **Rescission of contract:** One spouse alone may rescind a contract to sell community realty (although a contract to buy arguably cannot be rescinded by one spouse after equitable conversion) . . . . [239]
      h. **Waiver by court:** A court may dispense with the joinder requirement where consent has been arbitrarily refused or cannot be obtained and the proposed transaction is in the community's best interest . . . . [240]
      i. **Effect of nonjoinder:** An instrument signed by one spouse alone is voidable by the nonjoining spouse . . . . [241]
         (1) **Limitations period:** The nonjoining spouse must sue a bona fide purchaser within *one year of recordation*. If unrecorded, suit apparently must commence within five years . . . . [242]
         (2) **Post-dissolution relief:** Where relief is granted during marriage, the transaction will be set aside entirely. If granted after dissolution, it is set aside only as to the plaintiff's half interest. Arguably, a *good faith buyer* can rescind the entire transaction . . . . [243]
            (a) **Restitution required:** The plaintiff must make restitution for consideration paid by a grantee for that portion of the conveyance set aside . . . . [245]
            (b) **Remedy against grantor spouse:** A nonjoining spouse may have a cause of action against the conveying spouse who knew of objections to the conveyance . . . . [246]

D. **RESTRICTIONS ON MANAGEMENT POWERS—GIFTS OF PROPERTY**
   1. **In General:** Absent *written consent*, one spouse may not transfer community property subject to equal management for less than "fair and reasonable value" [248]
   2. **Transactions Covered by Restrictions:** Two types of transactions are covered: (i) a unilateral gift *with* donative intent; and (ii) unilateral nondonative transfers without fair or lawful consideration. A mere moral obligation does *not* constitute sufficient consideration . . . . [249]
   3. **Possible Exception for Trifles:** At least one state (Washington) has excepted small gifts to friends and relatives, small charitable contributions, tips, etc. . . . . [252]

	4.	**Possible Exception for "Business Gifts":** A strong argument can be made for a reasonable business gifts exception to the rule .... [253]
	5.	**Finding of Estoppel, Waiver, or Ratification Unlikely:** Estoppel, waiver, and oral ratification are probably no defense to a suit based on the written consent statute. But if both spouses act as *co-donors*, no writing is required .... [254]
	6.	**Remedies for Violation of Section 1100(b):** An improper gift or sale for less than value is merely *voidable*; so the transferor spouse may not sue to recover property .... [255]
		a. **Amount of recovery:** During marriage, the transferee must return the entire asset; after dissolution, the plaintiff may recover *only* a half interest. A transferee should not be liable for *mesne profits* .... [256]
	7.	**Remedy Against Transferor Spouse:** A transferor spouse who was aware of objections to the gift is subject to suit by the nonconsenting spouse .... [259]
E.	**RESTRICTIONS ON MANAGEMENT POWERS—FIDUCIARY DUTY OF A SPOUSE**	
	1.	**In General:** Spouses have a fiduciary relationship to each other. Each spouse must manage community property in the highest good faith; neither may take unfair advantage of the other when acting as manager .... [261]
	2.	**Spouse Need Not Invest Like Trustee:** The managing spouse does not have to invest community property like a trustee, but does have a duty to make the community property productive. Also, a spouse must account for and hold as trustee all profit or benefit from a transaction that concerns community property that the spouse did not consent to .... [262]
	3.	**Usurping a Community Opportunity:** Where because of a community investment a spouse has an opportunity to make a further good investment, his use of separate rather than available community funds violates the duty of good faith. This duty continues after separation until a property division at divorce ...... [263]
	4.	**Spouse's Duty to Account:** Where a spouse takes control of community property shortly before separation or divorce, he or she must account for it. By statute, one spouse may at any time require the other to fully disclose all assets and debts affecting the community, or even the spouse's separate assets and debts .... [264]
	5.	**Remedies for Violating Fiduciary Duty:** A spouse may recover damages for breach of the other's fiduciary duty and may enjoin threatened breaches. Such actions can be commenced at dissolution and during the marriage for up to three years from the date the spouse learns of the breach .... [266]
		a. **Alternative remedy:** In lieu of dividing community and quasi-community property 50-50, the court may value the portion of divisible property that would have been awarded to the spouse who purposely misappropriated the property and award offsetting property to the wronged spouse, even if this results in an unequal division of assets .... [267]
F.	**RESTRICTIONS ON MANAGEMENT POWERS—INCOMPETENCY OF ONE OR BOTH SPOUSES**	
	1.	**Equal Management Property:** If one spouse becomes incompetent, the other (sane) spouse has exclusive control over equal management community property and apparently even over community property subject to the incompetent spouse's primary management. This applies even though the incompetent spouse has a conservator .... [270]
	2.	**Dual Management Transactions:** If one spouse is incompetent, a dual management transaction (*e.g.,* a gift of community property) requires court approval *or* joinder in or consent by the sane spouse and the incompetent's conservator .. [272]

III. **LIABILITY FOR DEBTS**

   A. **GENERAL RULE**
   1. **Community Property Liable:** Generally, all community property is liable for a spouse's debts regardless of who has management and control of the assets.

		Text Section
	By statute, one spouse's quasi-community property is liable whenever community property is liable, but this raises some constitutional concerns	[273]
2.	**Nondebtor's Separate Property Generally Not Liable:** Separate property is liable for all of the **owner spouse's debts** but is usually not liable for debts incurred by the nonowner spouse	[274]

B. **EXCEPTIONS TO GENERAL RULE**

1. **Separate Property Liable for Necessaries:** One spouse's separate property is liable for a debt incurred for **necessaries of life** of the other spouse **while they are cohabiting**. If the spouses are living apart, liability of the nondebtor spouse is limited to credit purchases of "common necessaries." However, the necessaries rule does **not** apply where there is a formal written separation agreement .... [276]
   a. **Standard of life test:** If spouses are living together, liability extends to all necessaries (as opposed to only "common" ones). What is included as a "necessary" depends on the couple's standard of living .... [278]
   b. **Third party contracts:** Since 1985, a spouse's separate property is liable for contracts for necessaries made by third parties for the benefit of the other spouse .... [279]
   c. **Reimbursement claims:** The nondebtor spouse has a right to reimbursement for separate property taken by a creditor when nonexempt community or separate property of the debtor spouse was available .... [280]

2. **Community Property Not Liable for Premarital Obligations:** A spouse's community earnings for labor are **not** liable for any debts incurred by the other spouse before marriage. This exemption applies only as long as the earnings are kept in a bank account from which the other spouse has no right of withdrawal and into which no nonexempt community funds are commingled .... [281]
   a. **Child support and alimony:** Child support and alimony obligations are considered premarital debts for the purposes of the above exemption. The judgment date is irrelevant. *But note:* Other community assets **will be liable** for such debts .... [282]

C. **SPECIAL RULES FOR TORT LIABILITY**

1. **Community Torts:** Generally, the victim of a community tort can be required **first to levy on community property** before levying on the separate estate of the tortfeasor spouse .... [283]
   a. **Broad scope of community torts:** A community tort is one arising out of activity that could **benefit the community** including recreational activities of a spouse .... [286]
2. **Separate Torts:** If liability is **not** based on an act or omission involving an activity for community benefit, it is a separate tort and the **tortfeasor's separate property** is primarily liable .... [287]
   a. **Right to reimbursement:** If community funds are used to pay for a separate tort, the reimbursement right must be asserted within seven years after learning how the tort debt was paid. The statute is less susceptible to an interpretation that reimbursement is available when the victim of a spouse's community tort seizes the tortfeasor's separate property .... [288]
3. **"Combination" Torts:** If the activity benefits both separate and community estates, the tort is logically part community and part separate. However, the statute may compel community characterization .... [289]
4. **Spouses as Joint Tortfeasors:** If H and W are jointly liable, the tort should be treated as community no matter what the activity was .... [290]
5. **Scope of Priority of Liability Rules**: There is no priority of liability where the tort does not involve injury to person or property .... [291]

				Text Section

6. **Tort Liability of One Spouse to Other:** The tortfeasor spouse's separate property is primarily liable to the other spouse for personal injury tort liability. However, the debtor may use *insurance proceeds* to pay off an obligation, even if the insurance was purchased with *community funds*. The victim can then reach other community property with only the tortfeasor spouse's share viewed as paying the debt .... [292]

D. EFFECT OF SEPARATION OR DIVORCE ON LIABILITY FOR DEBTS
1. **Separation:** Separation of the spouses has no effect on debtor-creditor relations except that post-separation earnings of each spouse are separate property. Post-separation torts are likely to be separate rather than community (unless the activity was to preserve community property) .... [295]
2. **Divorce:** Property owned by the *obligor spouse* after division by the divorce court is liable on the debt that spouse incurred—even if the court ordered the other spouse to pay the debt .... [298]
   a. **Effect of assignment of debt:** Whether other property is liable on a debt depends on the assignment of the debt by the court. If the court assigned the debt to the *obligor spouse*, the community property awarded to the nonobligor spouse is generally *not* liable. If the court assigned the debt to the *nonobligor spouse*, all property owned after divorce by the nonobligor spouse *is* liable .... [299]
      (1) **Reimbursement:** If the court orders the nonobligor spouse to pay the creditor, but the creditor instead proceeds against the obligor spouse, the obligor spouse is entitled to reimbursement from the spouse who was ordered to pay the debt .... [302]
   b. **Post-divorce judgment:** If the nonobligor spouse has been ordered by the divorce court to pay the debt, his property can be subject to a judgment *only if* he was made a party to the suit .... [303]

E. ALIMONY PENDENTE LITE AND LUMP SUM ALIMONY
California statute sets orders of liability for support during separation and lump sum alimony, but not for periodic payments after divorce .... [304]

IV. DISSOLUTION OF THE COMMUNITY

A. DIVISION OF PROPERTY AT DIVORCE
1. **Separate Property:** California courts cannot award any portion of a spouse's separate property to the other spouse. However, a divorce court can divide property held in joint tenancy or tenancy in common by the spouses .... [306]
2. **Community Property:** A court generally divides property equally so that spouses each get *half of the value* in the aggregate .... [308]
   a. **Tenancy in common division disfavored:** An asset-by-asset division is preferred over the court making parties co-owners as tenants in common .... [309]
      (1) **Co-ownership of community pension interests:** Tenancy in common divisions are *not* disfavored when dealing with pensions because of the difficulty in valuing the community interest in pension interests where there are numerous conditions to enjoyment of the benefits. If the divorce court can fairly value the contract rights, it can award the pension to the employee spouse and community property of comparable value to the other spouse. Alternatively, it may declare the divorcing spouses to be co-owners of the future benefits under a fractional share formula .... [310]
         (a) **Diminishing community fraction of benefits:** Under fractional sharing, post-divorce labor decreases the community share of future payments (but not the dollar amount) payable to the nonemployee spouse .... [311]

				Text Section
		(b)	**Management and control:** The employee manages the pension after divorce, but owes a duty not to take unfair advantage of the former spouse	[312]
	b.		**"Equalizing" by promissory note:** Where an equal division is impossible or would impair the value of community property, a court may require the spouse receiving more than half to give the other spouse a promissory note	[316]
	c.		**"Equalizing" by assignment of debts:** A court can also equalize division by an assignment of community debts. It is net value received after deduction of debts each spouse is ordered to pay that must be equal	[320]
		(1)	**Where debts exceed assets:** Where this occurs, a court must assign the excess of debt as it deems just and equitable	[321]
		(2)	**Effect of one spouse's bankruptcy:** If one spouse obtains a discharge in bankruptcy of certain community debts, such debts must be treated as the other spouse's separate debts and cannot be considered in determining whether the spouses' shares of net community assets are equal	[322]
		(3)	**Debt payment as alimony:** A few courts have allowed an unequal division by labeling as alimony the obligation of a spouse to pay certain types of debts	[324]
		(4)	**Treatment of separate debts:** Each spouse is liable for his or her own separate debts, which are not considered in the division of community property. A "benefit" test similar to that employed regarding torts is used to decide if the debt is separate. An educational loan is ***presumptively*** a separate debt	[325]
	d.		**Valuing assets and debts:** *Market* (not face) value is used to make an equal division of community property. A ***promissory note*** will have value below face value if not secured or if the interest rate is low	[327]
		(1)	**Tax aspects:** The tax cost of converting an asset to cash is ignored in valuing assets, unless sale is actually ordered by the divorce court. Tax benefits and burdens created by the method of dividing the property or otherwise certain to occur *are* considered in valuing assets	[329]
		(2)	**Time of valuing assets:** Generally the time for valuing assets is at trial	[331]
	e.		**Exceptions to equal division rule:** Community personal injury damages generally are awarded to the victim spouse and are not considered in determining whether the community has been equally divided. Also where the net value of community and quasi-community is less than $5,000 and the defendant does not appear, all may be awarded to the spouse who does appear	[333]
	f.		**Out-of-state land:** If possible, a court should not alter ownership of out-of-state realty subject to division. Where necessary, it can be accomplished by ordering one spouse to execute a deed	[335]
3.			**Adjustment for Monies Owed One Spouse by the Other:** Equal division may be adjusted due to sums owed one spouse by the other for reimbursement for improvements, etc. Separate property is also liable on such claims. ***Reimbursement*** is also available where community funds were used to pay ***separate debts***. Debts may be part separate and part community for this purpose	[336]
	a.		**Separate use of community assets:** One spouse may also be awarded half of the community's reimbursement claim resulting from the other's separate use of community funds	[340]
4.			**Treatment of "Nondistributable" Community Assets:** Community assets that can be owned by only one spouse after divorce (*e.g.,* attorney's goodwill) must be awarded to that spouse. The court must value the community interest in the asset and award the other spouse community assets of equal value or, if necessary, a promissory note	[343]
5.			**Effect of Failure to Distribute Asset or Assign Debt:** After divorce, H and W are ***tenants in common*** of former community property not divided by the court	

or a property settlement contract. A failure to assign a community debt has the effect of making each former spouse ultimately responsible for half, although a creditor may proceed against all property of the obligor and perhaps all former community property now owned by the other ex-spouse .... [345]

B. **DEVOLUTION OF PROPERTY AT DEATH**
1. **Separate Property:** Separate property can be bequeathed as the decedent wishes. A surviving spouse takes at least one-third of any *intestate* separate property .... [347]
2. **Community Property:** Decedent may bequeath his or her *half interest* in each item of community property ("item theory"), with the exception of assets that a legatee could not own (*e.g.,* professional goodwill of survivor) .... [348]
   a. **"Election" by surviving spouse:** Survivor is put to an election if decedent's will seeks to bequeath the *survivor's* half interest in any community asset [350]
      (1) **Wills construed to avoid election:** If possible, a will is construed as acting only on decedent's half interest, but a *statement* that an asset is *decedent's separate property*, when it is in fact community, means the will seeks to dispose of the entire asset .... [351]
      (2) **Separate property:** Election is also required if a will seeks to bequeath separate property of the surviving spouse .... [354]
      (3) **No forfeiture of intestate succession rights:** Election against a will *forfeits* all benefits under the will but does *not* forfeit intestate succession rights .... [355]
      (4) **Will substitutes:** The election doctrine applies to will substitutes, *e.g.,* when decedent attempts to name a beneficiary of more than half of community life insurance proceeds .... [356]
      (5) **Method of election:** The survivor elects to abide by a will if she knowingly accepts benefits provided therein. A survivor's guardian or estate may make an election for the survivor .... [358]
   b. **Restrictions on surviving spouse's interest:** A decedent may not use an instrument having a primarily testamentary effect to burden the survivor's half interest in the community property. Such a burden *is* valid if the instrument has an inter vivos *business purpose* .... [360]
3. **Property Passing by Will Substitute:** For a spouse to pass to a beneficiary both community halves by will substitute, the other spouse must consent. If the designating spouse alters the designation, consent is revoked if the consenting spouse is alive. If the consenting spouse dies prior to the modification, the alteration is effective only as to the half interest in community of the modifying party .... [364]
4. **Ancestral Property Succession:** When a surviving spouse dies intestate without lineal descendants or a new spouse, some former community property (and former separate property of the predeceased spouse) is inherited by the surviving spouse's former in-laws; *i.e.,* the property is returned to the predeceased spouse's family line. *Note:* Legislation has limited the scope of the ancestral property doctrine .... [365]
   a. **Source of title:** An intestate's former in-laws claiming under the ancestral property statute have the burden of proving that the assets have their source in former community property or in former separate property of the predeceased spouse. *Tracing* through changes in form is permitted .... [371]

C. **ADMINISTRATION OF PROPERTY AND CREDITORS' CLAIMS AT DEATH**
1. **Property Required to Be Administered:** A decedent's property passing to someone other than her spouse must be administered in probate court. Decedent's separate property and her half of community property passing to her spouse need not be so administered unless the asset is in trust or the surviving spouse receives less than fee simple absolute interest .... [375]

				Text Section
		a.	**Election:** The surviving spouse may elect to have decedent's share passing to him (or even his half interest in the community) administered, so as to limit creditor claims for community debts	[376]
	2.		**Confirmation Proceedings for Community Property Passing to Surviving Spouse:** Community and quasi-community property not administered by probate can pass through confirmation proceedings to obtain proof of survivor's title	[378]
	3.		**Post-Death Management and Control of Community Assets:** The survivor spouse retains management over all community property not subject to administration	[381]
		a.	**Community realty:** Where community realty is going through administration, the survivor may assume management of it 40 days after the death. This gives the survivor full power to sell, lease, mortgage, etc. A devisee must file notice to prevent surviving spouse's management power and protect her devise	[382]
		b.	**Personal property:** Management of community personalty *cannot* be taken from the decedent's personal representative by the surviving spouse except where the personalty is comprised of community securities registered in the spouse's name only	[383]
	4.		**Liability for Debts at Dissolution by Death:** Death of a spouse will not decrease the amount of community property that can be reached by an existing creditor	[384]
		a.	**Where no probate proceedings occur:** Unless both halves of the community go through administration, a surviving spouse will be personally liable up to the amount of his interest in the community and quasi-community property on unpaid debts. However, a survivor's liability *cannot* be asserted by a creditor who fails to file a claim with the decedent's personal representative where *any* of decedent's property is subject to probate	[385]
			(1) **Offsets and defenses:** A surviving spouse is entitled to raise the same offsets and defenses that the decedent could have asserted against creditors	[387]
		b.	**Where probate proceedings conducted:** Claims presented to decedent's personal representative may be paid partly with the survivor's share of community property and partly with the administered property. ***Community debts*** probably are paid half with the survivor's community share and half with decedent's community share. ***Separate debts*** are paid by the appropriate separate estate. Debts that are neither community nor separate, including ***administrative expenses***, are paid with a pro rata share of decedent's separate estate and community property	[388]
	5.		**Death of Ex-Spouse:** Where the parties are divorced still owing an unassigned community debt, and H or W subsequently dies, the survivor is probably still liable to the creditor even though no claim was filed against the decedent's estate. The survivor's remedy is to file a contingent ***creditor's claim*** against the estate based on a potential right of reimbursement	[391]

V. RELATIONSHIPS SHORT OF VALID MARRIAGE

A. PUTATIVE MARRIAGES

	1.		**In General:** Legal rules similar to community property rules apply to invalid marriages where ***at least one*** of the "spouses" had a ***good faith belief*** in the validity of the marriage. However, if both partners know of the invalidity, their relationship is governed by the *Marvin* decision	[393]
		a.	**"Putative marriage" used to describe relationship:** An invalid marriage where good faith existed is referred to as a "putative marriage." Putative spouses are given considerable protection in California, although they do ***not*** receive all the benefits of a lawful marriage	[394]

  b. **Good faith presumed:** Good faith is presumed; thus, one arguing that *Marvin* rules should apply bears the burden of proving a lack of good faith .... [395]
  c. **Test for lack of good faith:** A *subjective* test applies first to determine the belief of the would-be spouse, after which the court will determine if the belief is *objectively reasonable* .... [396]
   (1) **No common law marriage in California:** California does not recognize common law marriages. A subjective belief that California does recognize such marriages will be held objectively unreasonable. However, if the parties contracted a common law marriage in a state where lawful, California will recognize it as *lawful* (rather than putative) ... [397]
   (2) **Spouse not in good faith:** Where one "spouse" has good faith and one lacks it, the latter can obtain no benefits under the putative marriage doctrine but must rely on the *Marvin* doctrine unless the quasi-marital property statute is construed contrary to civil law .... [400]
    (a) **"Quasi-marital property":** Property that would have been community or quasi-community property if the marriage were valid is "quasi-marital" property. It is divided 50-50 at annulment ...... [402]
 2. **Status During Putative Marriage of Acquisitions by Labor:** The law is unclear as to how property that would be community in case of a valid marriage is owned prior to annulment .... [403]
  a. **Property is community:** Under this approach, the property is treated as community for all purposes. However, courts have rejected this approach . [404]
  b. **Property is tenancy in common:** Some courts find that the putative spouses are tenants in common, at least as to acquisitions resulting from joint efforts .... [407]
  c. **Property arises from partnership:** A few courts have suggested a sort of "business partnership" wherein a putative spouse has an interest only in those acquisitions to which he or she contributed a joint effort .... [408]
  d. **Property is separate property of acquiring spouse:** The fourth approach concludes that all property rights in an acquisition that would have been community in a lawful marriage are separate property of the acquiring spouse .... [409]
  e. **Treatment of Social Security benefits:** A California putative spouse has the status of a wife (or husband, widow, etc.) for Social Security benefits if no lawful spouse makes a claim .... [410]
 3. **Remedies at Annulment of Putative Marriage:** If quasi-marital property at annulment is small in amount, a good faith "wife" rendering household services may sue the "husband" (even one in good faith) for the excess of the reasonable value of the service over the value of the support he provided .... [411]
  a. **Remedy should be neutral as to sex:** If the "husband" performed such services, he could probably sue the "wife" .... [412]
  b. **Defendant need not be in bad faith:** The defendant (usually the male) may be liable in quasi-contract even though he entered into the "marriage" in good faith .... [413]
  c. **Alimony available:** A good faith putative spouse may receive alimony pendente lite and post-annulment alimony .... [414]
 4. **Termination of Putative Marriage by Death of a "Spouse":** Where a surviving putative spouse was not the acquiring spouse, courts assure him or her a fair share—usually one-half of property treated as quasi-marital at annulment. Thus, the survivor has the same right as a lawful spouse to elect against decedent's will .... [416]
  a. **Surviving "spouse" has full intestate rights:** If no lawful spouse exists, a surviving putative spouse inherits intestate the same assets as a lawful spouse would have received .... [417]
  b. **Other death benefits for surviving "spouse":** A good faith surviving putative spouse can sue for the wrongful death of decedent (even if a lawful

spouse exists), obtain workers' compensation benefits as a widow or widower, and receive surviving spouse benefits under statutory plans (at least if no lawful spouse claims rights) .... [418]

B. COEXISTING BIGAMOUS MARRIAGES

1. **"Living Apart" Doctrine Usually Determines Result:** In most bigamous marriages, the twice-married person will have separated from the first spouse before "marrying" again. Under the doctrine, the first spouse has no claims on post-separation acquisitions by labor (except on intestate death), and the second spouse has no claims on acquisitions before the second "marriage" ..... [422]

2. **Equity Governs When Spouse Keeps Two Households:** A party maintaining two households can have a lawful and a putative spouse (or two putative spouses), both making claims on acquisitions while cohabiting with them. Where H cohabits with W-1 and putative W-2, W-1's earnings are community property co-owned with H. W-2's earnings (absent a contract) are her separate property and are probably not quasi-marital at annulment due to H's bad faith. H's earnings are both community co-owned with W-1 and quasi-marital property of union with W-2 .... [423]

   a. **Husband's earnings:** If H dies intestate, his earnings go half to W-1 and half to W-2; but if H leaves a will, some equitable share may go to his legatees .... [426]

C. NO PUTATIVE MARRIAGE ("*MARVIN*" RELATIONSHIPS)

1. **All Property Presumed Separately Owned:** In *Marvin*-type relationships (*i.e.*, both parties are aware that they are not married), acquisitions are each party's *separate property* unless there is a contrary express or implied agreement .. [431]

   a. **Express or implied contracts:** A contract between a cohabiting male and female to "share equally" is usually enforceable. They could be tenants in common or sharing could be postponed until they split up .... [432]

2. **Public Policy Limitations:** If monetary sharing is conditioned on the sharing of sexual favors, a contract is unenforceable .... [434]

3. **Duration of Contract:** In an *express Marvin* contract, the parties may agree to mutually support each other financially so long as both live or only so long as they live together. In the latter case, neither party would owe the other anything comparable to alimony after their breakup .... [435]

4. **Legal Status of Cohabitant:** For some purposes, such as the ability to maintain actions for wrongful death or loss of consortium, a couple in a *Marvin* relationship are legally strangers .... [436]

5. **Alternative Remedies for Cohabitant**

   a. **Quantum meruit:** If services were rendered with an expectation of a monetary award, a nonmarital partner may recover the reasonable value of household services rendered less the value of support received (probably subject to reimbursement if latter exceeds former). Recovery may be denied if sex was inseparable part of the arrangement .... [439]

      (1) **Advantages of noncontractual remedies:** Under quantum meruit, the prevailing party can levy on all property of the defendant. If an express or implied pooling contract is alleged, property of a type that would be separate in a lawful marriage will often be outside its scope .... [440]

   b. **Constructive trust:** A promise to hold in co-ownership, if fraudulent when made, allows the nonacquiring spouse to claim a share of ownership via constructive trust .... [441]

VI. CONFLICT OF LAWS PROBLEMS

A. SELECTION OF APPLICABLE LAW

A California court makes a choice of law on *each issue* rather than finding one state's law governs the entire case .... [444]

		Text Section

1. **Acquisitions by Nondomiciliaries:** If out-of-state law is chosen, reference to "separate property" of H or W will not likely mean the same assets that are separate property under California law .... [445]
   a. **Problems with nomenclature:** If earnings while domiciled in a common law state are called "separate" bylaws of that state, California courts, prior to dissolution, will probably treat such earnings as California *separate* property in determining debt liability under California law .... [446]
   b. **Change in form:** A change in form of an asset brought to California does *not* (prior to dissolution) alter property rights created by the state of domicile at the time of acquisition .... [448]
2. **Out-of-State Acquisitions by California Domiciliaries:** Out-of-state acquisitions by California spouses are classified as separate or community by California law in California courts, even where realty is at issue. However, a California *judgment* that attempts to directly change title to out-of-state land might *not be enforced* in the situs state .... [449]

B. **STATUTORY CHANGES—QUASI-COMMUNITY PROPERTY**
   1. **Quasi-Community Property Defined:** At end of marriage, California treats as community those assets acquired by H or W while domiciled out of state if the assets would have been community if acquired by California domiciliaries. Property that is community by the law of domicile at the time of acquisition but which would be separate under California law is treated as *community* when brought to California .... [455]
   2. **When Characterization Is Significant:** Characterization of quasi-community is significant mainly at dissolution by death or divorce .... [457]
      a. **Treatment of quasi-community property at divorce:** At divorce, quasi-community property is treated like community property for purposes of dividing assets. However, the quasi-community property approach is *not* used at divorce where California has only minimal contacts with the marriage; in that case, the law of domicile before separation is applied instead ...... [458]
      b. **Treatment of quasi-community property at dissolution by death:** At death, the quasi-community theory applies to decedent's separate property *except for out-of-state land*. The law of the situs governs the rights of H and W in such land .... [460]
         (1) **No mandatory election:** The survivor may claim half of the quasi-community property *without* forfeiting will bequests—unless the will specifies to the contrary .... [462]

VII. **CONSTITUTIONAL LAW ISSUES**

A. **SCOPE OF "SEPARATE PROPERTY" UNDER CALIFORNIA CONSTITUTION**
   The constitutional definition of separate property precludes a legislative narrowing of the present statutory definition of such property, but does *not* restrict *transmutations* by the spouses .... [464]

B. **EQUAL PROTECTION STANDARDS UNDER CALIFORNIA CONSTITUTION**
   Under the California Equal Protection Clause, sex discrimination is subject to a strict scrutiny test. Retention of the pro-female presumptions in Family Code section 803 may therefore be unconstitutional .... [467]

C. **DUE PROCESS ISSUES UNDER CALIFORNIA CONSTITUTION— RETROACTIVITY OF CHANGES IN COMMUNITY PROPERTY LAW**
   1. **Old Rule:** Legislative changes in community property laws could not apply to preenactment acquisitions, nor to post-enactment rents and profits therefrom or assets traced to preenactment acquisitions .... [469]

		Text Section
2.	**Rejection of Old Rule:** Legislative changes are now applied to preenactment property if such changes do not have the effect of taking a ***property right*** of a spouse (*e.g.,* equal management reform is retroactive)	[471]
a.	**"Taking" property at divorce:** Legislation changing spouses' property rights may be applied at divorce to preenactment acquisitions even if there is a "taking," where California has an interest in eliminating "rankly unjust" prior law	[473]
b.	**"Taking" property at death:** Legislation changing intestate succession laws and altering an owner's testamentary power can apply to preenactment acquisitions. However, legislation giving a spouse testamentary power over an interest not owned by him or her may not be retroactive	[476]
c.	**"Taking" during marriage:** The "modern" rule permitting a taking of property with due process has not been applied prior to dissolution (*i.e.,* during marriage). However, altering management and control over preenactment property and broadening creditors' rights to such property are not "takings" of property	[477]
d.	**Limit on police power:** Even at divorce, a statute is unconstitutional if its true effect is to void valid contracts or create a previously nonexistent debt owed by one spouse to the other rather than to provide for division of property	[478]

D. FEDERAL PREEMPTION UNDER UNITED STATES CONSTITUTION (SUPREMACY CLAUSE)

1.	**Test for Preemption:** State law will govern unless Congress has spoken with ***"force and clarity"*** to declare that a different rule should apply. Absent such congressional expression, preemption is found only if state law will substantially impair a significant federal interest	[482]
2.	**Examples of Federal Preemption**	
a.	**Armed services insurance:** State law is preempted to the extent that the policy and proceeds of armed services insurance purchased with community funds are ***separate property***. However, California holds that the preemption merely allows an insured to give away the proceeds (which are community)	[483]
b.	**Federal land grants:** These must be classified as separate or community as directed by federal statute. The inception of title approach, rather than a pro rata showing of title when ownership is acquired over a period of time, is often federally mandated	[486]
c.	**Federal retirement plans**	
(1)	**Social Security and Railroad Retirement benefits:** Social Security benefits and benefits under the federal Railroad Retirement Act (insofar as such benefits parallel Social Security benefits) are the ***separate property*** of the worker upon divorce	[487]
(2)	**Military retirement pay:** The U.S. Supreme Court held future military retirement pay had to be treated at divorce as separate property (*McCarty* case). However, Congress abrogated much of *McCarty* in enacting legislation that permits states to treat retirement pay as ***community property*** where the spouse is domiciled in the state (rather than living there merely because of military assignment). If the spouse is not domiciled within the state, *McCarty* governs, and the retirement pay is separate property	[491]
d.	**Federal bonds:** Bonds purchased with community funds are treated as the separate property of the spouse taking title, except to the extent that this would deprive the other spouse of property interests	[497]
e.	**E.R.I.S.A. pensions:** Marital property interests in private pensions generally are governed by state law, federal law (E.R.I.S.A.) notwithstanding	[501]

(1) **Management by laborer spouse:** One court has stated that E.R.I.S.A. preempts state law that allows a divorce court to enjoin ex-H from electing a pension payment that might be unfavorable to ex-W .... [502]
(2) **Terminable interest doctrine:** Despite Family Code section 2610, E.R.I.S.A.-governed pensions retain both aspects of the terminable interest doctrine. First, when the nonlaboring spouse (or ex-spouse following a divorce) dies, he or she cannot bequeath a community half interest in *future* pension benefits earned by the surviving spouse. Second, even though a pension plan participant earned the pension by his labors during marriage to his first spouse whom he divorced, there is no community interest in a widow's pension payable to his second spouse .... [503]
    (a) **Offsetting award barred:** The Supreme Court has held that state courts *cannot* correct the unfairness to a spouse caused by federal tampering with principles of equality by an offsetting award, *e.g.,* giving W testamentary power over whole assets of community property because of her loss of testamentary power over what would have been her half of future pension benefits under state law .... [504]
f. **Federal causes of action:** Federal, rather than state, law on putative spouses governs the right to bring certain federally created causes of action .... [505]
g. **Debtor's exemptions:** State law exemptions are preempted where a spouse owes federal taxes .... [506]
h. **Indian law:** Many federal laws prevent states from interfering with self-government of Native American tribes. Thus, a divorce court may be barred from distributing tribal lands by treating them as community property .... [507]

approach to exams

Most community property exam questions involve two issues:

(i) Classifying items of property as separate or community; and

(ii) Identifying a particular characteristic of the property—*e.g.*, who has management and control, for what debts is it liable, or how may it be distributed at divorce.

To analyze community property questions, ask yourself the following. (And while studying for your exam, be sure to review the chapter approach sections at the beginning of each chapter.)

1. ***Classification*** of the property may depend on one or more of a number of factors. The following issues should always be considered in this area:

    a. ***Was there a valid marriage?*** If not, was there a putative marriage? A ***"Marvin"*** relationship? Once the particular relationship is identified, the type of property created under it can be considered (*e.g.*, "quasi-marital" property at annulment of a putative marriage).

    b. ***Are there conflict of laws problems?*** If so, the doctrine of quasi-community property may apply. And remember that in a federal-state conflict, property may be deemed "separate" notwithstanding the fact that California would consider it community.

    c. ***When was the asset acquired?*** If acquired before marriage or after a separation, the property is probably separate. In answering this question, be sure to ***trace*** the asset through changes in form as far back as possible and consider any applicable presumptions, particularly when facts are hazy or appear to be in conflict.

    d. ***Was the asset acquired by gift, bequest, devise, or descent?*** If so, it is probably separate unless closer examination shows the acquisition was "onerous" (*e.g.*, the result of labor).

    e. ***Consider apportionment problems*** if the asset is traceable partly to separate assets (including separate labor) and partly to community assets (and/or labor). Be prepared to identify the apportionment ***remedy*** when mixed sources are involved: Pro rata vs. inception of title in mixed consideration cases; *Pereira* or *Van Camp* formulas where labor and capital of different classifications produce profits; reimbursement where post-acquisition expenditures result in an "improvement" rather than a "buy in."

    f. ***Is the classification process altered in any agreement of the parties***, including a pre-1985 oral implied transaction? Is the agreement valid? If the agreement is valid between H and W, does it bind third parties (such as creditors)?

    g. ***If the property would ordinarily be community***, is it nonetheless separate because it is a type of interest incapable of community ownership or because of a statute applied at divorce that treats property as community even though it was not community during the marriage?

2. Problems concerning ***management*** may be approached in the following manner:

Community Property—(i)

a. ***What is the normal rule of management for the type of property at issue*** (equal management for most community personalty, dual for transfers of community realty, etc.)?

b. ***Does the type of property involved fall under an exception***, such as primary management for single-spouse community business, and single-spouse management for interests in pension plans, and for community funds in a bank account in one spouse's name?

c. ***Does the nature of the transaction trigger a special rule of management***—e.g., a gift or sale of household items?

3. Regarding ***creditor's rights***, the general rule is that all community property and the ***debtor's*** separate property are liable for the debt. After considering the general rule, consider if any of the exceptions apply. Among such exceptions consider:

   a. Separate property of the nondebtor spouse is liable for ***"necessaries of life"*** while the spouses are cohabiting (or for "common necessaries" if the spouses are living apart);

   b. A spouse's segregated community ***earnings*** are not liable for pre-marriage debts of the other spouse;

   c. The "pecking order" of liability when the creditor is a ***tort victim*** of Husband or Wife; and

   d. The preemption of state law immunities where the ***federal government*** is the creditor.

4. ***Dissolution problems*** may be different at death and at divorce:

   a. ***Item theory*** (and possible spouse's election) applies only at death, whereas certain separate property tort recoveries and assets having a shared community-separate ownership during marriage are treated as community property at divorce.

   b. ***Debts*** take on community and separate status at divorce under a statute that has fixed rules, based on the time of contracting, that do not use the community or separate benefit test. Certain debts, such as costs of probate administration, are at death prorated and treated as part separate, part community.

INTRODUCTION

Community property involves co-ownership of property by a husband (H) and wife (W) in a form somewhat similar to a partnership. Under the English common law approach to marital property, H is the sole owner of his earnings during marriage—although for some purposes (such as purchasing family necessaries) W may be his agent capable of obligating H's earnings by her contracts. Under this traditional approach, the court at divorce may order H to pay over a fair part of accumulated earnings to W, and at H's death, W may be entitled to a "forced heir's" share (often one-third) of such earnings. During marriage, however, W does not share ownership of such property; and if she dies before H, she cannot bequeath any of it.

In a community property state, on the other hand, W is co-owner by law of one-half of H's earnings accrued during marriage and cohabitation, just as H owns one-half of W's earnings. In eight of the nine community property states (including California), W has "equal management" power over H's community earnings in *most* (but not all) situations (as does H over W's earnings). Usually, if H's earnings are subject to equal management, they can be reached by W's creditors. In California, upon judicial dissolution of the marriage (divorce), H and W each becomes owner of one-half the community property in value. When a married person dies, he or she can bequeath a one-half interest in the community property. Thus, the community property system goes much further than the common law system in treating the spouses as marital *partners*.

This Summary is based on the community property law of California. The laws of other community property states differ in varying degrees from the law in California. In decreasing order of similarity to California, these states are Nevada, Idaho, New Mexico, Arizona, Washington, Louisiana, Wisconsin, and Texas. At certain points, the Summary mentions rules of law developed in these other states which—although inconsistent with *present* California case law—would work well in the California system and should commend themselves to California courts in the future.

A note on terminology: Statutes such as the California Family Law Act of 1970 have sought to substitute the word "dissolution" for "divorce" in the family law vocabulary. [*See, e.g.,* Cal. Fam. Code §310] Unfortunately, the word "dissolution" has long been a generic term that encompasses a dissolving of the husband-wife community by divorce *or* by death of a spouse. To avoid using the cumbersome term "judicial dissolution" to refer to divorce—in order to distinguish it from dissolution in the broad sense—this Summary continues to use "divorce" as a short term for "judicial dissolution." "Dissolution" continues to mean a dissolving of the community by either judicial dissolution (divorce) or death. Similarly, the traditional term "annulment" is used in the Summary in place of the cumbersome statutory term "judgment of nullity of marriage." [*See* Cal. Fam. Code §2250]

I. CLASSIFYING PROPERTY AS COMMUNITY OR SEPARATE

chapter approach

Probably 90% of all law school and bar examination questions on community property involve the classification problems found in this chapter. To answer such questions you should use the following approach:

1. The first thing you will usually need to do to answer a classification question is to identify the applicable ***presumptions***. (This must be done before you try to apply the facts to the specific rules of classification.) Especially consider the general ***pro-community presumption***, but don't overlook special presumptions regarding transfers to W before 1975 and concerning joint tenancy recitals in deeds (as to which the presumptions are different during marriage and at divorce).

2. If you find the pro-community presumption is applicable to the facts in your question, consider whether it may be ***overcome*** by proof of separate ownership. You should look for separate ownership by applying the facts (*e.g.,* the property was acquired by gift) to the basic rules of classification (*e.g.,* a gift is separate property). But remember to consider the exceptions to these basic classification rules (such as a gift traceable to labor can be community property).

3. Note that the classification rules can be ***altered by agreement*** between the spouses, and be aware of the ***special exceptions*** to the normal classification rules (*e.g.,* exception regarding educational degrees and licenses to practice, for "earned expectancies" (*e.g.,* tips), and unusual treatment of portions of tort recoveries that ought to be, but are not, separate property under basic tracing principles).

To organize your analysis of the above issues, formulate a master list of the various sources of a community classification vis-a-vis a separate classification (such as tracing the alleged community property to the separate labor of a separated spouse or to an inheritance, etc.). In this way, you can determine the actual status of various items of property. Keep in mind that often a problem creates a situation where an asset is partly separate and partly community due to tracing to multiple sources or applying various apportionment formulas.

After organizing the sources of classification, look at the facts of your question. For each event in the question, consider the legal issues triggered by that event. For example, if the parties separate for a period of time, this may mean different rules may apply to a tort recovery, or the normal approach to apportionment situations may be reversed by the separation, etc.

Finally, in constructing your answer, be creative; for example, consider treating various privileges of one spouse that aren't usually thought of as community property as possibly being capable of community ownership, or look for pre-1985 implied transmutations. But always keep in mind the overriding policies of community property law: the equal sharing of gains by husband and wife, while continuing to recognize separate ownership.

(*And note:* The materials on federal preemption in chapter VII often must be worked into the classification process.)

gilbert LAW SUMMARIES
CHARACTERIZATION OF PROPERTY AS SEPARATE OR COMMUNITY

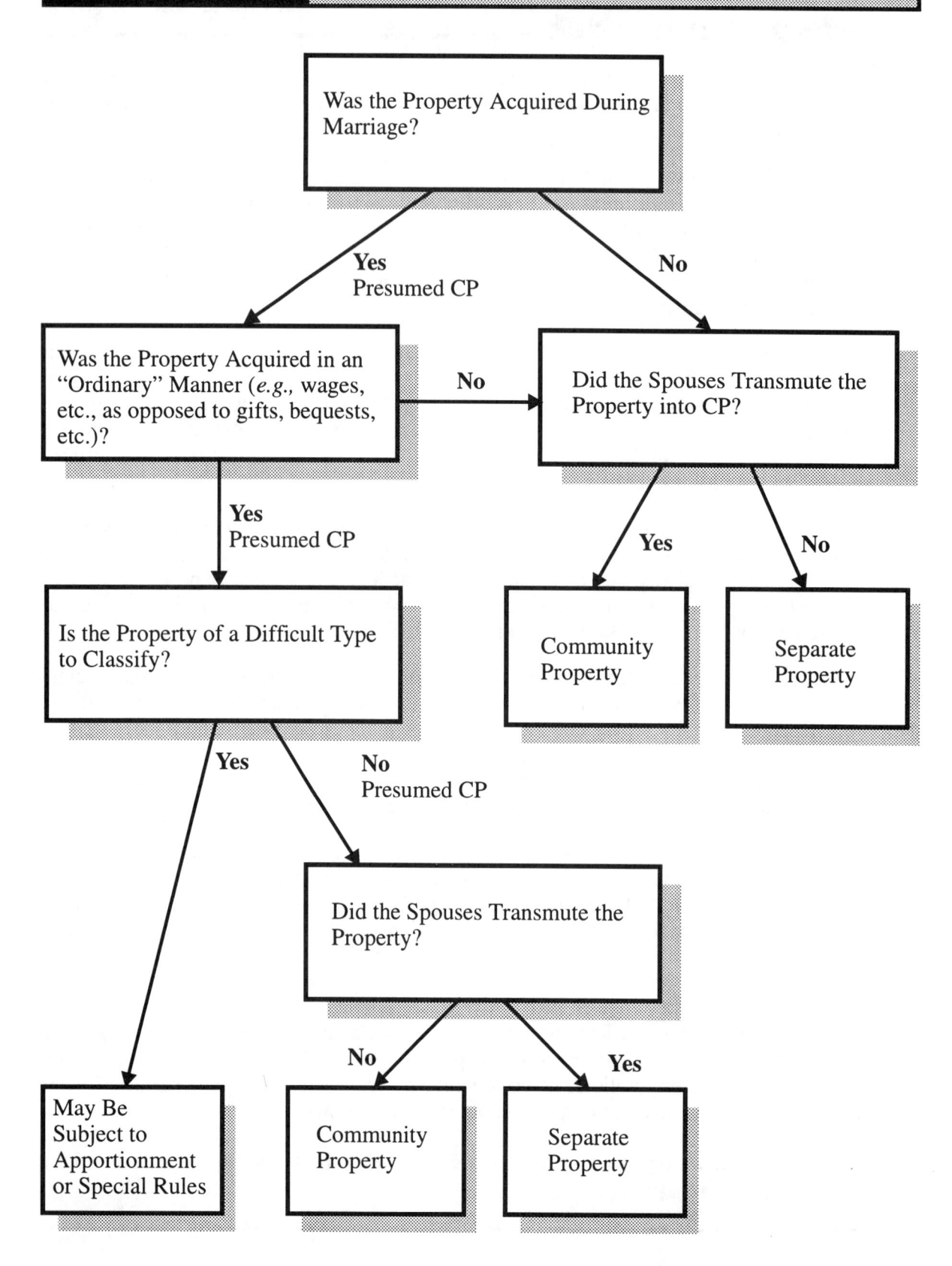

Was the Property Acquired During Marriage?

— **Yes** / Presumed CP →

Was the Property Acquired in an "Ordinary" Manner (*e.g.,* wages, etc., as opposed to gifts, bequests, etc.)?

— **Yes** / Presumed CP →

Is the Property of a Difficult Type to Classify?

- **Yes** → May Be Subject to Apportionment or Special Rules
- **No** / Presumed CP → **Did the Spouses Transmute the Property?**
  - **No** → Community Property
  - **Yes** → Separate Property

— **No** (from "Ordinary Manner") → **Did the Spouses Transmute the Property into CP?**

— **No** (from "Acquired During Marriage") → **Did the Spouses Transmute the Property into CP?**
- **Yes** → Community Property
- **No** → Separate Property

4—Community Property

A. BASIC STATUTORY FRAMEWORK

1. **Statutory Definition of Community Property:** [§1] The California Family Code states that except as provided in statutes defining separate property, "all property, real and personal, wherever situated, acquired by a married person during the marriage while domiciled in this state is community property." [Cal. Fam. Code §760]

2. **Statutory Definition of Separate Property:** [§2] The principal definitions of separate property are found in California Family Code sections 770 and 771. "Separate property" is defined as "[a]ll property owned by the [married person] before marriage," and that "acquired afterwards by gift, bequest, devise or descent." The *"rents, issues, and profits* of the [separate] property" are likewise separate. [Cal. Fam. Code §770] (*See infra,* §§33, 40-42 regarding "bequest" and treatment of gifts to H and W jointly.) Furthermore, "[t]he earnings and accumulations of a spouse and the minor children living with, or in the custody of, the spouse, while living separate and apart from the other spouse, are the separate property of the spouse." [Cal. Fam. Code §771]

B. PRESUMPTIONS RESPECTING OWNERSHIP [§3]

The first step in classifying property as separate or community is to decide whether any *presumptions* respecting ownership apply. Most such presumptions are rebuttable, but in many cases they may determine the outcome of the case. For example, when no one can offer evidence as to whether disputed items are separate or community (*e.g.,* probate proceedings after H and W are dead), or when rules of law applicable to the facts in question are uncertain, the presumption may control.

1. **Types of Presumptions:** [§4] There is a broad "general presumption" in favor of community ownership, and this presumption applies in most cases. In addition, two special statutory presumptions apply in narrower fact situations: (i) a presumption of separate ownership by W in certain pre-1975 transactions (*see infra,* §§22-31); and (ii) a presumption against joint tenancy and tenancy in common at the time of divorce (*see infra,* §§190, 193).

    a. **Note:** These three presumptions directly concerning ownership should be distinguished from various judicial presumptions on subsidiary issues, such as family expenses (*see infra,* §55).

2. **Requirements for General Pro-Community Presumption:** [§5] The proof that must be presented by the party seeking a "community" classification of disputed property in order to rely on the general presumption of community ownership is unclear. California Family Code section 760 defines community property, and some cases have tried to link the presumption to that section. However, the presumption seems to be *not* prescribed by any statute and is actually a judicial creation. [Marriage of Lusk, 86 Cal. App. 3d 228 (1978)] Three tests that have been used are:

    a. **Acquisition during marriage as a prerequisite—"during marriage" test:** [§6] Even after *Marriage of Lusk,* a majority of decisions declare that the general presumption of community ownership does not arise until proof has been received that the asset in question was "acquired during the marriage." However, that phrase in section 760 is merely part of the *definition* of community property and need not be read as a prerequisite for the general pro-community presumption. To the contrary, the general presumption could well operate ***to presume that the asset was acquired during the marriage***, as a minority of cases do.

    (1) **During marriage test primarily dicta:** [§7] The notion that a pro-community presumption arises only after proof that the asset at issue was acquired during marriage has generally been stated as dictum. Only one case has actually denied a community classification because of failure to prove acquisition during marriage. [Fidelity & Casualty Co. v. Mahoney, 71 Cal. App. 2d 65 (1945)—no evidence whether the dollar H had in his pocket two months after marriage came from pre- or post-marriage paycheck]

    (2) **Change in form may meet "during marriage" test:** [§8] Note that even under the "during marriage" test, a change in the *form* of the asset supplies a new acquisition date that should raise the pro-community presumption. [Bone v. Dwyer, 74 Cal. App. 363 (1925)]

        (a) **Example:** W marries H in 1989. In 1993, W is known to possess an emerald ring, but there is no evidence as to when she first acquired it. In 1997, W trades the ring for an oil painting at an antique fair. In 1999, the marriage is dissolved, and the oil painting must be classified as separate or community property. Since the painting was acquired in 1997, it is presumptively a community asset even though the ring would not have passed the "during marriage" test.

        (b) **Authority contra:** *Fidelity & Casualty Co. v. Mahoney, supra,* is contra on this issue, where money had been spent during marriage to buy life insurance for an airplane flight and the insurance proceeds were at issue. The court did not see that the change in form of the asset (from cash to an insurance contract) resulted in a "during marriage" acquisition date.

  b. **"Possession" test:** [§9] Where there is no proof as to the time of acquisition of an asset, a few cases have held that proof that either spouse ***possessed*** the asset during marriage will give rise to the general pro-community presumption. [Lynam v. Worwerk, 13 Cal. App. 507 (1910)]

  c. **"Possession plus long marriage" test:** [§10] Finally, another case has held that the general presumption can apply (despite failure to show acquisition during marriage) if the evidence shows possession of the property by either spouse at the end of a long marriage. [Estate of Caswell, 105 Cal. App. 475 (1930)]

3. **Possible "Unlimited" Presumption:** [§11] Some community property states use a pro-community presumption of ownership that arises when one party asserts that an asset is community property. Unlike most California case law, this presumption attaches without any preliminary proof. [*See, e.g.,* Krattiger v. Krattiger, 463 P.2d 35 (N.M. 1969)] Note, however, that *Marriage of Lusk* (*supra,* §5) would support such an approach, since it uncouples the presumption from the wording of Family Code section 760. Moreover, one older California case, while reciting the "during

marriage" test, effectively applied the unlimited presumption by holding that the burden rests on the person asserting that property is separate to prove that fact. [Wilson v. Wilson, 76 Cal. App. 2d 119 (1946)]

    a. **Exam tactic:** If the facts of a question show acquisition during marriage, you should state that this raises the pro-community presumption. If the facts do not show the time of acquisition, note that the "during marriage" test is most often said to be the law, but there are a few cases that use the possession during marriage test or even the unlimited presumption.

4. **Acquisition While Living Separate and Apart:** [§12] If the facts show acquisition by H or W after separation but before divorce, an asset could be either separate property under Family Code section 771 (*supra,* §2) or community because pre-separation community funds were used as consideration. There is no definitive holding, but cases imply that where the source of consideration is unknown, the pro-community presumption still applies even though the spouses were separated. A contrary holding based on the likelihood that section 771 applies would be just as logical.

    a. **Effect of "tracing back":** [§13] If the unlimited general presumption is adopted, it should apply in cases of an acquisition after separation but before divorce upon an allegation that the post-separation acquisition was purchased with pre-separation property. Alternatively, proof that the property allegedly given in exchange was acquired during marriage would meet the "during marriage" test for the presumption, while proof that it was possessed in that period would meet the "possession" test. Then the pro-community presumption would carry over to the post-separation acquisition upon *proof* of the exchange that traces it back to the (presumptively) community asset.

5. **Acquisition After Dissolution:** [§14] On occasion, a court must determine whether an asset acquired after dissolution of the community has a source in former community property. The mere allegation of such a source should not raise any presumption in this situation. Thus, to obtain the benefit of the pro-community presumption, a party must *show* that the consideration for the post-dissolution acquisition was itself acquired during marriage, possessed during marriage, or possessed at the end of a long marriage. [Estate of Adams, 132 Cal. App. 2d 190 (1955)]

6. **Effect of Contrary Evidence on General Presumption:** [§15] In California, a presumption is not evidence that the trier of fact can weigh against actual proof suggesting a contrary fact. [*See* Cal. Evid. Code §600] Thus, if *all* the evidence received is contrary to the presumption of community ownership, a directed verdict that the asset is separate property must be returned.

    a. **Allocating ultimate burden of proof:** [§16] The general pro-community presumption is based on public policy, and therefore where there is evidence both in support of community ownership and to the contrary, the ultimate burden of proof is on the party claiming separate ownership. [Cal. Evid. Code §605] That party must establish separate ownership by the preponderance of the evidence even if the other party generally bears the burden of proof (*e.g.,* because he is the plaintiff).

(1) **Standard:** [§17] The California Supreme Court has unequivocally held that the burden of proving separate ownership can be met by a mere preponderance of the evidence. [Freese v. Hibernia Savings & Loan Society, 139 Cal. 392 (1903)] Nevertheless, some court of appeals cases incorrectly say that only clear and convincing evidence will meet the burden of proof. [*See, e.g.,* Nevins v. Nevins, 129 Cal. App. 2d 150 (1954)]

b. **Result where general presumption does not arise:** [§18] If no general presumption arises (as where one of the more restrictive preliminary "tests" is applied and not met), the burden of proof would be governed by the normal rules of evidence.

(1) **Example:** During marriage, W gives Sister a necklace. After W dies, H sues Sister to recover half the value of the necklace on the ground that the necklace was community property and he did not consent to the gift. (*See infra,* §248, on unilateral gifts of community assets.) The court applies the "during marriage" test, and there is no evidence as to when W acquired the necklace. Hence, H does not benefit from the pro-community presumption, and he will probably lose the suit because he is unable to meet his burden of proof as plaintiff to establish the elements of his cause of action.

7. **Exception to Pro-Community Presumption:** [§19] California Family Code section 802 provides that where a person dies more than four years after divorce, "the presumption that property acquired during marriage is community property" (of the former marriage) *does not* apply to the assets in the person's estate.

a. **Application:** [§20] Section 802 applies only to property to which the decedent had "title" at death. Thus, it is directed at the surviving ex-spouse who claims against decedent's estate, that an asset not divided at divorce was former community property still half owned by the surviving ex-spouse. Section 802 in effect presumes the property was during marriage separate property of the decedent.

b. **Proper interpretation of statute:** [§21] Although section 802 refers only to the "during marriage" test for the pro-community presumption, the legislature probably intended no such restrictive interpretation. Accordingly, section 802 should be broadly construed so that the four-year rule applies to *any* form of pro-community presumption invoked against decedent's estate.

C. SPECIAL PRESUMPTIONS

1. **Transfers to Married Women:** [§22] In addition to the general pro-community presumption, there is a *special* presumption favoring separate-property classification for transfers to married women in writing *prior to 1975*. [Cal. Fam. Code §803]

a. **Historical background:** [§23] Under early California law, a married woman had no ownership rights in so-called community property. In 1889, the California legislature sought to alleviate this unfairness and bolster a wife's claim to separate ownership by abolishing—as to her—the rule that in a community property system, record "title" does not affect ownership. Under this statute, "title" in a wife's name raised a presumption of separate ownership by her.

b. **Operation of special presumption when wife is the only transferee:** [§24] Under section 803, the pre-1975 "instrument in writing" required for the pro-wife presumption will name the title holder. If W is the named transferee without qualification, there is a presumption that the asset is her separate property.

   (1) **Compare:** If Grantor deeds Blackacre "to Mary Jones to be held as community property," the special presumption does not arise.

c. **Presumption when wife is not the only transferee:** [§25] If the pre-1975 written instrument names W and one or more other transferees as owners, section 803 presumes that W's interest in the cotenancy is her separate property.

   (1) **Transfer to both spouses:** [§26] Where H is named as transferee along with W, and the instrument *describes them as husband and wife* but does not specify the form of co-ownership, the asset is presumed to be community property under section 803. But if the two are *not* so described, the pro-wife presumption attaches to W's interest and the general pro-community presumption attaches to the interest to which H has "title." [Dunn v. Mullan, 211 Cal. 583 (1931)]

      (a) **Examples:** If a deed conveys Blackacre to "John Jones and Louise Jones," or to "John and/or Louise Jones," without disclosing that John and Louise are married, W is presumptively a three-fourths owner of Blackacre (half as her separate property and one-fourth as a member of the community) while H is presumptively one-fourth owner. However, a conveyance to "Mr. and Mrs. John Jones" does describe the transferees as husband and wife, and each would be a one-half owner of the property. [Cardew v. Cardew, 192 Cal. App. 2d 502 (1961)]

d. **Exception to "pro-wife" special presumption—where wife has commingled property:** [§27] Between 1951 and 1975, W had management over her own community earnings provided she did not allow them to be commingled with property managed by H. Moreover, if before 1975 W commingled her community earnings with her *own* separate property in a bank account with a passbook or deposit card naming W alone as owner, the pro-wife special presumption would mean—if uncommingling were impossible—that the entire account was W's separate property. To avoid this result, an exception to the special presumption is recognized in this and any other situation where the presumption in concert with W's management power could be used to convert community assets into W's separate property. In such cases, the *general pro-community presumption* will apply. [Marriage of Mix, 14 Cal. 3d 604 (1975)]

   (1) **Note—case contra:** In one case, W took her pre-1975 earnings and invested them in land, taking title in her name alone. The court held that notwithstanding the fact that it was known that the source of the acquisition was W's *community earnings*, the special presumption of separate ownership by W still applied. [Marriage of Ashodian, 96 Cal. App. 3d 43 (1979)] This decision required presuming an agreement by H to convert the community funds into W's separate property (*see infra*, §171). The holding is probably overturned by the 1985 Statute of Frauds for transmutations (*see infra*, §174).

e. **Overcoming pro-wife special presumption:** [§28] Except for one situation (discussed below), the special presumption for a wife's pre-1975 acquisitions is *rebuttable.* Notwithstanding *Ashodian, supra,* proof that community funds (or other community assets) were used to pay for the acquisition should dispel the presumption (although if H put the "title" in W's name, an inference of gift might arise; *see infra,* §182). [Wells v. Allen, 38 Cal. App. 586 (1918)]

(1) **Limitation:** [§29] When the pro-wife presumption arises but evidence of community ownership is received, the special presumption converts to a rule placing the burden of proof on the party seeking a community characterization (even if that party is the defendant).

(2) **Presumption conclusive as to purchaser from a married woman:** [§30] The pro-wife presumption for pre-1975 acquisitions is conclusive in favor of a purchaser or encumbrancer—one who pays W reasonable value for the asset (or a lien on it)—unaware that it is not W's separate property. This rule is designed to prevent H or those claiming under him from upsetting transactions by W alone under her pre-1975 "title" even if she did not have power of disposition (*e.g.,* because it was community realty, pre-1975 H-managed community personalty, or H's separate property despite the form of "title").

(3) **Constitutionality of pro-wife presumption:** [§31] Since bona fide purchasers are protected by the conclusive presumption, there may be constitutional objections to continuing the pro-female rebuttable presumption in *any* situation. Such gender discrimination is judged by a "strict scrutiny" test under the state constitution. [Sail'er Inn v. Kirby, 5 Cal. 3d 1 (1971)] For example, suppose W acquires property in her own name in a pre-1975 instrument but never deals with it (*i.e.,* merely holds it). Since W in this situation has taken no action in reliance on the presumption, there seems to be no reason why it should apply in post-1974 litigation between the spouses.

2. **Special Presumption Against Joint Tenancy and Tenancy in Common at Divorce:** *See infra,* §§190, 193.

D. **OVERCOMING PRO-COMMUNITY PRESUMPTION BY PROOF OF SEPARATE OWNERSHIP** [§32]

The general presumption in favor of community ownership is rebutted by evidence showing separate ownership. The following discussion on overcoming the general presumption assumes that a pro-community presumption has arisen—either because an "unlimited" presumption is applied after a community status was alleged, or because one of the restricted versions of the presumption is adopted and the party seeking a community classification has *proven* acquisition or possession during marriage.

1. **Proof of Acquisition by Inheritance, Devise, or Bequest:** [§33] Under California Family Code section 770, property received by one spouse alone at any time by will or intestate succession is separate property. In certain cases, however, such acquisitions received during marriage may be shown to be "onerous" (*i.e.,* acquired by labor or other community consideration) or traceable to a community consideration. If so, the property would be a community asset (or tenancy in common if received after divorce and not divided in the divorce decree; *see infra,* §345).

a. **Example:** During marriage, W contracts to supply nursing care for her father ("F") if he will bequeath her his entire estate. Her acquisition under F's will is community property except to the extent of services rendered after dissolution of marriage or while living separate and apart from H. This is so even if W would have been her father's sole intestate heir, since he contracted away the power to disinherit her. [Frymire v. Brown, 94 Cal. App. 2d 334 (1949)]

b. **Bequest to both spouses:** [§34]   A devise or bequest to H and W as co-owners should presumptively create a community interest if H and W receive the property during marriage; and the burden of proof should rest with the party alleging that the testator intended H and W to hold the property as tenants in common or joint tenants. However, there are no California cases on point.

c. **Effect of tracing:** [§35]   Even if the item at issue was acquired with cash or other property during marriage, it will be separate property if the consideration given can be traced back to a bequest, inheritance, or other source of separate property. (*See* discussion of tracing, *infra,* §50.)

   (1) **Example:** H's son died with a will leaving all of his property to X. H was the son's sole intestate heir. H filed a will contest that was settled by X agreeing to convey certain interests in oil wells to H. Although H "bought" the oil rights during marriage through the settlement agreement, the consideration was his abandonment of any rights he may have had as his son's heir (*i.e.,* H inherited the right to contest the will). Hence, the oil rights were H's separate property. [Estate of Clark, 94 Cal. App. 453 (1928)]

2. **Proof of Acquisition by Gift to One Spouse Alone:** [§36]   If the property was acquired during marriage and before separation, a donative intent by the transferor will have to be proved to establish separate title on a theory of gift.

   a. **Example:** X owned a valuable watch that he lost in a public park. During marriage, H finds the watch and reports the discovery to the police, who in turn advise X. Out of pure laziness, X never contacts H to recover his property, and the time for X to claim the watch expires. In this situation there is no donative intent on X's part, and the watch is therefore community property.

   b. **Partial donative intent:** [§37]   Suppose H's uncle owes H $1,000 on a loan by H of community funds. If the uncle repays H $2,000 in gratitude for making the loan, there is some donative intent (*i.e.,* to the extent of the excess over principal and interest owed)—and this sum should be considered H's separate property.

   c. **Remunerative gifts:** [§38]   Where a donor makes a gift to one spouse in the sense that he has no enforceable obligation to part with title, yet his motive is to show appreciation for services rendered, the asset is community property on the theory it is really the fruit of a spouse's labor. Thus, where H was a key employee at a company that had no retirement plan and the company gave H for no consideration an interest worth $400,000 in realty, the remunerative gift doctrine was applied; the acquisition was community. [Downer v. Bramet, 152

Cal. App. 3d 837 (1984)] (*See also infra*, §210, concerning tips acquired by a waiter, porter, etc.)

- d. **Where donative intent is unclear:** [§39] Where there is substantial doubt as to donative intent because the "donor's" motive seems to be advancement of his own interests, the general pro-community presumption should still apply.

    (1) **Example:** Where W is "given" a kitchen appliance in return for answering an easy question in a radio "telephone quiz" show, the pro-community presumption is not rebutted.

3. **Acquisition by Gift to Both Spouses as Co-Equal Donees:** [§40] If a donor makes a gift to both spouses (in equal shares) during marriage, and there is no proof that the donor intended them to hold as tenants in common or joint tenants, California will characterize the acquisition as community property. [Marriage of Gonzales, 116 Cal. App. 3d 556 (1981)—where W's father purchased house and put title in names of both H and W, held to be a gift to the community]

    a. **Wedding gifts:** [§41] Gift cards traditionally name W as the recipient, but if the donor intends that H and W co-own the property (as when H's aunt gives family diamonds with a card naming W as donee), such intent controls.

        (1) **Impact of time of gift:** [§42] Suppose H's aunt—intending that H and W co-own the diamonds as community property—delivers them to W before the wedding that establishes the community. Ownership must be a tenancy in common because of the acquisition before marriage unless Aunt's delivery was conditional upon, and title would not pass until, the marriage.

4. **Proof of Acquisition While Spouses Are Living Apart:** [§43] California Family Code section 771 provides that "the earnings and accumulations of a spouse and the minor children living with, or in the custody of, the spouse, while living separate and apart from the other spouse, are the separate property of the spouse." Note, however, that pre-separation community earnings are not converted to separate property upon separation of the spouses, and that profits subsequently obtained from them would also be community assets under the tracing doctrine (*see infra*, §50).

    a. **Avoiding rule by tracing:** [§44] When one spouse receives an asset after separation, ownership of it can be community, notwithstanding section 771, if it can be traced to a pre-separation community source. *Example:* H performs labors in May, H and W separate in June, and H is paid for the labor in July. The money is community as traceable to community labor. However, layoff benefits or other unemployment insurance benefits received during separation will usually be separate property of the recipient spouse on the theory they are in lieu of wages that would have been paid during the period of separation and unemployment, even if community labor was necessary to qualify the spouse to receive the benefit. [Marriage of Flockhart, 119 Cal. App. 3d 240 (1981)]

    b. **Intent of spouses governs:** [§45] The intent of the spouses governs whether they are living apart under section 771. For example, the spouses may live physically apart for many years and not even see each other; but if they consider this separation temporary and their marriage still viable, section 771 would not apply and acquisitions during the separation may be community property. [Makeig v. United Security Bank & Trust Co., 112 Cal. App. 138 (1931)]

(1) **Permanent separation required:** [§46] Section 771 should not apply until at least one spouse regards a separation as permanent, since most couples regard a separation at the onset as temporary pending a possible reconciliation. [*See* Marriage of Baragry, 73 Cal. App. 3d 444 (1977)]

(2) **Unilateral intent sufficient:** [§47] Section 771 applies where one spouse believes the marriage is finally dead even though the other spouse believes the pair will reconcile. [Marriage of Hardin, 38 Cal. App. 4th 448 (1995)] This is the result because one spouse's view is sufficient to establish the irreconcilable differences upon which divorce can be granted.

c. **Apportionment of income during section 771 separation:** [§48] If section 771 is triggered and (prior to divorce) either H or W operates a business that uses community capital, an apportionment of income (*i.e.,* a return on separate labor and a return on community capital) is required. (*See infra,* §75.)

d. **Effect of reconciliation:** [§49] One case holds that a reconciliation—even after a divorce suit is litigated nearly to completion—means that the separation is not permanent and hence section 771 *never applied to the separated spouses*. [Marriage of Jaschke, 43 Cal. App. 4th 408 (1996)] This unsettling rule means that until a divorce is final, no third party can rely on H's or W's post-separation acquisition as being separate property no matter how defunct the marriage appears, because reconciliation is always possible. A better rule would provide that reconciliation is not proof per se that for some time period one spouse considered the marriage dead, thus triggering section 771. Under such an improved rule reconciliation could not change property that was separate under section 771 into community property.

5. **Establishing Separate Ownership by Tracing to Pre-Marriage Source:** [§50] As noted earlier, separate ownership of an asset acquired during marriage can be established by tracing back the consideration paid to a pre-marriage (or other separate) source. Such tracing through changes of form—*e.g.,* sale and reinvestment, trade, condemnation, accidental destruction and replacement with insurance proceeds—can begin with a known item of pre-marriage property and move forward in time, or begin with property on hand at dissolution or during marriage and trace backward in time. A change of form does not change ownership; and the profits generated (without labor) are treated as part of the capital that produced them.

a. **Example:** Before marriage, H owns shares of stock in Z Corp. After marriage, H sells the stock and uses the proceeds (plus retained dividends on the shares) to purchase Blackacre. The state subsequently condemns Blackacre and pays H $50,000 for the property, which H uses to purchase a valuable painting. The painting is stolen shortly thereafter, and H is paid $50,000 by the insurer. These insurance proceeds would be considered H's separate property by tracing back to the original source, the pre-marriage Z Corp. stock. (The character of the funds used to insure the painting should be irrelevant; *see infra,* §131.)

6. **Commingling and Uncommingling of Assets:** [§51] "Commingling" refers to the mixing together of fungible separate and community assets—usually money—without earmarking. Commingling itself does not change the character of separate property to community [Thomasset v. Thomasset, 122 Cal. App. 2d 116 (1953)], but the pro-community presumption usually makes the commingled mass presumptively community. The party seeking to establish separate property status has the burden of "uncommingling" the funds into separate and community shares.

   a. **Uncommingling where no withdrawals:** [§52] Uncommingling is often easy when no withdrawal has been made from the commingled mass. Where each known deposit is still present and can now be withdrawn, each can be given its initial classification (separate or community).

   b. **Test for other situations—"drawer's intent":** [§53] The current judicial test for uncommingling where withdrawals have been made is the "drawer's intent" test applied in *Marriage of Mix* (*see supra*, §27).

      (1) **Example:** Suppose W has deposited $5,000 of community property and $5,000 of her separate funds in a bank account. W later withdraws $2,000 from the account, making a contemporary entry that the withdrawn funds were community money. Under the "intent" test, $5,000 of W's separate funds will be held to remain in the account; and the pro-community presumption that initially attaches to all the money in the account (because acquired or possessed during marriage) is overcome.

      (2) **Self-serving testimony of drawer intent may suffice:** [§54] In *Mix, supra*, W testified at divorce that she intended all funds she withdrew from a commingled account (and subsequently invested in successful projects) to have been her separate property. The court found that such self-serving, after-the-fact testimony was nevertheless sufficient to establish the drawer's intent! However, where the separate funds, adequate to make the investments at issue, are spread among several bank accounts, mere evidence of intent to use separate funds will *not* suffice. It must be shown which bank account was drawn upon and that it contained at the time enough separate money to implement the alleged intent. [Marriage of Marsden, 130 Cal. App. 3d 426 (1982)]

   c. **"Family expense" doctrine:** [§55] Where there is no direct evidence of drawer intent in withdrawing funds from a commingled account, it will be presumed that *community funds* were withdrawn to pay for expenses of maintaining the household. [Huber v. Huber, 27 Cal. 2d 784 (1946)] This is known as the "family expense" doctrine.

      (1) **Flexible application of doctrine:** [§56] What constitutes a "family expense" depends on the relative wealth and customary standard of living of the family (*i.e.,* H, W, and any children supported by them). For wealthy families, the costs of a maid, gardener, country club dues, trips abroad, etc., are presumed to have been paid for by community funds. [Hicks v. Hicks, 211 Cal. App. 2d 144 (1962)]

      (2) **Total recapitulation barred:** [§57] Prior to *See v. See,* 64 Cal. 2d 778 (1966), when community funds in a commingled account were not sufficient to cover family expenses, courts simply treated a draw on separate

funds as a loan that would be automatically repaid at the time of the next community deposit. *See v. See,* however, held that in such cases the withdrawal of separate funds by the owner thereof constitutes a ***gift***. Under *See,* therefore, there is **no automatic repayment** from subsequent community deposits; and the spouse relying on the "family expense" accounting method of uncommingling must establish either that there were no such "gifts" or the amount to be deducted from total family expenses on account of such gifts. The spouse cannot just rely on total family expenses exceeding total community deposits as proof that there is no community money in the account; *i.e.,* there can be no "total recapitulation" accounting.

    (a) **Exception:** [§58] *See* does not apply—and automatic reimbursement is presumed—where the funds used to pay family expenses or other community debts are ***separate property under the "living apart" rule*** in California Family Code section 771 rather than separate as an inheritance, something owned before marriage, etc. [Marriage of Epstein, 24 Cal. 3d 76 (1979)]

(3) **Rationale behind *See v. See* is questionable:** [§59] In *See,* the commingled separate funds were H's, and at the time of the withdrawals H was exclusive manager of the community property. Since (generally speaking) only H at that time could spend and obligate the community funds, he was therefore responsible for dipping into separate monies to pay family expenses. Under post-1974 equal management, on the other hand, W can obligate community funds even in a bank account managed by H. Moreover, at the time *See* was decided, H's separate estate had a statutory duty to support W but not vice versa (except in unusual circumstances)—an obligation stressed by the court in explaining why H was not entitled to reimbursement. Today, however, California Family Code section 4301 places the co-equal duty of support on W; and the automatic reimbursement inherent in total recapitulation accounting—which causes H and W to split family expenses—is consistent with the philosophy of section 4301.

(4) **Present view of *See v. See*:** [§60] Despite the significant changes in law noted above, the state supreme court repeatedly reiterates the *See* no-reimbursement rule as being good law. [*See, e.g.,* Marriage of Buol, 39 Cal. 3d 751 (1985)] In none of the cases, however, was it urged that because of spending by the other spouse, the separate property owner seeking reimbursement was forced to dip into his or her separate funds to pay a community debt. Since the court in *Epstein, supra,* §58, realized donative intent was unlikely when the spouses were separated and one of them drew on separate funds to pay family expenses (*e.g.,* clothing for their children), it may also conclude donative intent is improbable in the situation described above, where one spouse's spending during cohabitation necessitates the use of the other's separate funds.

(5) **Criticism:** [§61] Even at the time *See* was decided, its reasoning appears to have been faulty. There was apparently non-liquid community property on hand when the bank account was temporarily out of community cash, and there was an expected flow of community income. Thus, H

undoubtedly could have borrowed money from a bank on community credit (the borrowed funds would have been community; *see infra,* §96) to pay family expenses while community funds were exhausted. Had H done this, the community would have had to pay interest to the bank. The total recapitulation theory, on the other hand, would have given the community an interest-free loan from H's separate estate.

    d. **Result where intent cannot be proved or inferred:** [§62] There may be situations in which drawer intent cannot be proved or presumed but it is obvious that separate property forms some part of the assets in dispute. For example, assume that H commingles $10,000 of separate property and $10,000 of community property. In four subsequent withdrawals of $5,000 each, H buys stock in four different companies, and H dies without indicating his intent in making the withdrawals. There are no California decisions squarely on point on this issue, but other courts have suggested various solutions:

      (1) *Treat each withdrawal as a pro rata portion of community and separate* [Duncan v. United States, 247 F.2d 845 (5th Cir. 1957)];

      (2) *Assume that the community property is drawn out first* [Welder v. Welder, 794 S.W.2d 420 (Tex. Civ. App. 1990), *no writ*];

      (3) *Assume that the most successful investments* were made with the $10,000 of *community funds* (the most logical way to give effect to the pro-community presumption);

      (4) *Hold on the basis of the pro-community presumption that all the investments are community property* (the result implied in a few California cases such as *Falk v. Falk,* 48 Cal. App. 2d 761 (1971)); or

      (5) *Give all the investments to the community* but *reimburse* H's separate estate for its $10,000 contribution (*see infra,* §§103-128).

7. **Rents or Profits from Separate Capital:** [§63] Rents and profits from separately owned capital, generated without applying community labor, are 100% separate property, due to tracing to the capital. But where labor of either spouse plays a part in generating the gain, it will be apportioned into separate and community components by one of two formulae:

    a. **The *Pereira* formula:** [§64] The approach developed in *Pereira v. Pereira,* 156 Cal. 1 (1909), takes the value of the separate capital and calculates an annual return on it at a particular interest rate over the period for which apportionment is sought. This gives the total separate return, with all remaining profits being community-owned—*i.e.,* the separate return is fixed and the community return "floats." Where profits are unusually large, the community benefits by use of the *Pereira* formula, but if profits are small, the entire gain may be classified as separate.

      (1) **Appropriate interest rate under *Pereira*:** [§65] The legal rate of interest is presumptively the correct rate under the *Pereira* formula, but a party may show that a higher or lower rate is appropriate in a particular case due to the nature of the capital. For example, a higher interest rate has been used when the separate-property claimant establishes such an

interest cost of borrowing money to replace the separate-property capital that he supplied to the business. [*See* Marriage of Folb, 53 Cal. App. 3d 862 (1975)—12% rate used where H developed raw land that was his separate property]

(2) **Compound interest allowed?** [§66] Gain determined by *Pereira* to be separate property is usually retained in the business several years before apportionment is made. Arguably, compound interest rather than simple interest should be calculated. *Marriage of Folb, supra,* stated that a court has discretion to do this in a proper case to do "substantial justice" for the separate estate, but as yet no reported decision has done so.

(3) **Result where profits vary over time:** [§67] Situations may arise in which the overall gain on separate capital is small over time (and might therefore be considered entirely separate property if viewed in the aggregate), yet there was a substantial gain in one particular year. One California case has held that a court should not look into "oscillations in growth or decline" of a business, but only at the overall value at the end of the marriage. [Marriage of Denney, 115 Cal. App. 3d 543 (1981)] However, Nevada has held that large gains in any *one year* would create some community interest, which if retained in the business would not be offset or eliminated by prior or subsequent years of small gain. [Cord v. Neuhoff, 573 P.2d 1170 (Nev. 1978)]

  (a) **Example:** In *Denney,* H's separate business had the same value at divorce as it had when H and W were married. W sought to prove that at one point during the marriage, the business had become worthless and that its value at divorce was due solely to community efforts in raising its value from zero. Contrary to the approach in Nevada, the court refused to look at this fluctuation in the value of the business during the period of the marriage.

  (b) **Compare—bankruptcy:** [§68] Bankruptcy will often terminate the status of a separate business. If the business is revived after bankruptcy, it will be 100% community property (unless it employs separate capital such as machinery that survived bankruptcy as exempt from creditor's claims). [Marriage of Winn, 98 Cal. App. 3d 363 (1979)]

(4) **Effect of distributions from business:** [§69] All sums withdrawn from a business by the managing spouse and earmarked as *salary* ought to be classified as community property, since the managing spouse has treated them as such (*see infra,* §172). If the *Pereira* formula would otherwise make all or part of such funds separate, their designation as "salary" would constitute a gift to the community. (The 1985 Statute of Frauds for transmutations (*see infra,* §174) does not apply to classifications made where community and separate interests have been "combined"—the situation in these apportionment cases. [Cal. Fam. Code §852(d)]) On the other hand, withdrawals earmarked as "profits"—or "dividends" in the case of an incorporated business—should be tested under the *Pereira* approach (or the competing *Van Camp* formula, below) to

determine if these apparent rents and profits from separate capital contain any community element.

- b. **The *Van Camp* formula:** [§70] The second approach to apportioning retained earnings, developed in *Van Camp v. Van Camp*, 53 Cal. App. 17 (1921), places a value—usually per year—on the community labor given to the business. The resulting "fair salary" figure is the community share of the gain, while all remaining earnings are separate property. Under the *Van Camp* formula, therefore, the community share is fixed and the separate share "floats," so that *Van Camp* is favorable to the community where the gain is small and favorable to the separate estate where the gain is large in comparison to the amount of capital and labor involved.

    (1) **Effect of "salary" payments or other withdrawals:** [§71] Under *Van Camp*, the amount of community gain from earnings remaining in the business is determined by deducting from the community share of gain (computed pursuant to the *Van Camp* formula) the total of all withdrawals earmarked "salary" and non-earmarked withdrawals used for family expenses. [Owens v. Owens, 219 Cal. App. 2d 856 (1963)]

    (a) **Note:** If the amount of withdrawals earmarked "salary" exceeds the reasonable return to the community calculated under *Van Camp*, the difference could still be classified as community because the laboring spouse has voluntarily labeled and treated the excess as a return for community labor. This will cause a transmutation from separate to community property (*see supra*, §69) of a larger separate property return than the laboring spouse might otherwise have had under *Van Camp*.

    (b) **And note:** Payment of *some* salary to the laboring spouse does not bar use of the *Van Camp* formula to *increase* the community return for labor. [Tassi v. Tassi, 260 Cal. App. 2d 680 (1972)] Neither does payment of a salary that is fair under *Van Camp* prevent the court from applying *Pereira* to obtain a community return greater than the salary. [Marriage of Dekker, 17 Cal. App. 4th 842 (1993)]

    (2) **Effect of retaining community earnings in business:** [§72] Where community earnings are retained in the business, they can be regarded as new additions to capital, so that in future years capital cannot be considered solely separate property. The "floating" share of total gain viewed as return on capital would have to be apportioned into community and separate shares. (Alternatively, fairness to the community might be attained by calculating simple, or even compound, interest on the retained earnings—although this would mix some *Pereira* logic into a *Van Camp* apportionment—and deducting this sum from the "floating" separate property share of total gain.) Such relief has not been sought in a reported California case.

- c. **"Compromise" formula for apportioning gains:** [§73] One tax case, *Todd v. McColgan*, 89 Cal. App. 2d 509 (1949), adopted an approach to apportionment midway between the *Pereira* and *Van Camp* formulae. Under *Todd*, the court first calculates a fair return under *Pereira* for the separate capital and a fair salary under *Van Camp* for the community labor. If "A" equals the *Pereira* return for the separate estate and "B" equals a fair return for the community under *Van Camp*, apportionment between the separate and community estates is then made as follows:

$$\left(\frac{A}{A+B}\right) \times \text{Total Gain} = \text{Share for Separate Estate}$$

$$\left(\frac{B}{A+B}\right) \times \text{Total Gain} = \text{Share for Community Estate}$$

d. **Which test should be applied?** [§74] For no apparent reason, the compromise formula in *Todd* seems out of favor with the courts, although it was mentioned in *Dekker* (*supra*) as an available approach. Instead, courts apply either the *Pereira* or the *Van Camp* formula, depending on whether separate capital or community labor was the chief contributing factor to the gain in the matter at hand. [*See, e.g.*, Beam v. Bank of America, 6 Cal. 3d 12 (1971); Marriage of Lopez, 38 Cal. App. 3d 93 (1974)] (That the business is incorporated is disregarded in making an apportionment.)

(1) *If community labor was the chief contributing factor,* the court would use the formula most favorable to that estate—*i.e., Pereira* where the gain is great, and *Van Camp* where the gain is small compared to similar-type investments.

(2) *If separate capital was the chief contributing factor,* the court should likewise apply the formula most favorable to the separate estate—which would mean *Van Camp* where the gain was relatively large and *Pereira* where the gain was relatively small.

(3) *If the gain is average in amount,* the only apparent guideline is the mandate of *Beam, supra,* to choose the formula that will achieve "substantial justice." The general presumption favoring community property would suggest that where neither labor nor capital can be considered the chief contributing factor, the formula more favorable to the community should be used. Remember that "substantial justice" might be achieved by adjusting the *Pereira* interest rate up or down from legal interest and/or by compounding the interest. Similarly, some flexibility in the *Van Camp* formula could be obtained by calculating simple or compound interest for community earnings retained in the business.

e. **"Reverse apportionment"—for cases involving community capital and separate labor:** [§75] Since a spouse's labor while living "separate and apart" under California Family Code section 771 is separate labor generating separate gains (*see supra*, §43), but separation does not convert community capital to separate property, nor change the rule that profits from capital have the same characterization as that capital, some sort of "reverse" *Pereira-Van Camp* apportionment is necessary in most divorce situations involving a community-owned business. [Marriage of Imperato, 45 Cal. App. 3d 432 (1975)] Of course, if the capital was part community and part separate, apportionment would also be required in this situation.

(1) **Example:** Suppose H and W own a community business with $200,000 in capital assets. The spouses live separate and apart for a year before divorce, during which time H alone works at the business and withdraws $20,000 in gains, leaving an additional $40,000 in gains for that year retained in the business.

 (a) *If the divorce court applies a "reverse"* **Pereira** *formula* in apportioning these gains, the community would receive a fair interest return on the $200,000—perhaps $18,000 based on a 9% interest factor. The $20,000 H withdrew would be treated as separate salary, leaving $22,000 separate and $18,000 community retained earnings for the year in question.

 (b) *Alternatively, a "reverse"* **Van Camp** *formula* would give the separate estate a fair salary (say, $40,000), and the balance of the gain ($20,000) would be regarded as community property.

(2) **General guidelines for "reverse" apportionment:** [§76] Presumably, courts will consider whether the separate or community contributions were the chief factor contributing to the gains that must be apportioned and will adopt the formula that favors that particular estate. If separate labor was the chief contributing factor, "reverse" *Pereira* should be used if the gain is relatively large and "reverse" *Van Camp* if it is relatively small. If capital was the chief contributing factor, "reverse" *Van Camp* would be used if the gain is relatively large (to hold the separate return on labor to a fixed amount) and "reverse" *Pereira* would be applied if the gain is small.

8. **Establishing Separate-Property Share in Mixed-Consideration Cases:** [§77] Both the community and the separate estate of one or both of the spouses may contribute consideration toward an item of property acquired during marriage. In such cases, each estate (community or separate) that contributes consideration applied before or at the time title to the property is acquired is credited with a pro rata share, and the property is co-owned as a tenancy in common (although the community portion thereof is community-owned). [Ortega v. Ortega, 118 Cal. App. 2d 589 (1953)]

 a. **Example:** During marriage, H uses $2,000 of his separate property and $3,000 in community funds to buy an oil painting. The painting is owned 40% by H's separate estate and 60% by the community, so that H effectively has 70% ownership and W 30%.

 b. **Purchases by installment contract:** [§78] When payments are made over time, and title does not vest in the buyers until a specified sum has been received by the seller, each item of consideration paid by way of installment is treated in forming the cotenancy.

 (1) **Example:** In 1974, H (while single) contracts to buy Blackacre from Vendor. The contract terms require H to pay Vendor $800 per month for 20 years, at the end of which time Vendor will deliver to H a deed to the property. For five years, H uses separate funds to make payments; he then marries W and uses community funds to make payments for the remaining 15 years. When title to Blackacre passes, a percentage of the land will

be owned as H's separate property and a percentage as community property. [Vieux v. Vieux, 80 Cal. App. 222 (1926)]

(2) **Criticism:** In cases like the previous example, the courts have treated the $800 per month paid in 1974 as buying the same share of cotenancy title as the final $800 payment in 1994. This ignores the fact that $800 in 1974 was worth considerably more in purchasing power than $800 in 1994 (due to inflation).

   (a) **Comment:** Lost interest on the early payments (*i.e.*, what could have been earned by investing the same $800 in a bank savings account or certificate of deposit) is likewise ignored, but this seems more reasonable. The fractional share purchased with an $800 payment in 1974 does grow in value over time if the land was a sound investment. Moreover, such contracts normally give the buyer a right of possession before title passes, and this benefit can be viewed as a benefit to H in lieu of interest on funds paid to the seller.

(3) **Determining ownership of contract before title passes:** [§79] If the marriage is dissolved before title to property passes under an installment contract, the court must determine how the *contract* is owned. The right to obtain title upon making the remaining installment payments will likely be a valuable property right if the land has increased in value since the purchase contract was made. Although no reported case has dealt with the problem, the court presumably would make a pro rata division based on the monies paid in at the time of dissolution. Thus, if the community is dissolved after $4,800 of H's separate property and $3,200 of community funds have been paid to the vendor to *reduce principal* owing, the contract would be owned 60% by H's separate estate and 40% by the community. Note that each payment alters the fractional ownership (unless the payment *itself* is composed of both community and separate funds in the same proportion as the contract is then owned).

(4) **Only payments of principal considered in making pro rata division:** [§80] Only so much of each installment payment as discharges the principal or basic purchase price is considered in determining the fractional interests of the separate and community estates. Sums paid for interest, insurance, or taxes on the property do not "buy in" to title. [*See* Marriage of Moore, 28 Cal. 3d 366 (1980)—a mortgage case considered applicable] The installment contract will specify (for income tax purposes) what the interest rate is even though no technical loan is involved.

   (a) **Comment:** Amortization schedules prepared for income tax treatment of installment contract payments show the great part of the earliest payments is interest. Thus, in the hypothetical above where a total of $8,000 was considered in determining the community and separate ownership of the contract, the total funds paid on the contract were probably six, seven, or eight times that amount.

(5) **Alternative approach—inception of title doctrine:** [§81] Under the doctrine of inception of title, ownership of an asset acquired by consideration furnished over a period of time is governed by the marital status of

the transferee *at the beginning of the period* (*e.g.*, when a contract for installment purchase is made). If H is the transferee and is then single, title when acquired will be separate even though the great bulk of consideration paid was community property. The nonacquiring estate gets reimbursement (without interest) for its contributions.

(a) **Doctrine generally rejected in California:** [§82] Because results under the inception of title doctrine tend to be unfair to the community estate, California has—with certain exceptions noted below—rejected the doctrine in favor of the pro rata shared-ownership rule, under which payments from community funds subsequent to entering into the contract make the community a co-investor with the separate estate. The community thus shares in any profits the purchase may generate, and also shares the loss if there is a drop in value.

(b) **Doctrine applies where land is acquired by labor:** [§83] Where title to property is acquired over a period of time by *labor*—*e.g.*, occupying land to obtain adverse possession title or occupying and improving government-owned land to obtain title under homesteader-type statutes—California courts have used the inception of title doctrine rather than pro rata sharing. [Siddall v. Haight, 132 Cal. 320 (1901)—adverse possession; Estate of Rupley, 174 Cal. App. 2d 597 (1959)—government land grant] To obtain title by adverse possession, the occupier must pay taxes [Cal. Civ. Pro. Code §325]; and if separate title were obtained, such payments probably would be viewed as an "improvement" of an inchoate title, with reimbursement to the community for the amount paid. Homestead cases necessarily involve improvements to the property—possibly paid for with community funds and/or erected with community labor—which would also give rise to reimbursement (*see infra*, §§103-128).

1) **Criticism:** There seems to be no logical reason why community consideration in the form of money will "buy in" to a title acquired over time while community *labor* necessary to acquiring such title will not. Thus, where the property was acquired by labor and has appreciated in value, the community should ask the court to apply pro rata sharing principles.

(c) **Doctrine applied to lease renewal:** [§84] In *Marriage of Joaquin*, 193 Cal. App. 3d 1529 (1987), H acquired before marriage a five-year leasehold with an option to renew for five years. During marriage, and after having used community funds to pay some of the rental obligation, thus keeping the option alive, H renewed for five years. At divorce, because the stipulated rental was well below market value, it was important to determine whether the community had an interest in the renewed leasehold. Applying the inception of title doctrine, the court held that it was entirely H's separate property. The pro rata approach could have been used by viewing the right of renewal as purchased by all rentals H paid on the initial leasehold—before marriage with his separate funds and after marriage with community funds.

c. **Apportionment of pension benefits:** [§85] Many employed spouses participate in pension plans, earning retirement benefits by their labor or frequently by payroll deductions of specific sums. Such plans usually require that the employee work for the employer for a specified period of time (*e.g.*, 5, 7, or 20 years) before such pension benefits *vest*. Where the employed spouse is married and cohabiting during a portion of the time that pension benefits are earned, and single (or living separate and apart) for part of such time, a pro rata apportionment is used to determine the respective interests of the community and separate estates. Inception of title is not used even if labor alone earns the pension. Most courts form the pro rata fraction based on the ***time*** (*e.g.*, number of months or years) of participation in the plan while single (and separated) as compared to the time of participation while married. [*See, e.g.*, Marriage of Freiberg, 57 Cal. App. 3d 304 (1976)]

   (1) **Defined benefit plans:** [§86] In a defined benefit plan, the participant earns the right to specified benefits after a certain amount of time on the job. Neither the employer nor the employee-participant makes any specified periodic contribution on the participant's behalf, and no account is kept in the participant's name. The specified benefits (once matured) must be paid even if plan investments have been unsuccessful. In such defined benefit plans, a day on the job in 1979—insofar as it earns future benefits—is worth no more or less than a day on the job in 1999, and "time" apportionments therefore make sense.

   (a) **Exception:** [§87] A "time" apportionment may not be made where the defined benefit plan by its terms uses a different measure than time on the job to qualify H or W for benefits. In one case, retirement pay was based on "points" earned during military service (*e.g.*, one point per each day of active duty, points for attending reserve training sessions, etc.). The court had to determine marital status of the spouse (H) when he earned each point and apportion on a "point" basis. [Marriage of Poppe, 97 Cal. App. 3d 1 (1979)]

   (2) **Defined contribution plans:** [§88] Under a defined contribution plan, an account is kept for each employee-participant and periodic contributions—payroll deductions contributed by the employee and/or contributions by the employer as consideration for the employee's labor—are paid into the account. Earnings on investment of funds in the account are recorded periodically (*e.g.*, once a year).

   (a) **"Money" apportionments of defined contribution plans:** [§89] An apportionment of defined contribution benefits based on money can be made. However, it would seem inappropriate simply to total all the contributions of community funds (or funds traceable to community labor) and compare this amount with total separate contributions to form the pro rata fraction, since contributions many years ago will have generated considerably more earnings than more recent contributions. Instead, the yearly earnings themselves should be characterized as community, separate, or a portion of each, and these totals should then be added to contributions to form the pro rata fraction.

1) **Example:** In one case of defined contribution where additions to the plan were based on company profits, the community interest was calculated by obtaining the value of employee H's interest at the date of separation while adding to that the amount of appreciation (*e.g.*, through interest or other profits made on the investment) of that sum from the time of separation to the date of division of property. [Marriage of Behrens, 137 Cal. App. 3d 562 (1982)] Note that if unusually large profits of the company had resulted in very large additions to the plan in H's name during the period of separation, W would have fared much better had a "time" apportionment been made.

(b) **"Time" apportionments of defined contribution benefits:** [§90] Even though the fact that apportionments based on money contributed are possible with respect to defined contribution plans, the courts usually have used "time" apportionments here as well. This achieves a kind of rough justice, since monthly contributions in early years (often a percentage of salary) are likely to be smaller and the earnings thereon larger, while recent monthly contributions are likely to be larger and the earnings thereon (generated over a shorter period of time) smaller. Even so, where one spouse demands a "money" apportionment and furnishes the necessary information for that computation, the court should use the latter method of apportionment for a more accurate division of proceeds between the separate and community estates.

(3) **Incentive stock options:** [§91] "Time" apportionments are made to determine community and separate interests in stock options awarded to an employee spouse based on labor over time that include community labor (the employee was married and cohabiting with his spouse) and separate labor (he was unmarried or living separate and apart). In these cases, the issue is whether the option was awarded in part to compensate for prior service or solely to entice the employee spouse to stay with the company from the time the option was awarded until it becomes exercisable. The employer's intent governs here (including, if the option is partly a bonus for work already performed, how far back in time the apportionment period extends). [Marriage of Nelson, 177 Cal. App. 3d 150 (1986); Marriage of Hug, 154 Cal. App. 3d 780 (1984)]

d. **Apportionment of life insurance:** [§92] The cash surrender value of a whole-life insurance policy will be subjected to a "money" pro rata apportionment where some premiums have been paid with separate funds and some with community funds. For example, if H has spent $5,000 of community funds and $2,500 of his separate funds over the years to pay premiums and at divorce the cash surrender value of the policy is $9,000, two-thirds of this value would be community property. [McBride v. McBride, 11 Cal. App. 2d 521 (1936)] Cases have treated a dollar paid many years ago as earning the same share of the policy value as a dollar recently paid. However, a strong argument can be made that earlier payments should be worth more than later payments of the same amount, since the early payments generate greater earnings, which in turn cause the investment value of the policy to grow.

(1) **Death benefits**

    (a) **Spouse healthy enough to be reinsured:** [§93]   Older cases applying pro rata apportionment to death benefits, based on the total of separate and community funds used to pay premiums, are no longer followed. Instead, for an insured spouse who remains healthy enough to obtain a new policy, the death benefit coverage is treated as a series of distinct contracts. The type of funds used (separate or community) to pay the premium for the present period of coverage controls classification of the contract and of death benefits paid if the insured spouse dies during the time period. [Marriage of Spengler, 5 Cal. App. 4th 288 (1992)]

        1) **Policy not property?** [§94]   One case implies that if at the time of divorce the insured spouse is healthy enough to be reinsured under a new policy, an existing term policy, acquired with community consideration in money or labor on a job providing life insurance as a fringe benefit, is either not property at all or has a value of zero. [Lorenz v. Lorenz, 146 Cal. App. 3d 464 (1983)] This result is clearly incorrect. If the policy is awarded to the insured spouse at divorce and she dies before the end of the period of coverage acquired with community consideration, the insurer must pay out valuable benefits. The value of the contract at divorce can be determined based on mortality tables showing the chance of death of the insured during the remainder of the term of coverage.

    (b) **Spouse not healthy enough to be reinsured:** [§95]   A feature of term life insurance is that paying the premium for a period of coverage entitles the insured to continue coverage even though he has become so ill he would not be eligible to buy insurance initially (*e.g.,* because it is very likely he will die soon). If the insured dies during a term that began after he became uninsurable, benefits paid are apportioned under the pro rata approach, based on all community and separate funds used to pay premiums. [Estate of Logan, 191 Cal. App. 3d 768 (1987)] If divorce occurred, the policy itself would be part community, part separate.

9. **Establishing Separate Interest in Credit Acquisitions:** [§96]   Borrowed money or items purchased with borrowed money may have to be characterized as separate or community property at various times—*e.g.,* at dissolution by death or divorce, or when a creditor levies execution. Items purchased on credit are treated as if the buyer had "borrowed" money from the seller and then used the money to purchase the property in question. In California, characterization in such credit transactions turns on the state of mind of the credit vendor or the lender; *i.e.,* did she expect to be repaid with community or separate funds? If the lender indicates that she was relying on both sources, the loan proceeds are ***not apportioned***. Rather, the court determines which source was ***primarily*** relied on; and this controls classification of ***all*** the proceeds. [Ford v. Ford, 276 Cal. App. 2d 9 (1969)]

    a. **Contrary authority:** [§97]   One court has stated that the primary reliance test is wrong and that the presumption of community ownership of loan proceeds and credit acquisitions during marriage can be overcome only by proof that the lender relied *solely* on separate assets of one of the spouses for repayment. [Marriage of Grinius, 166 Cal. App. 3d 1179 (1985)] The subsequent sections in this Summary discussing credit acquisitions assume, however, a primary rather than sole reliance test will be employed.

b. **Effect of security:** [§98]   If a spouse encumbers separate property as security for the loan in question, the pro-community presumption is rebutted and the loan proceeds will be presumed to be separate even if the proceeds are acquired during marriage. [Gudelj v. Gudelj, 41 Cal. 2d 202 (1953)] However, this pro-separate property presumption may itself be rebutted. Thus, if the value of separate security is much less than the debt, the lender may be relying primarily on community wealth.

c. **Where security is item acquired on credit:** [§99]   Credit vendors often take a security interest in the asset being purchased. If the lender (by reason of an agreement or an anti-deficiency judgment statute) can look only to this security for payment of the debt, the "lender intent" test cannot supply a classification—since the lender is relying on the very asset that requires classification. One possibility here is to characterize the entire acquisition according to the nature of the down payment. Where no anti-deficiency judgment statute applies, the court can characterize the purchase on the basis of the other property that the vendor could reach should the security of the purchased asset prove to be inadequate.

d. **Effect of other spouse's signature on loan document:** [§100]   Suppose H seeks a loan and the lender demands W's signature as well on the promissory note. Since H alone could obligate the community (*see infra*, §273), it may well be that the lender was looking primarily to W's separate property (which her additional signature obligates) for repayment; and if so, the acquisition would be her separate property. In any case, decisions such as *Ford v. Ford, supra*, indicating that W's signature has *no* effect, seem incorrect unless the lender misunderstands community property law.

e. **Effect of repaying loan:** [§101]   Under the "creditor's intent" test, the manner in which a loan is repaid is irrelevant in characterizing the assets at issue (although it may well have a bearing on reimbursement claims; *see infra*, §§103-128). Thus, for example, if the lender relied primarily on H's separate property for repayment, the credit acquisition will be considered separate even if the loan is actually repaid with community funds. This rule has not been applied, however, in recent cases of *realty* acquired by purchase money mortgage financing (*see infra*, §111).

f. **Criticism of California approach to classifying credit acquisitions:** [§102] Where consideration for a purchase is mixed (part separate and part community), ownership of the property is generally apportioned between the two estates. (*See supra*, §77.) Thus when a lender relies on both separate and community funds for repayment, there is no reason why the credit acquisition should not also be apportioned. Moreover, looking to lender's intent in these situations creates uncertainty and tends to encourage litigation. Texas has what appears to be a more workable rule, namely that the pro-community presumption can be overcome only where the lender was limited by law or contract to reaching separate property in obtaining repayment. [*See* Dillard v. Dillard, 341 S.W.2d 668 (Tex. Civ. App. 1960), *writ ref'd n.r.e.*]

10. **Calculating Separate Interest in "Improvement" Cases:** [§103] Pro rata sharing of ownership in cases where separate and community funds are combined to obtain title (discussed previously) must be distinguished from expenditures with respect to a title already obtained—*i.e.*, "improvement" situations. In this latter type of case, the post-title expenditure usually does *not* "buy in" to title and the pro rata apportionment rule is therefore not applied. Rather, the "improving" estate usually has a right to reimbursement from the improved estate. [Wheeland v. Rodgers, 20 Cal. 2d 218 (1942)]

   a. **Example:** Suppose W owned Blackacre before marriage. After marriage W uses community funds to build a house on the land. The improved land is all W's separate property, but the community has a claim for reimbursement against W for the community funds spent on the house. Conversely, had W used separate funds to build a house on community-owned land, the realty would all be community with W's estate probably having a right of reimbursement. At divorce, the right to reimbursement can be lost only by written waiver. [Cal. Fam. Code §2640] At a death dissolution, it is unclear whether there is a presumption that W's use of separate funds was a gift to the community or whether the party opposing reimbursement must prove W had donative intent. (*See infra*, §122.)

   b. **Theory—fixtures doctrine:** [§104] The common law of fixtures—that an accession to real property takes on the same ownership characteristic as the realty improved—is relied on in refusing to recognize any ownership rights in the estate paying for the improvement. [*See* 50 Cal. L. Rev. 844 (1962)]

      (1) **Minority view:** [§105] An occasional case rejects the fixtures doctrine and holds that a house paid for with community money but built on separate land would be a community house. [Long v. Long, 88 Cal. App. 2d 544 (1948)]

      (2) **Alternative approach:** [§106] One case used yet a third theory—a "buy in" to title. As an example, if W's separate land cost $10,000 and a house was constructed thereon with community funds of $90,000, the improved realty would be considered 90% community and 10% separate. [Marriage of Sparks, 97 Cal. App. 3d 353 (1979)] *Sparks*, however, indicated that the "reimbursement" approach would be used where the expenditures were not great in comparison to the value of the realty at the time of the expenditure.

         (a) **Approach in Arizona:** [§107] In Arizona, the improving estate is credited with a 90% fractional share of *value* in the *Sparks* situation (*supra*). [Drahos v. Rens, 717 P.2d 927 (Ariz. 1985)] But rather than buying in to a share of title, the percentage claim of the improving estate is a flexible right to reimbursement. In the hypothetical above, if the property doubles in value after the house is built, the reimbursement claim increases to $180,000. If overall value fell, the reimbursement claim would shrink. If the property were rented out after the house was built, the *Sparks* theory means rentals are 90% community, but in Arizona, they would be 100% separate, as building the house did not change ownership. The Arizona approach simplifies management of the improved property by recognizing only one estate as the actual owner.

c. **Scope of improvement doctrine:** [§108]   The improvement doctrine is involved not only when tangible assets are affixed to realty but also when taxes levied on the property are paid and probably when sums are paid for major rehabilitation or even upkeep. [Estate of Turner, 35 Cal. App. 2d 576 (1939)] Application of community labor to separate realty (*e.g.*, constructing an irrigation system) could also be viewed as raising an improvement issue, at least in nonbusiness situations. (Such labor applied to an ongoing separate ***business*** would probably require *Pereira-Van Camp* apportionment; *see supra*, §§63-76.)

d. **Effect of right to reimbursement on creditors:** [§109]   An early California case held that creditors of a debtor spouse stand in the shoes of the debtor spouse with respect to reaching the improved estate. Thus, creditors cannot levy on the debtor spouse's right to reimbursement until the debtor spouse could exercise that right—*i.e.*, at dissolution of the marriage. [Peck v. Brummagin, 31 Cal. 440 (1886)] Courts today would probably follow this view or, alternatively, hold that the right of reimbursement is too contingent to be subject to execution. Under the *Sparks* case's buy-in approach, however, the improving estate aquires a share of the title on which a creditor can levy (*i.e.*, in *Sparks*, H's creditor to whom community but not W's separate property is liable).

   (1) **Where intent to defraud creditors:** [§110]   If an improvement was made with actual intent to defraud creditors or under circumstances rendering the improving estate insolvent, the buy-in theory rather than reimbursement is applied so there ***will*** be a present property interest to levy on. [*See* Estate of Barreiro, 86 Cal. App. 764 (1927)]

e. **Treatment of mortgage payments:** [§111]   Mortgage payments, like tax payments, help to remove an encumbrance from land and logically come within the improvements doctrine. Older cases have applied the doctrine in this area [Wedemeyer v. Elmer, 33 Cal. App. 2d 336 (1939)]; but a contrary line of authority dealing with purchase money mortgages treats the payment of the portion of a mortgage that reduces ***principal*** owing on the debt (but not interest) as buying in to title [Giacomazzi v. Rowe, 109 Cal. App. 2d 498 (1952)]. These latter cases have relied on the pro rata sharing rule for installment contract payments made before title passes (*supra*, §§77-78), and apparently have overruled older authorities such as *Wedemeyer*. [*See also* Marriage of Moore, *supra*, §80]

   (1) **Effect is shifting of title:** [§112]   The effect of using a buy-in approach seems necessarily to be a shifting of title each time a mortgage payment is made. The original consideration initially fixes the title as community or separate (or a fractional amount of both, if there is mixed consideration), and later mortgage payments alter the title.

      (a) **Example of calculating community buy-in:** Where one spouse, say H, acquires property while single, by mortgage financing, and later marries and begins using community funds to make mortgage payments, the pro rata interests are calculated as follows according to *Marriage of Marsden* (*see supra*, §54):

1) *Step (1):* Calculate the percentage of the original purchase price paid by community payments of ***principal***. Thus, if the purchase price was $100,000, and $20,000 of community funds have been used to reduce the principal indebtedness, the community-separate ratio is 20% to 80%, and the separate estate is treated as paying in $80,000, regardless of the cash outlay, because it alone was liable on the original promissory note secured by the mortgage.

2) *Step (2):* Add the amount of appreciation in value between the time of purchase and the time that community money is first used to make a mortgage payment (if known) to the separate interest. So, if by the time of the first community payment the value of the property is $140,000, add $40,000 to the $80,000 already credited to the separate estate. If this appreciation figure is not calculable, skip step (2).

3) *Step (3):* Divide the post-marriage appreciation (or all appreciation if step (2) is skipped) between the separate and community estates using the fractional shares calculated at step (1). *Note:* The appreciation value found in step (2) is ***not*** added to the step (1) payments. [Marriage of Frick, 181 Cal. App. 3d 997 (1986)]

4) *Step (4):* Total the various separate and community values and reduce the separate estate's value by the amount of loan unpaid (if any).

(b) **Amount of pre-marriage appreciation ignored in classifying rents?** [§113]   Since under *Frick* (*supra*), the value of pre-marriage appreciation is ignored in apportioning post-marriage gain, pre-marriage appreciation apparently is not a proprietary interest of the separate property estate during marriage. (By the same logic, pre-marriage appreciation would also be ignored in apportioning rents into community and separate shares if the property were rented out rather than occupied by the spouses.) It has not yet been determined whether the *Frick* right to assert ownership of pre-marriage appreciation is secured during marriage by a lien on the property. It is likely that the treatment of pre-marriage appreciation in cases of acquisition by mortgage-financing will be extended to cases where acquisition is by installment land contract (*see supra,* §79).

(c) **Effect of 1983 statute:** [§114]   Section 2640 of the California Family Code, passed in 1983, provides that where ***separate*** funds are applied to pay off a mortgage on property with a title showing most forms of co-ownership by the married couple (*but see infra,* §126), the remedy is reimbursement (without interest, and not to exceed the property's value at the time of divorce) to the separate estate. Section 2640 applies only when calculating community and separate interests ***at divorce***. Courts continue to use the buy-in to title approach, discussed above, when the issue arises at death of a spouse or during marriage. Note that section 2640 is prospective only (*see infra,* §478).

(2) **Equitable result:** [§115]   Although based on a misconception that purchase money mortgage payments are no different from installment contract payments, the buy-in approach reaches a fair result. In the above hypothetical, for instance, the community will share in any inflationary increase in value of the property, which certainly seems preferable to a mere right to reimbursement for mortgage principal paid. The buy-in is also fair to creditors of the other spouse (W), since the community payments create an actual property interest they can levy on if the property is not exempt.

f. **Amount of reimbursement under improvement doctrine:** [§116]   California law is unclear as to the amount of reimbursement to which the improving estate is entitled when a buy-in to title does not occur (as it does in modern mortgage payment cases). Some cases hold that the proper amount is value added, but not to exceed the amount spent (without interest). [Noe v. Card, 14 Cal. 577 (1860)] Thus if $10,000 were spent to build a swimming pool but the pool adds only $7,500 to the market value of the property, $7,500 is the amount owed in reimbursement by the improved estate. Yet if the value of the property increased by $12,500, reimbursement would be limited to $10,000.

(1) **Date for determining value added:** [§117]   The same older cases hold that value added is determined at dissolution of the community. Thus if H used $2,000 of community funds in 1975 to put a new roof on his separately owned house but at divorce in 1994 this improvement added only $100 to the value of the property (*e.g.*, because a new roof was again needed), H's estate would owe only $100 reimbursement to the community.

(2) **Criticism:** [§118]   The value-added measure of reimbursement was borrowed from Louisiana and Texas, where rents and profits from separate property are community owned and hence the community might benefit financially from the improvement. That approach is inappropriate in California (where rents and profits of separate property are separate) unless the community is the improving estate and has enjoyed use of the property. A better approach would be to measure reimbursement by the amount spent plus interest and then offset this amount with any benefits the improving estate had enjoyed in using the property (*see infra*, §121).

(3) **Contrary approach:** [§119]   In one case, W had used community funds to improve her separate land that she rented out. The evidence showed that she and H had agreed that the community was not making a gift to W. The court implied an *interest-free* loan from the community to W. [Marriage of Warren, 28 Cal. App. 3d 777 (1972)] However, the decision seems wrong. The spouses knew that W was using the community funds to help generate separate gains for herself. One would expect the community to participate in the gain in some way. This would be achieved if the implied loan earned legal interest for the community.

(4) **Recovery where constructive fraud at issue:** [§120]   When reimbursement is ordered because the fixture doctrine would otherwise work a constructive fraud on the improving estate—as where H himself uses

community funds to improve his separate property without any agreement to repay the community—the proper measure of reimbursement has been said to be the *greater* of the amount spent or value added. [Marriage of Warren, *supra*] It is unclear when value added is measured—apparently at the time of reimbursement.

g. **Reducing reimbursement via offset:** [§121] In *Marriage of Reilley*, 196 Cal. App. 3d 1119 (1987), a separated spouse ("H") used post-separation separate property earnings to construct improvements on community property. The value added was less than the amount spent. No gift was presumed (*see infra*, §123), and the amount to be reimbursed was the value added (the lesser amount). However, the court said in dictum that unusual equitable factors might call for a higher reimbursement award. The court also seemed to be implying that if H and W had not been separated and both had lived in the house, the amount of reimbursement would have been the *greater* of the amount spent or value added (*see supra*, §120). But in this case, the result may be supportable based on an offset from the normal reimbursement amount based on H's having separately lived in and used the addition to the house (although he claimed it was for the children when they visited him). Where the community pays loan interest, taxes, and insurance on a separately owned house, reimbursement is not granted, because of the offset theory, if the community occupied the premises. [Marriage of Moore, *supra*, §80]

h. **Uncertainty as to when gift will be presumed:** [§122] Before a wife had management powers over community property, the law presumed a gift when her husband used separate or community funds (or labor) to improve her separate property or used his separate funds to improve community property. [Dunn v. Mullan, *supra*, §26] This presumption might apply in certain situations today not covered by the special rules discussed below.

   (1) **Special rule for mortgage payments on realty titled in names of both spouses:** [§123] Suppose W uses her separate funds to make a mortgage payment on land titled in H and W. This will in part buy in to a share of title (*see supra*, §111) if no gift were found. Even a finding that W had no donative intent cannot overcome the *presumption of gift* arising from the form of title. Only an actual agreement (oral or written) with H that no gift was being made would overcome the presumption. [Marriage of Lucas, 27 Cal. 3d 841 (1980)] This same logic could apply when W uses her separate funds to improve in any way property titled in H's name alone: There is a presumptive gift to the community or, if the date on the instrument is pre-marriage, to H's separate estate.

   (2) **Rule inapplicable at divorce:** [§124] By statute, the *Lucas* presumption of gift does not apply at divorce to improvements in the form of separate property "contributions to acquisition" of property titled in any form of co-ownership or property that is community although titled in the name of only one spouse. [Cal. Fam. Code §§2581, 2640] At divorce in these situations, only a *writing* signed by the contributor spouse can establish a gift. Moreover, the normal rule that such a contribution buys in to title does not apply. The remedy is reimbursement of the contributed separate funds, without interest, not to exceed the total value of the property at the time of divorce. The same rule applies to payments for improvements in kind (*e.g.*, adding a swimming pool) but *not* to payments

for maintenance, taxes, and insurance, and not, significantly, for the interest component of mortgage payments (rather, only for the amount thereof that increases equity). [Cal. Fam. Code §2640]

(a) **Tracing on sale of property:** Suppose H contributed $60,000 of his separate funds to buy Blackacre, taking title in the name of both spouses. Later Blackacre was sold for $300,000, and the proceeds were used to buy blocks of $100,000 worth of stock in three corporations, A, B, and C. According to *Marriage of Walrath*, 17 Cal. 4th 907 (1998), under section 2640, H now has a right of reimbursement at divorce of $20,000 assertable against each block of stock. But if the value of the stock in A Corp. should fall to $10,000, H loses $10,000 worth of reimbursement (because section 2640 caps the reimbursement claim at the value of the affected property at divorce). H cannot recoup this loss based on the values of B and C Corps.

(b) **Applicable rule unclear:** Expenditures not covered at divorce by the statutes cited in this section could (i) be subject to the older presumption of gift, now gender neutral, which is overcome by proof of donative intent; (ii) be governed by the stronger *Lucas* presumption of gift that only a spousal agreement can rebut; or (iii) create a right to reimbursement unless donative intent is proved.

(3) **Statute of Frauds inapplicable:** [§125] In situations where California Family Code section 2640 does not apply (*see supra*, §124), an *oral* statement by a spouse making improvements or mortgage payments that a gift *is intended* is effective even though it involves a transmutation (*e.g.*, of H's separate funds into community land when H pays taxes on it) because the Statute of Frauds applicable to most interspousal transmutations does not by its terms apply to cases involving a combining of separate and community assets (or of W's separate property and H's separate property). [Cal. Fam. Code §852(c)]

(4) **True joint tenancy deed:** [§126] If a deed to spouses recites a joint tenancy and adds the words "and not as community property," the asset, even at divorce, is joint tenancy property (as it is if the spouses have a "side" agreement in writing to that effect). Section 2640, with its rejection of the presumption of gift, does *not* apply. If separate funds of one spouse are used to make a mortgage payment on property titled in this way [*see* Cal. Fam. Code §2581], the *Lucas* rule governs even at divorce, and there is a presumption of gift so strong that only an express contrary agreement can rebut it, proof of lack of donative intent being insufficient.

i. **Uncertainty as to whether lien arises:** [§127] In most community property states, the right to reimbursement arising when there is no buy-in to title is secured by an implied-in-law lien on the improved property (an important remedy if the improved estate is insolvent). [*See* 44 Wash. L. Rev. 379 (1969)] However, no California case has recognized such a lien.

j. **Presumption when source of improving funds is unknown:** [§128] Where the source of funds used to improve property is unknown, most decisions outside California presume that the funds used were of the same character as the improved estate. [*See, e.g.*, Lawson v. Ridgeway, 233 P.2d 459 (Ariz. 1951)]

(An occasional non-California case applies the normal pro-community presumption even to monies spent to improve separate property. [*See* Gregory v. Gregory, 223 So. 2d 238 (La. 1969)]) The one California case on point holds that there is no presumption at all [Seligman v. Seligman, 85 Cal. App. 683 (1927)], which apparently means that the estate seeking reimbursement must prove the nature of the funds spent [Marriage of Frick, *supra,* §112].

11. **Determining Separate Interest in Tort Recoveries**

    a. **Property damage recovery:** [§129] Under basic tracing principles, recovery from a tortfeasor for damage to property takes on the same character as the property damaged; *e.g.,* if W's separate car is wrecked, recovery on a judgment for this loss is also her separate property. [Scoville v. Keglor, 27 Cal. App. 17 (1938)] The same tracing concept would be used to characterize damages paid in eminent domain proceedings as separate or community property.

    (1) **Business property:** [§130] If business property is tortiously damaged, some of the damages recovered may be for lost profits. Such damages should take on the character that would have attached to earnings under *Pereira-Van Camp* apportionment or reverse *Pereira-Van Camp* (where community capital is damaged and the spouses are living separate and apart; *see supra,* §§63-76). However, the portion of the award going to the estate that would have performed labor probably should be adjusted downward, since the loss being compensated is lost *opportunity* to earn gain, not the gain itself (*i.e.,* the labor was not in fact rendered and could have been devoted elsewhere).

    (2) **Insured property:** [§131] Regarding the proceeds of insurance, there is a split of authority. The better view is that where recovery is paid by an insurer on a casualty loss policy taken out by one spouse, tracing principles apply so that the proceeds have the same separate or community character as the asset damaged. The insurance premiums would be treated as an improvement (protecting the property from loss just as payment of taxes protects it from loss due to tax sale). [Belmont v. Belmont, 188 Cal. App. 2d 33 (1961)]

    (a) **Another approach:** [§132] In one case where H had used his separate funds to purchase casualty insurance on property co-owned by H and W, the court traced the insurance proceeds for a loss to the insurance *contract* and the funds used to pay premiums rather than to the damaged property. [Russell v. Williams, 58 Cal. 2d 487 (1962)]

    b. **Personal injury damages:** [§133] Under present California law, the starting point in classifying recovery ordered by a court or received under a settlement agreement on account of a tortfeasor's having caused personal injury damages to one spouse is the time when the tort occurred—*i.e.,* when the cause of action arose.

    (1) **Tort occurring before marriage:** [§134] Technically the pro-community general presumption applies to personal injury damages *received* by a spouse during marriage, but these can be traced back to the cause of action, which is also a form of property. If the recipient-spouse can show he

or she owned the tort cause of action before marriage, the presumption is dispelled by the tracing process, and the damages are also separate property of the victim.

- (a) **Possible exceptions:** [§135] Note, however, that if a portion of the tort recovery is for lost earnings and the period of disability extends into the time when the victim was married and cohabiting, some part of this recovery for lost earnings is logically community (since it is received to replace what would have been community earnings). Likewise, recovery for medical expenses (*e.g.,* doctor bills, ambulance fee) could arguably be community, especially if community funds were used to pay them before tort damages were received. (*But see infra,* §143, indicating that no apportionment may be allowed.)

(2) **Tort occurring during separation:** [§136] Where the spouses are living separate and apart at the time of the tort, the cause of action is the separate property of the victim. [Cal. Fam. Code §781(a)(2)]

- (a) **Limited statutory right to reimbursement:** [§137] Section 781(b) provides that if the *spouse of the victim* has used his or her separate property or community property to pay medical or other expenses generated by the accident, a right to reimbursement (apparently without interest) arises. Reimbursement is equally warranted where the *victim spouse* has used community funds to pay such expenses; and the courts will undoubtedly permit reimbursement in such instances, even though section 781(b) does not specifically provide for it.

- (b) **Effect of loss of community profits:** [§138] Suppose the separated victim spouse had been applying his or her labor to make community capital productive before the injury. The injury rendered the capital unproductive. Under the "reverse apportionment" approach, *supra,* §75, the lost profits would have been partly community. It is unclear whether California Family Code section 781(a), in declaring that the time of the tort governs classification, bars a community classification of such lost profits. If so, fairness suggests the courts should fashion a reimbursement right for the community to correct the illogical classification mandated by section 781(a).

- (c) **Dividing cause of action at divorce:** [§139] Even if part of the damages in an action arising during separation could be community, principles of civil procedure against splitting a cause of action (plus fairness to the tortfeasor as potential defendant) will require the divorce court to award all of the tort cause of action to the victim spouse. At most a portion of it could be *valued* as community property for purposes of ascertaining if an equal division of the community has been made.

(3) **Tort occurring during marriage and cohabitation:** [§140] If the cause of action arises during marriage and cohabitation, it (and damages received under it) is presumptively community property. Logically, at

least portions of the recovery could obtain a separate classification by tracing back beyond the cause of action and the time it arose to the victim's body, something he or she obviously owned before marriage and was separate property. For example, if the victim's leg was sheared off in the accident, monies received because of such a loss would be, if tracing of this type were allowed, separate property of the victim.

(a) **Is there a statutory bar to tracing?** [§141] California Family Code section 2603 states that "'community property personal injury damages' as used *in this section* means all money or other property received or to be received by a person in satisfaction of a judgment for damages for his or her personal injuries or pursuant to an agreement for the settlement or compromise of a claim for such damages, if the cause of action for such damages arose during marriage but is not separate property" under California Family Code section 781(a)(2) (*see supra,* §136). The section referred to above is a provision for division of such damages (or potential damages) *at divorce.* It would seem, then, that section 2603 does not affect the classification process when the issue arises at some other time.

(b) **Case law refusal to trace to right of personal security:** [§142] In most community property states, even though the tort occurs during marriage, that portion of the award for pain and suffering is the victim's separate property by a process of tracing back to a "right of personal security" owned before marriage. [*See* Soto v. Vandeventer, 245 P.2d 826 (N.M. 1952)] California has never adopted this theory; the difficulty with it is that the right traced to is not property—not something "owned" before marriage—in that the legislature was free to vary the law of tort before an injury was suffered.

(c) **No apportionment at all allowed?** [§143] When, however, the victim seeks to trace to the lost leg, something owned before marriage, and the classification is not governed at divorce by section 2603 (*see supra,* §141), the only apparent bar to successful tracing is dictum in some cases that the cause of action cannot be broken down into part community, part separate, so long as the spouses are married. [Washington v. Washington, 47 Cal. 2d 249 (1956)] No reason why apportionment should be denied has ever been given, and California does apportion gains in many other contexts (*e.g.,* the *Pereira-Van Camp* apportionment rules). Therefore, where the victim does seek to trace to something owned before marriage (such as the lost leg), there is reason to believe that future decisions will allow a logical classification that apportions the damages.

(d) **Treatment at divorce:** [§144] As indicated, section 2603 labels *all* the personal injury damages on hand or yet to be received community property at divorce (*see supra,* §141). However, it goes on to call for an award of such assets in most instances as if they were separate rather than community property (which must be divided 50-50 at divorce). Section 2603 requires that all the damages be awarded to the victim spouse "unless the interests of justice require another disposition" or unless the recovery "has been commingled with other assets of the community." The statute provides that the "interests of justice" notwithstanding, the victim spouse must be awarded at least half of the funds on hand that had been paid as tort damages.

1) **Reimbursement claims:** [§145] Suppose community earnings of H or W or separate funds of the nonvictim spouse were used to pay medical expenses of the victim spouse after a tort that occurred during marriage and cohabitation. If the recovery to the victim included sums on account of such expenses (which would otherwise go to the victim at divorce under section 2603), the community estate or the separate estate of the nonvictim spouse may claim reimbursement (apparently without interest) or ask for an apportioned award under the "interests of justice" proviso.

2) **Criticism:** [§146] Section 2603 is so broadly worded that it presumptively directs distribution of all the personal injury damages to the victim spouse notwithstanding that some portion of such recovery was paid for lost earnings before the spouses separated. Hence, courts should frequently use the "interests of justice" clause to subject such portions of personal injury awards to ordinary equal division at divorce.

3) **Effect of expenditure:** [§147] Suppose that a personal injury recovery included sums for lost earnings during marriage as well as pain and suffering, etc., and that some of the funds have been spent for food, rent, or other "wasting" assets that cannot be traced. The law presumes community funds are used for these "family expenses" (*see supra*, §55). Since section 2603 presumptively treats recovery for pain and suffering, lost future earnings, and future medical expenses as separate property at divorce, it seems equitable to presume that the family expenses were paid with that portion of the award attributable to lost earnings during marriage and cohabitation.

4) **Uncommingling:** [§148] The proviso of section 2603 concerning commingling should bar separate property treatment of a damages award for pain and suffering only where uncommingling is impossible. Thus, if the victim puts $50,000 awarded to her for pain and suffering into a bank account with $50,000 of her earnings and no withdrawals are ever made, surely one-half of the account can be awarded to her under that statute and is not subject to the 50-50 division rule for ordinary community property.

(e) **Where recovery is received after dissolution by death:** [§149] The death of the *nonvictim* spouse converts a cause of action for the surviving spouse's personal injuries from community property (if the tort occurred during marriage and cohabitation) to the survivor's separate property. [Flores v. Brown, 39 Cal. 2d 622 (1952)] Presumably the decedent's estate could assert half of a community right to reimbursement against subsequent recovery for community funds spent for medical care and/or lost community earnings (if compensated in the award received).

   1) **Death of victim does not change classification:** [§150] The death of the victim spouse prior to recovery will not change characterization of any recovery his or her estate may obtain on a cause of action surviving death.

(4) **Recovery by one spouse from the other:** [§151] California Family Code section 781(c) provides that all recovery for personal injury that one spouse receives from the other by judgment or settlement is the separate property of the recipient in every case.

   (a) **Criticism:** This rule can have absurd consequences. For example, if W negligently injures H and H recovers money for lost earnings that would have been community property, such sums are immune from W's creditors and H can keep all of such monies (plus half of W's community earnings) at divorce. He can pass them all by will to a third party at his death. This imposes a very harsh penalty on the negligent spouse.

   (b) **Treatment of insurance proceeds:** [§152] Where one spouse recovers personal injury damages from the other and a significant part thereof would be community property absent section 781(c) (*e.g.,* the tort occurs before separation), the real payor will almost certainly be a liability insurance company—since spouses living amicably together are not likely to sue one another except to collect insurance proceeds. Nevertheless, section 781(c) seems to encompass such insurance payments, since it provides that damages paid "by or *on behalf of*" the tortfeasor spouse are the separate property of the recipient.

      1) **No reimbursement claim on premiums:** [§153] Since tracing to the community insurance contract is barred by section 781(c), the community likewise should not be able to claim reimbursement for the amount of premiums paid on the insurance policy in question. While the premiums purchased a separate recovery for the victim spouse, they also bought protection for the community against tort liability to third parties; the community has therefore received what it paid for.

(5) **Imputed negligence:** [§154] Suppose H is injured by the acts of D, who is 80% the negligent cause of H's injuries, and W, who is 20% at fault. Under California Civil Code section 1431.2, a tortfeasor like D is jointly and severally liable for 100% of economic damages (*e.g.,* lost earnings, reimbursement for medical bills) even though his liability for noneconomic damages (*e.g.,* pain and suffering) cannot exceed 80% (the amount of his fault). With respect to D's liability for economic damages, Family Code section 783 has been construed to bar imputing W's negligence to plaintiff H to reduce H's recovery to 80% under the rule of comparative negligence, even though recovery is community property which the negligent W will co-own. [Lantis v. Condon, 95 Cal. App. 3d 152 (1979)]

c. **Recovery for loss of consortium:** [§155] Each spouse has a cause of action against a tortfeasor who injures the other spouse so that she or he cannot engage in marital sex. [Rodriguez v. Bethlehem Steel Corp., 12 Cal. 3d 382 (1974)] This recovery ought to be community property, since the right invaded depends on marriage, and recovery cannot be traced to any separate property right. Whether such recovery would be viewed as "personal injury damages" at divorce under California Family Code section 2603 (*see supra,* §141) is not settled.

d. **Workers' compensation awards:** [§156] Workers' compensation benefits recovered by a spouse injured on the job have been held ***not*** to be personal injury damages under Family Code sections 2603 and 781. [Marriage of Fisk, 2 Cal. App. 4th 1698 (1992)] Hence, they are classified not on the basis of when the injury occurred, but rather under "in lieu" tracing theory (*see infra,* §161). *Fisk* says the benefits are ***100%*** in lieu of post-injury lost wages and in no way are intended to compensate for pain and suffering or to reimburse for medical care paid, for example, by community funds. Since pre-separation medical expenses are clearly community debts, in *Fisk* W received for the community no reimbursement from H's workers' compensation damages paid after separation for medical expenses paid with community funds; they were a proper source of payment. (The result may be technically correct but seems unfair.)

(1) **No tracing to payroll deductions:** [§157] In one case, nonvictim W contended that the workers' compensation award H received was traceable to community labor or payroll deductions that made him eligible for payments. The court held that this kind of direct tracing was improper. [Marriage of Robinson, 54 Cal. App. 3d 682 (1976); *and see infra,* §161—"in lieu" tracing, which occurred in Marriage of Robinson]

e. **Private disability contracts:** [§158] Where a spouse has purchased with community funds (and probably, too, when he has acquired by payroll deductions) a private, nonstatutory contract to pay disability benefits if he becomes unable to work, subsequent benefits are apportioned. Payments received in lieu of lost wages that would have been received after divorce or separation but for the disability are separate property. Payments for lost wages that would have been community are, of course, community. Additionally, where payments extend beyond the disabled worker's normal retirement age, they are viewed as in lieu of pension benefits and are community because the consideration paid was community. [Marriage of Saslow, 40 Cal. 3d 848 (1985)]

(1) **Mixed consideration contracts:** The theory developed in term life insurance cases, that each insurance-coverage period acquired by making a premium payment (*see supra,* §93), applies to that portion of disability insurance benefits received that is in lieu of lost earnings and not a form of investment for retirement. Thus, if H used community funds for 20 years for disability coverage, then made one premium payment with separate funds and became disabled during the period of coverage the payment acquired, all benefits received in lieu of lost earnings are H's separate property. [Marriage of Elfmont, 9 Cal. 4th 1026 (1995)]

(2) **Convertible benefits:** [§159] Many pension plans, both statutory and by private contract, provide that if a worker must retire for disability reasons,

he can convert his longevity pension benefits into disability benefits at a higher level. At divorce, future benefits are again apportioned: So much as the worker would have received at his earliest retirement age is treated as a longevity pension (and will be 100% community if all consideration was community labor or money); the balance is separate property if it appears to be awarded in lieu of lost earnings. [Marriage of Stenquist, 21 Cal. 3d 779 (1978)] Arguably, if the injury occurred before separation, the excess sums the retired worker receives after his expected retirement date are community property personal injury damages subject to section 2603 (*see supra,* §§141, 144) and a division "in the interests of justice."

(3) **Contracts providing for severance pay:** [§160]   Although not involving any protection against tortious injury, a contract providing severance pay upon loss of a job is similar to a disability benefit contract. One case held that a payment of a lump sum upon loss of his job by H after he had separated from W was separate property, as a payment in lieu of separate earnings he was giving up. This was so, held the court, even though the amount of payment was based on years worked on the job (*i.e.,* tied directly to community labor). [Kuzmiak v. Kuzmiak, 176 Cal. App. 3d 1152 (1986)] A contrary decision found the severance award earned by the community. [Marriage of Horn, 181 Cal. App. 3d 548 (1986)]

(a) **"In lieu" tracing:** [§161]   What the court did in *Kuzmiak* can be called "in lieu" tracing. That is, the court traces not to the funds paid or other consideration that created the contract, but rather to what the payment *is in lieu of* (in *Kuzmiak,* post-separation separate earnings). Such in lieu tracing is finding increasing acceptance in the courts. In cases where the consideration was community and in lieu tracing results in separate property classification for funds paid out (as in *Kuzmiak*), consider the possibility of the community's asserting a reimbursement claim based on unjust enrichment of the separate estate.

1) **Statute of Frauds inapplicable:** Apparently, the in lieu tracing theory allows classification of payments as separate property even when 100% of the consideration is paid with community funds. As in *Elfmont, supra,* the intention of the spouses is a significant factor in applying the in lieu tracing doctrine. The doctrine operates as a judge-made exception to the special Statute of Frauds for transmutations (*see infra,* §175), because the statutory exception for mixed-consideration cases (*see infra,* §178) does not apply to these situations.

f. **Recovery for wrongful death:** [§162]   Although the "time of injury" test (as opposed to a tracing approach) has been applied to wrongful death recoveries received by a spouse [Cervantes v. Maco Gas Co., 177 Cal. App. 2d 246 (1960)], the characterization should properly depend on the nature of the claim. Thus, a plaintiff spouse who clearly establishes that the wrongful death award was based on what the decedent would have provided that spouse alone as separate property—*i.e.,* as gifts—should be able to rebut the presumption that a cause of action arising during marriage is community property. It seems particularly foolish to classify a recovery H obtains for wrongful death of his father or of his child by a prior marriage as community property co-owned by W just because the death occurred during H's marriage to W.

(1) **Effect of separation or divorce:** [§163]   If the wrongful death of a child occurs after separation of the spouses, each parent proves his or her own damages and recovery of each is separate property. [Christiana v. Rose, 100 Cal. App. 2d 46 (1950)] If the death occurs during marriage but recovery is obtained after divorce (or after dissolution of the community by death), the recovery should likewise be characterized as separate property. [Flores v. Brown, *supra,* §149; Washington v. Washington, *supra,* §143] (This assumes that divorce courts will consider section 2603's rules regarding "community property personal injury damage" (*see supra,* §141) inapplicable to wrongful death recoveries.)

(2) **Imputed negligence in wrongful death cases:** [§164]   Where wrongful death recovery is community property (*e.g.,* because no attempt is made to show that the award was in lieu of separate property gifts that decedent would have made to the plaintiff), negligence by the plaintiff's spouse will likely be attributed to plaintiff in applying the comparative negligence doctrine. Section 783 (*see supra,* §154) probably would bar the damages reduction only in a case where the ***married person*** (rather than a relative) is injured.

(a) **Effect of transmutation:** [§165]   A post-tort agreement by the negligent spouse that any recovery will be separate property of the plaintiff (nonnegligent) spouse will not eliminate reduction of damages under the comparative negligence doctrine where the agreement is made ***after*** the cause of action arose. [Kesler v. Pabst, 43 Cal. 2d 254 (1954)] However, a contract made ***before*** the cause of action arises that all acquisitions (or even just all acquisitions via tort law) of H and W would be separate property of each would make negligence of the nonplaintiff spouse irrelevant.

E. **ALTERING STATUTORY AND CASE AUTHORITY BY HUSBAND-WIFE AGREEMENT**

1. **In General:** [§166]   The various rules for classifying property as community or separate are not mandatory but may be altered by agreement between the spouses. [Cal. Fam. Code §721] In addition, rights conferred on a spouse by law may be unilaterally waived by him or her.

2. **Antenuptial Agreements:** [§167]   California's version of the Uniform Premarital Agreement Act ("U.P.A.A.") provides that contracts made before marriage affecting marital rights in property (both real and personal) must be in writing and can be amended or revoked only by a writing. [Cal. Fam. Code §§1611, 1614] Prior to 1985, when unwritten transmutations were recognized, a similar Statute of Frauds was always avoided by the courts by finding either a post-marriage reaffirmance of the oral agreement [Woods v. Security First National Bank, 46 Cal. 2d 697 (1956)] or a post-marriage "ratification" by conduct [Estate of Wahlefeld, 105 Cal. App. 770 (1940)]. Still another case held that H was estopped to invoke the Statute because W "relied" on the agreement in marrying H! [Estate of Sheldon, 75 Cal. App. 3d 364 (1977)] Because unwritten transmutations are now prohibited (*see infra,* §173), the reaffirmance and ratification devices to avoid the Statute of Frauds for

antenuptial agreements are now unavailable. It remains to be seen if the courts will recognize a weak estoppel doctrine as a basis for avoiding the U.P.A.A.

- a. **Unconscionability:** [§168] The U.P.A.A. section applicable to all provisions of a premarital contract indicates that unconscionability will void a promise only if there was no full disclosure of pertinent facts to the aggrieved spouse. [Cal. Fam. Code §1615]

- b. **Public policy limitation—must not promote divorce:** [§169] Even if an antenuptial agreement appears to be one-sided (*e.g.*, H agrees that W's earnings will be separate property but his own will be community), such contracts are based on the consideration of marriage, and the apparent one-sidedness will not render them void per se. An antenuptial contract that "promotes divorce" is invalid as against public policy. [Marriage of Dawley, 17 Cal. 3d 342 (1976)] It is not precisely clear what this means, although a contract giving W 80% of all H's separate and 80% of all community property at divorce would probably be void under this limitation.

    - (1) **Example:** In *Marriage of Noghrey,* 169 Cal. App. 3d 326 (1985), the court held void as promoting divorce H's promise to pay W at divorce the greater of $500,000 or half his estate (which included his extensive separate property). The U.P.A.A. says that an antenuptial contract can provide how property will be divided at divorce or death of a spouse, but a note adds that such provision must not be "in violation of public policy."

- c. **Alimony can be waived:** [§170] The U.P.A.A. as drafted by the Commissioners on Uniform Laws specifically allowed a spouse to waive alimony except to the extent that this would make the party after the divorce dependent on welfare assistance. The California legislature eliminated the provision authorizing waiver of alimony when enacting the California version of the U.P.A.A. According to *Marriage of Pendleton,* 62 Cal. App. 4th 751 (1998) (petition for review in California Supreme Court filed), this statutory change left it to the courts to apply public policy, and in the contemporary context of no-fault divorces, a waiver of alimony in an antenuptial agreement is ***not per se void***. Whether the courts will void the waiver to the extent it forces a divorced spouse onto welfare rolls remains to be seen.

    - (1) **Waiver of support after separation:** *Pendleton, supra,* does not address contractual waivers of the duty each spouse owes the other ***during*** marriage. It is established, however, that ***after they separate***, spouses may contract to waive the benefits of the support duty. [Marriage of Epstein, *supra,* §58] Indeed, California Family Code section 4302 provides that such a waiver by each spouse is ***implied*** in a separation contract that does not refer to a continuing duty of support.

3. **Postnuptial "Transmutations":** [§171] During marriage, the spouses may change the status of any or all of their property, presently owned or thereafter acquired. Such changes—from separate to community, from community to separate or from the separate estate of one spouse to the separate estate of the other—are referred to as "transmutations" and can be accomplished by contract or gift. A transmutation that is neither a contract (because there is no consideration) nor a gift (because no asset capable of delivery is involved) is also recognized—*e.g.,* H signs a writing stating

"I agree that my wife's future earnings will be her separate property." [Estate of Raphael, 91 Cal. App. 2d 931 (1949)]

a. **Older rule—no formalities:** [§172] For many years, no formalities were required for effective postnuptial transmutation. For example, the statement "what is mine is yours and what is yours is mine" was held sufficient to transmute separate into community property. [Durrell v. Bacon, 138 Cal. App. 396 (1934)] The transmutation took effect as soon as the agreement or statement was made and required no deeds, delivery, change of possession, etc. If intended to apply to assets not yet acquired, the transmutation acted upon them at the instant of acquisition [Wren v. Wren, 100 Cal. 276 (1893)]; and evidence corroborative of the oral declaration was not required [Woods v. Security First National Bank, *supra*, §167]. Finally, an oral agreement transmuting real property was *valid notwithstanding the Statute of Frauds*, since the source of acquisition—rather than "title"—governed whether property is community or separate and, said the courts, because it was "fully executed" when made. Contracts already performed are not subject to the Statute of Frauds. [Woods v. Security First National Bank, *supra*, §167] In sum, transmutation was easy to achieve. To create a joint tenancy, however, a writing was required.

   (1) **Pre-1985 "treatment" of property may supersede contract:** [§173] In one tax case, H and W executed a written antenuptial contract providing that they would live separate in property (*i.e.*, each would own his or her acquisitions as if unmarried). Later, the spouses worked together at a business and "treated" the earnings as co-owned. Despite the antenuptial contract, the tax court held that such earnings were community property. [Springer v. Commissioner, 36 T.C.M. 782 (1977)] Conversely, where H treated separate property as community in filing federal income tax returns, he nevertheless was permitted at a pre-1985 dissolution to establish by nonwritten evidence that there was no separate-to-community transmutation (just a tax fraud). [Estate of Neilson, 57 Cal. 2d 733 (1962)]

b. **Post-1984 transmutation—writing required:** [§174] Effective in 1985, Family Code section 852 requires, with limited exceptions, a writing with an "express declaration that is made, joined in, consented to, or accepted by the spouse whose interest in the property is adversely affected" in order for a transmutation to be valid. The statute applies to both real and personal property. Legislative history suggests that the lawmakers were serious about eliminating oral or implied transmutations; thus, it is unlikely that the courts will avoid section 852 by finding an unwritten transmutation "fully executed" or by finding a weak estoppel. However, the part performance doctrine, generally applicable to oral dealings in realty, could apply.

   (1) **Writing must be unambiguous:** [§175] In a leading case, H designated a trust that he controlled as beneficiary at his death of community-owned retirement benefits. W signed a form that said: "I hereby consent to the above designation." This was held too ambiguous to be the "express" declaration section 852 requires. Neither could extrinsic evidence be received to make it express. (W was dying of cancer and had previously divided up all other co-owned property so that there would be no community property when she died.) [Estate of MacDonald, 51 Cal. 3d 262 (1990)] The writing must show that the alleged transmuter knows

that she has or may have a property interest affected by the document. In dictum, the court said that the following would suffice if signed by W on a bank account funded with community money: "I give my husband 'any interest I have in the funds deposited in this account.'"

(2) **Exceptions:** [§176] The old law applies to pre-1985 transmutations. Also, section 852(c) excludes from its writing requirement "a gift between the spouses of clothing, wearing apparel, jewelry, or other tangible articles of a personal nature used solely or principally by the spouse to whom the gift is made and that is not substantial in value taking into account the circumstances of the marriage."

(3) **Statute inapplicable to "mixing" situations:** [§177] No writing is required where ownership changes due to a mixing of community and separate funds. [Cal. Fam. Code §852(d)]

    (a) **Example:** H uses community funds to make a mortgage payment on land in his name, all prior payments having been made with H's separate funds. The community acquires a pro rata share of ownership despite no express writing (*see supra,* §111).

(4) **Writings in signed will:** [§178] A mere statement of characterization in a will cannot be a transmutation; *e.g.,* "Blackacre is community property, and I leave my half interest to . . . " (when in fact, H had inherited the land). [Cal. Fam. Code §853] Even a precise statement that meets the *MacDonald* test ("Blackacre is my inherited separate property but I hereby transmute it to community property and devise my half to . . . ") may not be immediately effective, because a will does not have legal effect until the testator dies.

4. **Situations in Which Transmutation May Be Inferred or Presumed**

  a. **Traditional gifts:** [§179] If one spouse "gives" the other a present on a holiday, birthday, anniversary, etc., in the traditional sense of wrapping the present and including a greeting card, under both pre-1985 law and section 852's exception clause (above), this may be enough for a transmutation by the donor spouse from community property (or the donor's separate property) to donee's separate property (or from the donor's separate property to the community). However, such a traditional gift is not conclusive of an intent to transmute, but merely offers an *inference* of such intent that the trier of fact may or may not draw. [Estate of Walsh, 66 Cal. App. 2d 704 (1944)] The burden of proof is on the party claiming that there was a gift-type transmutation creating separate property; and if the burden is not met, the nature of the funds used to purchase the asset "given" to the spouse would control classification of the property.

    (1) **Criticism:** The uncertainty as to when a traditional "gift" has worked a transmutation—with the law inviting the trier of fact to draw whatever inferences it wishes—helps to foster litigation. When a creditor of one spouse seeks to levy execution, the debtor spouse as donor of previous gifts may well "recall" an intent to transmute (or not to transmute, whichever defeats the levy), which the creditor will have problems disproving. More definite rules in this area would help to clarify when a transmutation has occurred and create a more fair and efficient marital property system.

(2) **Gift should be presumed:** [§180]   There would be more certainty if rather than permitting an inference to be drawn, the law raised a presumption of transmutation to the donee's separate estate when a personal gift covered by the exception clause in section 852 is made. Many cases have *presumed* a gift rather than just allowing an inference to be drawn when a spouse used community funds under his control to improve separate property of the other or used his own separate funds to improve community property. [*See* Shaw v. Bernal, 163 Cal. 262 (1912)] This rule may still apply as to improvements despite the substantial changes in the law of management and control since it was formulated. (*See supra*, §§122, 124.) The rule could reasonably be extended to birthday gift situations.

b. **Effect of recitals in pre-1985 deeds:** [§181]   In community property states (unlike common law states), recitals in deeds of a married person are not presumed to be true but are—at most—admissions of those parties signing the instrument. Thus where a deed delivered to H during marriage recites that H takes the property as his separate estate, and the deed is signed *only by the grantor*, the recital has no legal effect. It does not establish that H in fact used separate money for the purchase, nor does it prove that W transmuted community property to H's separate estate. [Tolman v. Smith, 85 Cal. 280 (1890)] The same rule would apply to a recital that H's separate property had been used to make the purchase.

(1) **Caveat regarding pre-1975 instruments:** [§182]   Recall that in pre-1975 instruments, the mere naming of W as grantee raises a presumption that the property conveyed is her separate property. (*See* discussion *supra*, §§22-23.)

(2) **Effect of grantee's own signature:** [§183]   Obviously, the effect of a recital of separate ownership by H cannot be altered by the fact that H (as well as the grantor) may have signed the deed (*i.e.*, deed of indenture). Such a signature would of course show H's intent, but it would not indicate the source of funds used or show W's intent—and only W can unilaterally transmute community funds into H's separate property.

(3) **Effect of wife's signature:** [§184]   If W signed the deed to H containing the recital that the property was separately H's, this should be enough evidence under pre-1985 law to conclude W has given up all interest in the property she might have based on consideration paid. However, under post-1984 law (*see supra*, §175), the writing is not sufficiently "express" to work a transmutation because it does not indicate W's awareness that she had an interest in the consideration paid.

(4) **Recital of joint tenancy:** [§185]   Pre-1985 case law was inconsistent in treating a recital of joint tenancy in a deed to both spouses delivered during marriage. The cases *presumed* from the recital that the spouse had made a transmutation agreement to change the funds used to buy the property (presumptively community) to joint tenancy property—even where one of the spouses (or both) did not sign the deed. [*See* Tomaier v. Tomaier, 23 Cal. 2d 754 (1944)] Proof that the funds used for the acquisition in question were not themselves joint tenancy property was not sufficient to rebut the presumption of a joint tenancy. However, proof that the

spouses did not understand the difference between joint tenancy and community property *would* overcome the presumption, since the parties could not agree to alter community funds to a form of which they were not aware. [Hansford v. Lassar, 53 Cal. App. 3d 364 (1975)]

(a) **Unilateral intent insufficient:** [§186] The courts held that the presumption arising from a recital of joint tenancy in a deed not signed by both spouses was not rebutted by proof that one of the grantee spouses did not intend a transmutation. [Machado v. Machado, 58 Cal. 2d 501 (1962)] This may be a sound rule where the other spouse is shown to have reasonably believed that a transmutation was occurring. (*See* Contracts Summary.) But if the evidence indicates that through the fault of neither spouse there was never a "meeting of the minds" to transmute, the trier of fact should be able to find that there was no transmutation. A rule that the presumption can be overcome only by showing the spouses in fact *agreed* that the community status would *not* terminate is illogical in demanding more than proof that there was no transmutation.

(b) **Criticism of presumption:** [§187] No reason appears for presuming a transmutation from a recital of joint tenancy but not from a recital of separate ownership by one spouse. The issue in both cases should be whether it is probable that the spouses agree with the recitation in the deed. Moreover, with the reform of probate proceedings in the 1970s, whatever practical reasons once existed for favoring joint tenancy ownership because of its right of survivorship no longer seem to be present.

1) **Persons harmed by presumption:** [§188] The old rule regarding a joint tenancy recital deprives the first spouse to die of the power of testamentary disposition over half of the property in question, unless the spouse is astute enough to sever the joint tenancy before death. Creditors of either spouse are harmed: Joint tenancy is half the separate property of each spouse, and the creditor of one spouse alone can reach only half, whereas *all* the community property could be reached (*see infra*, §273). (Creditors do have standing to rebut the joint tenancy presumption, and have succeeded by showing that the couple did not know the difference between joint tenancy and community property. [Hansford v. Lassar, *supra*]) Finally, the surviving spouse loses the tax benefit of a stepped-up basis given the survivor's half of appreciated community (but not joint tenancy) property by I.R.C. section 1041(b)(6).

(c) **Effect of 1985 Statute of Frauds:** [§189] Section 852 (*see supra*, §174) states that an unsigned transmutation document may be valid if "accepted by the party whose interest in the property is adversely affected." Where community money is used and a joint tenancy deed taken, the loss of testamentary power and loss of management over half the property are likely to be held to be such an adverse effect. However, even if both spouses read the deed while receiving it and understand what a joint tenancy is, section 852 as interpreted in

MacDonald (*see supra,* §175) should bar finding a transmutation. The accepted deed will not disclose that the spouse's ownership interest in the funds used for the acquisition was also not in joint tenancy, and thus there will be no "express" writing showing the deed would work a transmutation. *MacDonald* indicates that extrinsic evidence cannot come in to prove that the deed worked a change of legal rights (in management and testamentary powers).

(d) **True joint tenancy deeds not severed by filing for divorce:** [§190] Family Code section 2580 provides that at divorce property conveyed by a deed reciting joint tenancy is ***presumed*** to be community property. In the case of a pre-1985 deed merely reciting joint tenancy ownership (and lacking language of transmutation), section 2580 has the effect of severing the joint tenancy when action for divorce is filed so that if a spouse dies while the action is pending the other does not take by right of survivorship. [Marriage of Hilke, 4 Cal. 4th 215 (1992)] Section 2580 does not apply and the filing for divorce does not work a severance, if the deed says the spouses take as joint tenants "and not as community property" or otherwise specifically states an intent to transmute community funds used for the acquisition into joint tenancy.

   1) **Right of reimbursement:** [§191] Where one spouse's ***separate*** property is used to buy just a ***part*** of property with title taken in the name of both spouses, even the most express statement in the deed that the separate property contributor intends a transmutation to community, joint tenancy, or tenancy in common ownership is sometimes not enough to eliminate all separate property rights. At divorce, the separate property contributor still has a right of reimbursement under Family Code section 2640 unless he or she has "signed" a waiver of the reimbursement right. Mere acceptance of a deed reciting such waiver is ineffective for lack of a signature. *Note:* Section 2640 applies only at divorce.

   2) **Exception for joint bank accounts:** [§192] California Probate Code section 5305 provides that the spouses' joint tenancy bank account is presumptively community property but that the presumption can be overcome by ***tracing to separate funds that were deposited*** into the account. Section 5305 controls joint tenancy bank accounts at divorce; sections 2581 and 2640 ***do not apply***.

      a) **Note:** Section 5305 also controls a joint tenancy bank account at a spouse's death. Under section 5305, the community presumption may be overcome and a spouse's right of survivorship can be preserved pro rata by tracing deposits to funds that were held in true joint tenancy.

(5) **Recital of ownership by married couple as tenants in common:** [§193] There is no authority on whether a transmutation will be presumed from

a recital in a pre-1985 deed not signed by the couple that they take as tenants in common. Whatever logic led to the pro-joint tenancy presumption could apply here, but the policy reasons—*i.e.,* promoting quick succession at death at a saving of probate costs—are not the same because there is no right of survivorship with a tenancy in common. This issue is important when a creditor strikes. However, at divorce, tenancy in common property is treated like community property. [Cal. Fam. Code §2650]

5. **Effect of Husband-Wife Agreement on Third Parties:** [§194] All transmutations that are valid between the spouses are also binding on third parties who become creditors *after* the transmutation occurs. [Kennedy v. Taylor, 155 Cal. App. 3d 126 (1984)—irrelevant that a formal transfer by deed that effectuated the pre-1985 oral transmutation occurred after H went into debt]

   a. **Title to land:** [§195] Unlike the statutes it replaced, the U.P.A.A. (*see supra,* §167) does *not* state that an antenuptial agreement affecting ownership to land (*e.g.,* by changing separate realty into community at the moment of marriage) must be recorded in the situs county to bind third parties. *But note:* The general recording act could be construed to have that effect insofar as land is affected. (*See infra,* §197.)

   b. **Existing creditors:** [§196] Persons who are creditors of a spouse at the time of a transmutation are not bound by it if it renders the spouse insolvent. Thus, where H and W transmute community property into two equal shares of separately owned property, H's existing creditors can have the transmutation set aside if his half of former community property that was wholly liable to the creditors is insufficient to pay them. [Wikes v. Smith, 465 F.2d 1142 (9th Cir. 1972)]

   c. **Reliance on record title:** [§197] A third party who initially deals with a spouse *after* transmutation and who actually relies on record title consistent with pre-transmutation (but not post-transmutation) ownership has been held entitled to avoid the transmutation agreement. Thus, a purchaser or secured lender actually aware that title to realty is in joint tenancy can rely on one spouse's being able to convey a half interest without joinder of the other. (This would be voidable if the property were community; *see infra,* §229.) An unrecorded agreement that the property remains community (having been bought with community funds) or a transmutation to the separate property of one of the spouses (even if she alone is in possession) cannot affect the rights of third parties relying on record title. [Kane v. Huntley Financial, 146 Cal. App. 3d 1092 (1983)]

F. **EXCEPTIONS TO NORMAL CLASSIFICATION RULES**

   1. **"Terminable Interest" Doctrine:** [§198] An old rule reducing the community interest in pension benefits was abrogated in 1986 by enactment of what is now California Family Code section 2610. Under prior law (called the "terminable interest doctrine"), an interest in a community pension earned by H and awarded to W would terminate at her death (unless all interest in the pension had previously been awarded to H at divorce, in which case W would have no interest to be terminated) even though retired H (or ex-H) was still alive and receiving a flow of benefits earned by the community. That is, W was deprived of testamentary power over her

share. Section 2610 restores it. Also under old law, if H remarried after being divorced from W and then died, W as an ex-wife had no interest in survivor benefits paid to the legal widow. The issue arose when the divorce court failed to award the survivor benefit to H alone so that there was no decree cutting off the ex-wife's interest. Today, in this situation an ex-wife can claim an appropriate fractional interest (it would be one half if H earned 100% of the pension rights during marriage and cohabitation with W) in the benefit for the surviving widow.

    a. **Exception—statutory pension plan:** [§199] Section 2610 has limited effect where a state statute creates the applicable terms of the pension plan and provides that only the legal spouse of the participant and not an ex-spouse has a right to post-death benefits. In such a case, the divorce court cannot award the participant's ex-spouse a share of post-death benefits. [Marriage of Cramer, 20 Cal. App. 4th 73 (1993)] This is because the specific statute directed to a particular pension plan prevails over the general section 2610. In a nonstatutory plan, the provision denying a divorcing spouse a community share of future death benefits would probably be void unless the participant's spouse signed a document expressly giving up the community interest protected by section 2610. (*See also infra,* §503—federal preemption can force California courts to adhere to terminable interest doctrine despite section 2610.)

        (1) **Remedy at divorce:** Where a state statute disqualifies the divorcing spouse from an award of future death benefits, section 2610 empowers the court to award the spouse more than a 50% share of lifetime benefits (that were community property) that the participant will receive after divorce to compensate for the loss of community-earned death benefits. Alternatively, a lump sum award to the spouse, or her estate if she is dead, would be an appropriate mode of compensation, and it could be made payable at the time of the participant spouse's death when the value of death benefits is known. [Marriage of Carnall, 216 Cal. App. 3d 1010 (1989)]

2. **Educational Degrees and Licenses to Practice:** [§200] A 1984 statute confirms prior case law holdings that, while college degrees and governmentally issued licenses to practice a profession are property for some purposes, they are ***not capable of community ownership***. [Cal. Fam. Code §2641] The statute provides, however, that at divorce the community is entitled to ***reimbursement*** for community funds used to educate or train one of the spouses so as to increase his or her earning capacity. Legal interest is payable on the sum reimbursed.

    a. **Calculating the reimbursement amount:** [§201] Reimbursement is to be reduced or eliminated if the community has "substantially benefited" from the spouse's education or training, although it is presumed (rebuttably) that there has been no such benefit from expenditures made less than 10 years before the divorce action is filed.

    b. **Unpaid educational loans:** [§202] At divorce, unpaid educational loans are classified as the ***separate debt*** of the educated spouse except to the extent there has been substantial benefit to the community from the education (subject to the 10-year presumption above). (*See infra,* §326.)

c. **Exclusive remedy:** [§203]   The statute says that reimbursement "pursuant to this section" (which deals solely with divorce) is the exclusive remedy for claims based on community expenditures increasing a spouse's earning capacity. This may mean that a court *cannot* order educated H to pay any reimbursement to W's estate when she *dies* days after he receives his medical degree following extensive community expenditures for his medical education.

d. **Distinguish business goodwill:** [§204]   The professional goodwill created by one spouse operating as a sole proprietor is community property to the extent that it is generated by labor during marriage and cohabitation. At divorce, therefore, it should be valued as community property and awarded to the professional spouse who developed it with an offsetting award to the other spouse. [Marriage of Fortier, 34 Cal. App. 3d 384 (1973)]

   (1) **Incorporated professional:** [§205]   If the business is incorporated, the value of the goodwill shows up in the value of the community-owned stock in the corporation and need not be separately valued. If the stock is subject to a buy-sell agreement between the professionals in the corporation at a fixed price that does not take account of goodwill, one case holds that that price governs the valuation; *i.e.,* goodwill of the corporation vanishes as a community asset. [Marriage of Aufmuth, 89 Cal. App. 3d 446 (1979)]

   (2) **Partnership:** [§206]   If the professional works in a partnership, the community interest is the spouse's contract rights arising out of the partnership agreement; the community has no interest in any specific partnership asset. [Cal. Corp. Code §15025(e)] Nevertheless, a partner's own goodwill will be valued at divorce as a community asset. [Marriage of Slater, 100 Cal. App. 3d 241 (1979)]

   (a) **Example:** In *Slater,* the physician H had a contract with his co-partners that if he ceased to be a partner, the others could buy out his interest for the value of the capital account and accounts receivable attributable to H, with no payment for goodwill. Despite this feature making the goodwill inalienable by H, the divorce court was ordered to value it on the assumption that H would remain in the partnership and the goodwill would attract patients.

   (b) **Comment:** *Slater* and all post-1979 pertinent cases suggest that *Aufmuth* (*supra,* §205) was wrongly decided. No logical distinction exists between an agreement fixing a price (that ignores goodwill) to pay a departing partner compared to a departing shareholder where the professional firm is incorporated. *Aufmuth* should have ignored the buy-sell agreement there.

   (3) **Treatment of goodwill upon remarriage:** [§207]   If the professional goodwill awarded H or W at divorce is property at divorce, it will still be property if and when the spouse remarries and continues to work at the profession. Arguably, this goodwill is part of the separately owned capital of the spouse's profession and should therefore be entitled to a return of capital under *Pereira* or *Van Camp* (*see supra,* §§63-76) in the same manner that tangible capital assets used in the profession generate some separate profits under an apportionment formula. But, after remarriage, as the

spouse renews contacts with former clients/patients and obtains work, his or her goodwill increasingly becomes an asset based on post-marriage labor. After a while, the spouse's separate interest should evaporate.

3. **Pensions with "Vesting" Requirements:** [§208]   Prior to 1976, nonvested interests in a pension plan were separate property even though earned by community labor or monetary contributions. This aberration was rejected in *Marriage of Brown*, 15 Cal. 3d 838 (1976).

4. **Earned Expectancies:** [§209]   Certain *earned* expectancies that do not look like true property rights can nevertheless be community property. For example, a community interest has been found in retirement pay that H would receive from the United States government as a result of working for the military while married to and cohabiting with W—even though H had no *contract* right to receive the pay (*i.e.*, Congress could have abolished the retirement pay program for those in the military). [Marriage of Fithian, 10 Cal. 3d 592 (1974)]

   a. **Tips or gratuities:** [§210]   "Tips" received by one spouse for services provided during marriage and cohabitation are community property (*see supra*, §38). The same result should apply to a year-end "bonus" paid as a reward for employee services.

   b. **Merit raises:** [§211]   Instead of a year-end bonus, an employee may receive an increase in salary for future labor with the employer's specific statement that the raise is a reward for meritorious service during the previous year. Suppose that in this situation the employee and spouse finally separate the day before the raise takes effect. Even though post-separation labor by the employee is a prerequisite to receiving the increased salary, it can be argued that the employee's right to be paid an amount in excess of the prior salary is community, as a return for pre-separation labor.

      (1) **Analogy to deferred compensation:** [§212]   In *Marriage of Skaden*, 19 Cal. 3d 679 (1977), H, an insurance salesman, had a right upon discharge to receive benefits calculated as a percentage of premiums paid on life insurance he had sold (during marriage). The court held that even if the discharge occurred after marriage, the benefits would have to be viewed as earned by labor expended selling insurance and not by being "discharged." By the same reasoning, the mere fact that a merit raise is not paid until after separation need not preclude an appropriate classification of the benefits.

      (2) **Gratuity given after divorce:** [§213]   Suppose at divorce W shows a long practice at the company where H works that suggests that sometime after divorce H is likely to be awarded a bonus based on performance that included a period when the spouses were married and cohabiting. Should the divorce court reserve jurisdiction to calculate a community interest in the event such a bonus is awarded? In a case where W had shown a history of recurrent bonuses awarded in the form of stock options, one court said no, concluding that "claims of a community interest in employee stock options granted to the employee spouse after dissolution of the marriage would appear too speculative and would lack the immediacy and specificity necessary for exercise of jurisdiction over them." [Marriage

of Hug, 154 Cal. App. 3d 780 (1984)] A similar, dubious holding was made concerning a regularly given but not contractually compelled year-end bonus paid to H after separation. [Marriage of Nelson, 177 Cal. App. 3d 150 (1986)]

    c. **Right to reinstate pension participation:** [§214] When a spouse participates during marriage in a pension plan and, upon withdrawing from it and removing community funds deposited, retains a right to redeposit the withdrawal and rejoin the pension program, that right is a community asset, and not a mere expectancy. [Marriage of Lucero, 118 Cal. App. 3d 836 (1981); *but see* Marriage of Forrest, 97 Cal. App. 3d 850 (1979)—contra]

gilbert LAW SUMMARIES — CHARACTERIZATION OF PROPERTY THAT IS DIFFICULT TO CLASSIFY

Type of Property	Characterization
Pensions in General	Apportioned CP/SP
Pensions Through Federal Government	*See infra*, §§501-504
Stock Options	Apportioned CP/SP
Life Insurance Proceeds	Trace to last premium
SP Property Insurance Proceeds	SP (but right of reimbursement for premiums paid from CP)
Tort Recovery Against Third Party	CP if cause of action arose during marriage (note divorce exception)
Tort Recovery Against Spouse	SP
Disability Pay	CP (to extent replacing marital earnings)
Severance Pay	Generally treat like disability pay
Education Degrees	Not CP (but right of reimbursement under certain circumstances)
Business Goodwill	CP

II. MANAGEMENT AND CONTROL OF PROPERTY

chapter approach

Exam questions involving management and control problems often appear in three fact situations: (i) where a creditor is seeking the marital property (so that the rules of law in chapter III as well as this chapter are implicated); (ii) where one spouse has attempted to convey community property without the consent of the other; or (iii) at dissolution, where one spouse claims damages from the other for mismanagement (*e.g.,* a gift of community property not consented to). When you see these situations or any problem regarding management and control, you should first identify whether a community asset at issue is subject to *equal, primary,* or *dual* management. Then cast about for some reasons why the normal rule should *not* apply (*e.g.,* W is estopped to assert that she did not join in a dual management transaction). And consider the *restrictions* on management powers concerning gifts, good faith dealing by a spouse, and incompetency.

The question may invite discussion of *remedies* for violations of the rules concerning management. If so, this gives you a chance to be creative, for often an aggrieved party has more than one remedy.

Always remember to keep your answer consistent with the policies at work:

—For *equal management,* recognize W as a true copartner of H, contrary to the historic rule giving him exclusive management power;

—For *primary management* (*i.e.,* of a community business), the promotion of commerce by assuring third parties they may deal with only one person; and

—For *dual management,* protection of the community against improvident acts.

A. SEPARATE PROPERTY

1. **In General:** [§215] Each spouse has *exclusive management* of his or her separate property. The owner-spouse may expressly or impliedly confer *agency power* on the other spouse to deal with such property.

2. **Concurrent Ownership:** [§216] Where the two spouses (or one spouse and the community) are concurrent separate owners of property (such as tenants in common), a separate interest in the property can be *sold* only by the owner-spouse. However, each co-owner has a right of enjoyment and use of the whole—and therefore a good deal of management power over all of the property. (*See* Property Summary.)

B. COMMUNITY PERSONAL PROPERTY

1. **Equal Management:** [§217] Equal management of all community personal property is the *basic* California rule. This means that either spouse without consent

of the other can sell an item of community personalty, make contracts with respect to it (*e.g.,* license another person to use it), and the like. [Cal. Fam. Code §1100(2)] In this summary, "management" refers to the power to deal with property in such manner; "control" means the power to prevent the other spouse from dealing by withholding a required consent.

   a. **Example:** To perfect a security interest in personalty under the U.C.C., a lender must file a financing statement giving the "names of the debtors." The term "debtor" includes the "owner of the collateral." [Cal. Com. Code §9105(1)(d)] If a lender giving credit to H names only H as debtor in taking community personalty as a security, the creditors of W are nevertheless bound because of H's equal management power over W's interest. [*In re* Biane, 20 Bankr. 659 (Bankr. 9th Cir. 1982)] (A dissent in *Biane* questioned how W's creditors were supposed to know that she was married or what her spouse's name was in order to determine what property liable on her debts was subject to a perfected security interest.)

2. **Exceptions**

   a. **Business managed by one spouse alone:** [§218] California Family Code section 1100(d) provides that "a spouse who is operating or managing a business or an interest in a business that is all or substantially all community personal property has the primary management . . . of the business or interest." This rule extends to community personalty that is part of a business also involving community real property.

      (1) **"Primary" management defined:** [§219] "Primary" management means exclusive management with one exception: The managing spouse must advise the other spouse in writing of any proposed sale, lease, exchange, or encumbrance of all or substantially all community personalty used in the business. If a transfer is made without notice when it should have been provided, the transfer itself is valid but the nonmanager spouse has a cause of action for damages. Since this spouse could not have vetoed the transfer after receiving notice, arguably there are no damages if the manager spouse convinces a court or jury that he would have made the transfer despite any arguments against it made by his spouse.

      (2) **Power to exclude:** [§220] If section 1100(d) is to be effective, it must mean that one spouse can exclude the other from joining in the operation of the business. Suppose, for example, that H runs an unincorporated flower shop and W wants to enter into a contract to supply flowers to a hotel chain, although she has never previously involved herself in the business. If W could simply declare herself co-manager and then make the contract, H would not have the primary management provided for in section 1100(d). Apparently, then, an announced intent by the other spouse to join in management has no legal effect until the operator-spouse consents.

      (3) **Establishing a one-spouse community business:** [§221] As long as a spouse acts in good faith (*see infra,* §261), that spouse can deprive the other spouse of equal management over community funds by transferring them to a business that is subject to section 1100(d). If the spouse could

not, that section would be limited to businesses having no capital assets or partly community businesses in which the capital assets are separately owned.

(4) **Effect on third parties:** [§222] Suppose W physically seizes an asset at H's flower shop (*e.g.,* a typewriter) and takes it to her own store, where she sells it to a third party who believes that it is community property over which W has management power. H can probably have the sale set aside on the ground that W lacked authority under section 1100 to make the sale, since the cases indicate that a third party deals with one spouse alone at his peril and takes the risk that the spouse lacked power to convey. [*See, e.g.,* Newell v. Brawner, 140 Cal. App. 2d 523 (1956)] Purchasers from one spouse alone must also beware of "mixed consideration" assets, since the buyer assumes the risk that the seller-spouse lacks authority to sell the separate fractional interest of the other spouse.

b. **Bank and savings and loan accounts:** [§223] A number of statutes provide that a bank or savings and loan account "in the name of a married person shall be . . . free from the control . . . of any other person." [*See, e.g.,* Cal. Fin. Code §851] These statutes provide an easy way to defeat equal management (although the nondepositor spouse is able to obligate such funds by credit purchases; *see infra,* §276). Nevertheless, they relieve banking institutions from the intolerable problem of determining whether funds deposited in the account are community or separate, in the event that the nonsignatory spouse seeks to withdraw "community" property from the account. However, the other spouse usually can obtain a court order adding the spouse's name to the account as a co-depositor (*see infra,* §233).

c. **Right to "seize control" of community assets:** [§224] By practical necessity, some community rights and properties may not lend themselves to equal management, and in such cases one spouse may be able to seize control of the right or property. As noted previously, an employee-spouse appears to have exclusive control over pension contracts (*see infra,* §§312-315). Similarly, if one spouse—say H—files a lawsuit in his name to recover what would be community damages, it is doubtful that a purported dismissal filed by W would have legal effect. And in situations where third parties are involved in continuing relationships with H or W, the courts are likely to find that one spouse has seized control (*e.g.,* if W hires X to do domestic chores around the house, it is doubtful that X must take orders from H or that H can fire X).

d. **Transactions requiring consent of both spouses:** [§225] Equal management does not apply to sales or encumbrances of community furniture, household furnishings, clothing of the nonacting spouse, clothing of the children, or "fittings" of the family dwelling. [Cal. Fam. Code §1100(c)] All such transactions require **written** consent of the nonseller spouse.

(1) **Effect of violating section 1100(c):** [§226] A sale or encumbrance without the consent required by section 1100(c) is ***void ab initio***, not merely voidable by the nonconsenting spouse. Hence, a buyer deals at his peril in taking household property. The nonseller spouse suing to recover the household items need not make restitution of community funds received for the household goods sold or pledged. [Dynan v. Gallinatti, 87 Cal. App. 2d 553 (1948)] Instead of pursuing the buyer of community

property, the nonconsenting spouse can, at least at divorce, compel the other spouse to account. (In one case however, the court held that H made a sufficient accounting simply by testifying that he spent the proceeds of a sale of community household furnishings on his own basic maintenance even though H and W were separated at the time. [Marriage of Cohen, 105 Cal. App. 3d 836 (1980)])

(2) **Oral consent of both spouses could suffice:** [§227]   Section 1100(c) does not require any writing signed by the selling or encumbering spouse. Thus, if *both* spouses deal with the buyer, written consent would not be needed.

C. COMMUNITY REAL PROPERTY

1. **General Rule—Equal Management:** [§228]   Ordinary day-to-day management of community realty is subject to the equal management rule. [Cal. Fam. Code §1102] Thus, one spouse acting alone may properly cut down a tree on the community realty, license an invitee to enter upon the property, and the like.

2. **Dual Management for Alienation:** [§229]   By statute, one spouse alone lacks the power to convey, encumber, or lease for more than one year community realty; in such transactions, both spouses "must join in executing any instrument" of conveyance. [Cal. Fam. Code §1102] Note that a spouse will not be permitted to avoid this rule by unilaterally conveying or encumbering a half interest in community property on the theory that it is his or hers alone.

   a. **Leasehold as realty:** [§230]   If the community owned a leasehold interest, both H and W would have to execute an instrument of assignment or sublease (unless the term was one year or less). [Cal. Fam. Code §700—leasehold is realty under all community property statutes]

   b. **Presumption of validity where one spouse signs:** [§231]   If one spouse alone signs the instrument but that spouse has "record title" to the community real property, section 1102(c) presumes a valid conveyance in favor of "a lessee, purchaser, or encumbrancer in good faith *without knowledge of the marriage relation*." Note that a good faith belief that the property is separate is not enough if the purchaser does not also believe that the grantor or lessor is unmarried.

      (1) **Interpretation of statute:** [§232]   The courts interpret section 1102(c) as creating a *presumption* that the property conveyed is the *separate property* of the grantor or lessor. [Mark v. Title Guarantee Trust Co., 122 Cal. App. 301 (1932)] The presumption can be overcome by proof that community funds were used to acquire the property. (Merely showing acquisition of the realty during marriage is probably not enough to rebut the presumption, however.) It seems unfair to defeat so easily the reasonable expectations of a buyer who paid fair value to a seller who had record title and represented himself as being unmarried.

      (2) **"Add-a-name" remedy:** [§233]   Where title to community property is in the name of one spouse and the other is concerned about operation of the presumption, there is a remedy in California Family Code section

1101(c), authorizing a court to order the titled spouse to change the title so that both spouses are named as owners. (The court's authority extends to personalty as well, but the existence of both names on the title to personalty would not alter equal management power, although it would create power where a spouse's name is added to a bank account containing community funds.) The add-a-name statute does not apply to interests of a general partner or shareholder in a professional corporation. Nor does it apply to any asset in a business subject to section 1100(d) (*see supra*, §218).

c. **Scope of joinder rule:** [§234]   Section 1102 is directed at conveyances involving an "instrument" and apparently does not apply to transactions where an interest in community realty passes because of nonwritten statements or conduct of H or W, either one of whom may act with respect to the property. [*See, e.g.,* Janes v. LeDeit, 228 Cal. App. 2d 474 (1964)—H's acts alone resulted in loss of community realty under doctrine of boundary by acquiescence] For this reason, judgment liens—which arise as a matter of law and not through an "instrument"—can encumber community realty even though one spouse alone was the judgment debtor.

   (1) **Mechanic's or materialman's liens:** [§235]   Likewise, the joinder statute will not apply to a mechanic's or materialman's lien on community realty. Even if the laborer is hired by a written contract, that is not an "instrument" that creates a lien.

d. **Oral consent may be sufficient:** [§236]   A spouse may be estopped to invoke section 1102 if he orally consents to the other spouse's conveyance and a third party acts in detrimental reliance on the consent. [*See* Vierra v. Pereira, 12 Cal. 2d 629 (1939)] However, reliance must be reasonable, and given the clear joinder rule of the statute, dispensing with a spouse's signature on the instrument will seldom be reasonable.

e. **Rule applies to commercial dealings:** [§237]   If one spouse were a real estate developer, the joinder statute still applies to sales of lots and houses in the ordinary course of the spouse's business unless the business is incorporated or a partnership, in which case the realty is not community owned.

f. **Rule not applicable to some encumbrances:** [§238]   In California, unlike some other states (including Nevada), one spouse alone can use community funds to buy realty. This means that at the time of acquisition one spouse alone can agree to encumber the property with a purchase money mortgage signed by that spouse only. The theory is that the mortgage does not encumber an interest in property owned by the community but rather that the vendor's retained security interest never passes to the community in the first place. [*See* King v. Uhlmann, 437 P.2d 928 (Ariz. 1968)—presumably good law in California]

   (1) **Caveat:** The theory excluding purchase money mortgages from the joinder statute is based on a conceptual fiction that is not even theoretically possible when one spouse alone borrows money from a third party (*e.g.,* a bank) and grants that party a mortgage at the moment when title is acquired. In this situation, section 1102 should apply.

g. **Rescission of contract:** [§239] If both spouses contract to sell community realty or to buy realty with community funds, can one alone rescind? The answer has been held to turn on whether equitable conversion has occurred. [Mamula v. McCulloch, 275 Cal. App. 2d 184 (1969)] In a *purchase* situation, one spouse alone could not rescind if equity views the title as having passed to the community. However, where a contract to *sell* community realty has been made by both spouses, rescission of it could not pass any interest in realty from the community to a third party—so one spouse alone should be able to rescind irrespective of whether an equitable conversion has occurred.

h. **Joinder waived by court:** [§240] California Family Code section 1101(e) authorizes a court order dispensing with the joinder requirement (without regard to the form of title to the community realty) where consent has been "arbitrarily refused" or cannot be obtained (*e.g.,* the other spouse is insane, has vanished, etc.) and the proposed transaction is in the best interest of the community.

i. **Effect of failure to join in conveyance:** [§241] A deed, lease, or mortgage of community realty executed by one spouse alone is not void; the nonjoining spouse may sue during marriage to avoid it in toto. [Droeger v. Friedman, Sloan & Ross, 54 Cal. 3d 26 (1991)] It is not clear whether the *grantee* has standing to rescind the transfer. If she knew that the vendor was married and thereby took the risk of nonjoinder, she probably should be bound. However, if she believed in good faith that the grantor was single (or conveying separate property of his) and if she paid fair value, the grantee ought to be able to rescind because her title is defective.

(1) **Limitations period to set aside transaction:** [§242] Where the record "title" at the time of conveyance was in the name of the signing spouse only, section 1102(d) requires that an action to void the transaction be commenced within one year of recordation of the instrument. (If the instrument is not recorded or title was not in the name of the signing spouse alone, the limitation period apparently is five years under California Civil Procedure Code section 318 for suits to recover land.) This relatively short statute of limitations gives some benefit to the buyer in nonjoinder situations. *But note:* The one-year period does *not* apply in favor of a transferee who knows that the grantor was married and that the grantor's spouse was supposed to join in the conveyance. [Byrd v. Blanton, 149 Cal. App. 3d 987 (1983)]

(2) **Post-dissolution relief:** [§243] Although a nonjoining spouse can have the real property transaction totally set aside while the marriage is on-going (*see supra,* §241), if the community has been dissolved by death or divorce at the time relief is granted, the plaintiff can recover only half the property (*e.g.,* an undivided half interest as tenant in common with the grantee). [*See* Trimble v. Trimble, 219 Cal. 340 (1933)]

(a) **Right of good faith buyer to rescind entire transaction:** [§244] If the buyer purchased the property in good faith (*i.e.,* did not know the vendor was married) and does not want to keep only half the property, the plaintiff arguably should be forced to void the entire transaction even if the community has been dissolved.

(3) **Plaintiff must make restitution:** [§245] A plaintiff spouse seeking to void the transaction must make restitution to the buyer (at least a buyer in good faith) of funds received by the community for the conveyance. [Mark v. Title Guarantee & Trust Co., *supra*, §232] The fact that the grantor spouse may have disappeared with the money is no defense to this right of the buyer.

(4) **Remedy against grantor spouse:** [§246] If the signing spouse acted in bad faith in making the conveyance without joinder, the nonjoining spouse probably has a cause of action against the grantor spouse as an alternative to suing to void the transaction. Damages may be difficult to calculate, but one measure might be the increase in value enjoyed by the realty after conveyance compared to the increase realized by investment of the funds obtained from the buyer.

(5) **Liability for damages:** [§247] Where a nonconsenting spouse has elected to avoid a *contract* to sell community realty made by the other spouse, the signing spouse may nevertheless be liable for damages if the contract is construed as containing an undertaking by him to obtain his spouse's joinder in a conveyance. Such a promise will not be ***implied***, however, even though the contract signed by H alone states that he and his wife are co-owners of the land. [Andrade Development Co. v. Martin, 138 Cal. App. 3d 330 (1982)] Note that if damages are awarded, execution may be had against community property including realty to the extent it is not exempt.

D. RESTRICTIONS ON MANAGEMENT POWERS—GIFTS OF PROPERTY

1. **In General:** [§248] Even when an item of community property is subject to equal management generally, California Family Code section 1100(b) prohibits one spouse alone from giving or transferring the item for less than "fair and reasonable value" absent the ***written consent*** of the other spouse. The statute says that the written consent rule "does not apply to gifts mutally given by both spouses." However, apparently, if W asks H if she can make a gift to her sister and H orally agrees, this is mere oral ***consent*** and does not constitute participation sufficient to eliminate the written consent requirement.

2. **Transactions Covered by Restriction:** [§249] Section 1100(b) covers two types of transactions: (i) a unilateral gift ***with*** donative intent, and (ii) unilateral nondonative transfers without fair or lawful consideration (as where H uses community funds to pay gambling debts that are legally unenforceable). [Novo v. Hotel del Rio, 141 Cal. App. 2d 304 (1956)]

    a. **What constitutes sufficient consideration:** [§250] The *Novo* case, *supra*, makes clear that a mere moral obligation will ***not*** suffice as consideration under section 1100(b). Thus, payments made by one spouse to a sickly relative whom the spouses are not legally obligated to support are gifts prohibited by the statute. Payment of a debt barred by the statute of limitations probably requires consent (even if payment improved the spouse's credit rating).

    b. **Note—statute is overbroad:** [§251] Under a literal interpretation of the statute, one spouse, say H, is entitled to relief if W, in immediate need of funds, sells an asset for the maximum price offered by the first potential buyer, if proof shows she could have obtained a significantly better price by advertising and negotiating with several possible buyers. Apparently her good faith is irrelevant, because the value received by her was not "fair." Perhaps the courts will find a more sensible construction.

3. **Possible Exception for "Trifles":** [§252] Under a rule similar to section 1100(b), the state of Washington has created a "trifles" exception that allows one spouse alone to make relatively small gifts on appropriate occasions to friends and relations, contribute small sums to church and charity, give tips to waiters, and the like. [Hanley v. Most, 115 P.2d 933 (Wash. 1941)] The exception is logical, and California hopefully would follow the same approach.

4. **Possible Exception for "Business Gifts":** [§253] Suppose H's unincorporated business makes annual gifts that are more than "trifles" to the United Way and to employees but does not obtain W's written consent. Section 1100(b) surely was not directed at this situation, and a strong argument can be made for carving out a "reasonable business gifts" exception to the rule.

   a. **Note:** If the business is incorporated or a partnership, the asset given will not be community-owned and section 1100(b) would not apply.

5. **Finding of Estoppel, Waiver, or Ratification Unlikely:** [§254] Since in 1977 the legislature specifically reenacted the written consent requirement after a two-year period of repeal, legislative intent would be defeated if a party could avoid section 1100(b) by showing an oral waiver or ratification by the nondonor spouse. Moreover, since a donee is not likely to rely to his detriment upon oral approval by the nondonor spouse, estoppel to invoke the statute should seldom arise.

6. **Remedies for Violation of Section 1100(b):** [§255] A gift of community personalty or a sale for less than fair value without written consent is *voidable*, not void. The donor spouse has no standing to set aside the transaction. It is unsettled whether a transferee who has agreed to pay less than full value can rescind the executory contract.

   a. **Amount of recovery:** [§256] If the nontransferor spouse sues the transferee before dissolution of the community, she can recover the full amount of the property. Probably, any consideration paid in the situation of a sale for inadequate consideration would have to be returned to the transferee, as in the case of unilateral sales of realty (*see supra,* §245).

      (1) **After dissolution of community:** [§257] If the community has been dissolved by divorce or death, the nontransferor spouse or her estate may recover only half the property. [Harris v. Harris, 57 Cal. 2d 367 (1962)] If the transferor spouse is dead, a quasi-testamentary disposition would be recognized with respect to the other half (although promised payment would still be owed in the case of an executory contract to sell for unfair value). If the nontransferor were dead, her will could effectively bequeath only a half interest.

(2) **Treatment of mesne profits:** [§258] The transferee should not be liable for fair use value or profits from the property during possession. Since the gift or sale was voidable and not void, the transferee had a lawful property interest when he possessed the item and took profits from it. (The same result should apply to one-spouse realty transfers later set aside under California Family Code section 1102; *see supra,* §241.)

7. **Remedy Against Transferor Spouse:** [§259] At least where the transferor spouse was not acting in good faith, the other spouse—rather than suing the transferee—may obtain a judgment for damages against the transferor spouse. Presumably this judgment would be the amount for which the transferee would be liable if he were the defendant, but the transferor spouse conceivably could owe more. For example, if the asset had dropped in value after the gift, the transferee need merely return the asset, but the transferor might be held liable for the value at the time of the gift.

    a. **Result where donor acted in good faith:** [§260] If the transferor spouse acted in good faith—*e.g.,* believed that the other spouse also desired that the low-priced sale or gift be made but neglected to obtain the required writing—it is not clear whether the transferor can be sued by the nontransferor spouse.

E. **RESTRICTIONS ON MANAGEMENT POWERS—FIDUCIARY DUTY OF A SPOUSE**

1. **In General:** [§261] California Family Code section 1100(e) provides that spouses have to each other a "fiduciary relationship" like that of persons in a confidential relationship (*e.g.,* attorney-client). Family Code section 721(b) states that each spouse must manage community property in "the highest good faith" and that neither spouse when acting as manager "shall take unfair advantage of the other." Section 721(b) also requires each spouse to account to the other for any profit made in a transaction affecting the community to which the other spouse had not consented. The fiduciary duties imposed by both section 1100(e) and section 721(b) continue after separation of the spouses until property is divided at divorce.

2. **Spouse Need Not Invest Like Trustee:** [§262] The strict duties of care defined in sections 1100(e) and 721(b) do not require a spouse to invest community property like the trustee of a family trust. Accordingly, a spouse is not barred per se from making high-risk investments or maintaining a nondiversified investment portfolio. Neither must the spouse segregate community from separate funds nor keep the kind of detailed records required of a trustee. [Williams v. Williams, 14 Cal. App. 3d 560 (1971)—although decided before the strict duties of sections 1100(e) and 721(b) were enacted, this should still be good law] However, the spouse does have a duty to make productive community property under his sole control (*see, e.g., supra,* §218). [Marriage of Mungia, 146 Cal. App. 3d 853 (1983)] And section 721(b) states that a spouse must account as and "hold as trustee" all profit or benefit from a transaction that "concerns the community property" that the other spouse did not consent to.

3. **Usurping a Community Opportunity:** [§263] Where because of a community investment a spouse has an opportunity to make a further good investment, his using separate funds to do so rather than available community funds violates the duty

of good faith. Thus, where H had withdrawn funds from a pension plan that was primarily a community asset but was free at any time to buy back into the plan, regaining valuable benefits at a relatively small cost, his use of separate funds to do so was wrongful. The divorce court declared the pension benefits community, while requiring W to reimburse H's separate estate for its contribution. [Marriage of Lucero, 118 Cal. App. 3d 836 (1980)]

    a. **Note:** This duty continues after separation until a property division at divorce. Thus, if one spouse learns of an investment opportunity during separation, she must advise the other spouse of it in writing. Apparently any gain made by the spouse who fails to give notice will be co-owned by the parties. [Cal. Fam. Code §2102]

4. **Spouse's Duty to Account:** [§264] Under the earlier rule of exclusive male management, H had a duty to account for community assets known to exist shortly before H and W separated but missing at the time of divorce. If H could not show that the assets were expended for community purposes, he was required to reimburse the community. [Marriage of Valle, 53 Cal. App. 3d 837 (1975)] This meant that W could collect the value of half of the missing assets from H's separate property and H's half of the community property on hand.

    a. **Rule under equal management:** [§265] Undoubtedly, the duty to account recognized under male management now applies to both spouses with respect to community assets over which a spouse had obtained exclusive management power and possibly also with respect to other community assets known to be in the possession of one spouse at the time the parties separate. By statute one spouse may at any time require the other to fully disclose all assets and debts affecting the community [Cal. Fam. Code §721(b)], or even the spouse's separate assets and debts [Cal. Fam. Code §2102—applicable after separation]. The duty includes providing access to pertinent records and books.

5. **Remedies for Violating Fiduciary Duty:** [§266] A spouse has a remedy to recover damages for breach of the above-described fiduciary duties and to enjoin threatened breaches. Family Code section 1101(a) and (g) allows suit for violation of any of the management statutes, and it can be commenced during marriage. The statute of limitations is three years from the date the plaintiff spouse learns of events giving rise to a remedy. The running of the three-year period does not bar raising the claim at divorce but apparently does bar asserting it at dissolution by death. [Cal. Fam. Code §1101(d)]

    a. **Alternative remedy:** [§267] Family Code section 2602 provides that the divorce court, in lieu of making a 50-50 division of community and quasi-community property, may invade the portion of divisible property that would have been awarded to a spouse who has "deliberately misappropriated" community and/or quasi-community property (defined *infra* in §269). The appropriate amount is awarded to the wronged spouse, and the result is an ***unequal*** division of divisible assets. Since "deliberate misappropriation" seems to require more proof of wrong than needed to show breach of the fiduciary duties described above, the alternative remedy under section 2602 often may not be useful. [*See* Marriage of Moore, *supra,* §80—H, while separated from W, spent large sums of community money on liquor and the court found no "deliberate misappropriation"]

(1) **Separate property immune:** [§268] Section 2602 does not authorize an award of the separate property of the wrongdoing spouse—although such property would certainly be liable for a judgment under section 1101 or on some common law basis of liability, such as fraud. [*See* Fields v. Michael, 91 Cal. App. 2d 443 (1949)]

(2) **Gifts of quasi-community property:** [§269] Property acquired by a spouse while living in a common law state before moving to California that would have been community property had the spouse been a Californian at the time of acquisition is quasi-community property. (*See infra*, §454.) For most purposes quasi-community property is treated as a spouse's separate property prior to divorce or the spouse's death. If after the move to California the spouse deliberately uses quasi-community property to make a substantial gift to a third party when inherited or other "pure" separate property was available for the gift, this could be found to be a "deliberate misappropriation" under section 2602. Probably no remedy is available to the spouse of the donor under any other statute or theory.

F. RESTRICTIONS ON MANAGEMENT POWERS—INCOMPETENCY OF ONE OR BOTH SPOUSES

1. **Equal Management Property:** [§270] If one spouse becomes incompetent, the other (sane) spouse has exclusive control over community property formerly subject to equal management and, apparently, even over community property subject to the incompetent spouse's primary management (such as a single-spouse business, *supra,* §218). [Cal. Prob. Code §3051] This applies even though the incompetent spouse has a conservator, except to the extent the competent spouse confers management power on the conservator. The conservator can, however, sue the managing spouse to enjoin actions taken in bad faith vis-a-vis the incompetent's half interest and to compel the manager spouse to apply funds to the support of the incompetent.

    a. **Both spouses incompetent:** [§271] If both spouses are incompetent, the conservator of each manages an undivided half interest in each community asset. [Cal. Prob. Code §3051(d)]

2. **Dual Management Transactions:** [§272] If one spouse is incompetent, a dual management transaction (*e.g.,* a gift of community property, alienation of community realty) requires court approval *or* joinder in or "consent" to the transaction by the sane spouse and the incompetent's conservator. If both spouses have conservators, each conservator must consent to or join in the transaction. [Cal. Prob. Code §3071]

[§§273-276]

III. LIABILITY FOR DEBTS

chapter approach

Exam questions in this area concern a creditor's rights to the property of the debtor and debtor's spouse. The basic rule is that *all* community property and the *debtor's* separate property are liable, but the separate property of the debtor's spouse is generally not liable for the debt.

Thus, after you have determined who the debtor is and thought about the general rule, you need to sort through the exceptions to the basic rule (*e.g.*, a debt for "necessaries"). You should also consider whether your answer is affected by the special rules for tort liability or whether a divorce or separation of the parties has affected liability.

In general, keep in mind that the basic rules are pro-creditor.

A. GENERAL RULE

1. **Community Property Liable:** [§273] The general rule concerning liability for debts is that all *community* property is liable for all debts of a spouse regardless of who has management and control of the assets at issue. [Cal. Fam. Code §910] Statutes then carve out a large number of exceptions to the general rule of liability (*see* below). The Family Code provides that one spouse's quasi-community property (*see supra*, §269; *infra*, §455) is liable in every situation in which community property is liable. [Cal. Fam. Code §912] However, this treatment of quasi-community property raises serious constitutional concerns (*see infra*, §480).

2. **Separate Property Generally Not Liable:** [§274] A spouse's separate property is liable for all of the *owner spouse's* debts. [Cal. Fam. Code §913(a)] Other than the general exemption statutes, there are no exceptions to this rule. Conversely, separate property is *not* generally liable at all for the debts incurred by the *nonowner spouse* alone. [Cal. Fam. Code §913(b)] (For the few exceptions to this rule, *see* below.)

3. **Note—Law Greatly Changed in 1985:** [§275] Section 910, above, is part of a broad reform of the law concerning liability for debts that became effective in 1985. These statutory changes apply to property of spouses whenever acquired, including property acquired before 1985. While the most important provisions of the reform legislation are discussed in this chapter, almost all cases involving pre-1985 debt collections from marital property need to be reexamined in light of the major changes in the law.

B. EXCEPTIONS TO GENERAL RULE

1. **Separate Property Liable for Necessaries:** [§276] Contrary to the general rule, one spouse's separate property *is* liable for a debt incurred for *"necessaries of life"* of the other spouse *while they are cohabiting*. If the spouses are living apart when the debt is incurred, separate liability of the nonobligor spouse is limited to credit purchases of "common necessaries," defined in a statutory note as items "necessary to sustain life." [Cal. Fam. Code §914]

a. **When doctrine does not apply:** [§277] The necessaries doctrine does not apply when a couple has separated pursuant to a formal agreement that does not require the spouse allegedly liable under the doctrine to support the other. [Cal. Fam. Code §4302] The statute apparently eliminates the duty to support only where there is a *written* separation agreement.

b. **Standard of life test:** [§278] If the spouses are living together (so that liability under the necessaries doctrine extends to all "necessaries" and not just "common" ones), what constitutes a necessary depends on the couple's station in life. [Wisnom v. McCarthy, 48 Cal. App. 697 (1920)] For example, for a couple used to living like the very wealthy, servants have been held to be a "necessary."

c. **Third party contracts:** [§279] A spouse's separate property is liable under the necessaries doctrine for contracts made by third parties for the benefit of the other spouse (*e.g.*, W's mother orders nursing care for the comatose W).

d. **Reimbursement claims:** [§280] If a creditor takes separate property of a noncontracting spouse under the necessaries doctrine when nonexempt community or separate property of the spouse in need was available, the spouse whose separate property is taken has a statutory right to reimbursement. [Cal. Fam. Code §914(b)]

2. **Community Property Not Liable for Premarital Obligations:** [§281] A spouse's community earnings for personal services rendered are not liable for any debts incurred by the other spouse *before* marriage. [Cal. Fam. Code §911] This exemption lasts only as long as the earnings are kept in a bank account from which the other spouse has no right of withdrawal and into which no nonexempt community funds are commingled. Commingling separate funds (that are not quasi-community property) into the account does not lose the exemption, but investing the earnings in some securities would have that effect.

   a. **Child support and alimony:** [§282] Child support and alimony obligations from a prior marriage are viewed as premarital debts for purposes of the above exemption, regardless of when a judgment for enforcement is rendered. [Cal. Fam. Code §915(a)] Thus, the nonobligor spouse's community earnings are not liable. (Pre-1985 law viewed such obligations as continuing and arising anew each time a periodic obligation became due, and thus they were not "premarital" debts.)

      (1) **But note:** Other community assets will be liable. If such assets (or the debtor's quasi-community property) are used by the debtor to pay the obligation or are seized by the alimony or child support creditor, the community is entitled to *reimbursement* to the extent that nonexempt separate property of the obligor spouse was available at the time community funds were applied to the debt. [Cal. Fam. Code §915(b)]

C. **SPECIAL RULES FOR TORT LIABILITY** [§283]

The general rule that all community property plus all of a debtor spouse's separate property is liable for the debtor spouse's debts also applies to tort liabilities. However, California Family Code section 1000(b) creates a "pecking order" of liability in this area that turns on whether a community or separate tort is involved. But note that to the extent a spouse's tort liability is satisfied by liability insurance proceeds, the "pecking order" statute does not apply.

1. **Community Torts:** [§284]   If liability is based on "an act or omission which occurred while the married person was performing an activity for the benefit of the community," liability shall be satisfied *first from community property* and then from the tortfeasor's separate property. [Cal. Fam. Code §1000(b)(1)]

    a. **Procedure:** [§285]   Presumably the tortfeasor spouse must invoke the protection of section 1000(b) by paying the judgment with community property subject to his management or identifying other nonexempt community property upon which the creditor can levy (*e.g.*, a community bank account in the other spouse's name). The creditor's only obligation would be to give the tortfeasor this opportunity before seizing the tortfeasor's separate property.

    b. **Broad scope of torts "for the benefit of the community":** [§286]   States where community property has long been liable only for "community torts" hold that a spouse's recreational activity during marriage (with or without the other spouse) is an activity for the benefit of the community. [*See, e.g.,* Reckart v. Arva Valley Air, Inc., 509 P.2d 231 (Ariz. 1973)—H negligently crashed airplane while taking flying lessons] California is likely to follow this same approach in applying section 1000(b).

    (1) **And note:** A tort incurred by one spouse's failing to keep up the couple's joint tenancy property is probably also a community tort, since both spouses (the community) are co-owners of the joint tenancy.

2. **Separate Torts:** [§287]   If liability is not based on an act or omission involving an activity for the benefit of the community, the tortfeasor's *separate property* is primarily liable and community property secondarily liable under section 1000(b)(2). The nontortfeasor spouse, given notice by the creditor, apparently has the burden of preventing a levy on community property by identifying separate property of the tortfeasor subject to execution.

    a. **Right to reimbursement:** [§288]   If community funds are used to pay for a separate tort, reimbursement can be awarded. The statute provides that "no right of reimbursement *under this section*" may be asserted more than seven years after the spouse claiming reimbursement learns how the tort debt was paid. [Cal. Fam. Code §1000(c)] The highlighted language implies that the statute creates a right of reimbursement when community funds are used to pay a separate tort obligation and vice versa. However, the statutory language is much less susceptible of the interpretation that reimbursement is available when the victim of a spouse's *community tort* seizes the spouse's *separate property* for payment.

    (1) **Note:** This section provides for a *seven-year* limitations period for reimbursement as compared with section 920, which applies a three-year limitations period for other reimbursement claims. (*See infra,* §341.)

3. **"Combination" Torts:** [§289]   Suppose X is injured by a hazard negligently created on land owned 40% by the community and 60% as H's separate property. Management of the land is an activity benefiting the community as co-owner, but it

seems inconsistent with the policy of section 1000(b) to make the community primarily liable for tort liability to X. Instead, liability could be considered 40% a community tort and 60% a separate tort for purposes of applying the priority rules in the statute.

4. **Spouses as Joint Tortfeasors:** [§290] If both spouses incur tort liability in an activity not benefiting the community (*e.g.,* they both attack and batter the party obtaining judgment against them), section 1000(b) should not force the creditor to levy on separate property. The community property is equally owned by the spouses, and is therefore an appropriate source for paying a debt on which both are equally liable.

5. **Torts Covered by Section 1000(b):** [§291] The "pecking order" rules of section 1000(b) may not apply to all tort liabilities. The statute by its terms applies to "liability for death or injury to person or property." Hence, there is some question whether it covers torts such as slander or invasion of privacy; and if it does not, the community property and the tortfeasor's separate property are equally liable to the victim. Note that conversion by embezzlement has been held to be an "injury to property" tort under section 1000. [Marriage of Stitt, 147 Cal. App. 3d 579 (1983)]

6. **Tort Liability of One Spouse to Other:** [§292] California Family Code section 782 provides that in the case of "injury to a married person" where one spouse is liable to the other in tort, community funds may not be used to pay the liability until the tortfeasor's separate property is exhausted. The same "pecking order" rule also applies to any sums that the tortfeasor spouse may owe by way of contribution to a joint tortfeasor who has paid the victim spouse more than his share of the liability.

    a. **Payment with community funds:** [§293] After the tortfeasor's separate property is exhausted, the victim spouse can reach community property (which then becomes the victim's separate property). Since the victim-spouse already owns half of the community property, the recovery from such property would logically be "two for one" (so that the tortfeasor's share is the sole payor); *e.g.,* if the remaining liability is $500, $1,000 in community assets would be required to satisfy it.

    b. **Insurance purchased with community funds:** [§294] Section 782 does "not affect the right to indemnity provided by an insurance or other contract to discharge the tortfeasor spouse's liability," even if the insurance was purchased with community funds. This clearly means that the insurer must pay on the contract even if the tortfeasor spouse has ample separate property to discharge the liability. It is less clear whether each dollar of insurance purchased with community funds discharges $1 of liability, or only 50¢ of liability (on the theory that the victim already owned half of what was received). The legislative intent behind section 782 suggests that each dollar received from the insurer discharges a full dollar of liability.

D. **EFFECT OF SEPARATION OR DIVORCE ON LIABILITY FOR DEBTS**

1. **Separation:** [§295] The fact that spouses begin living separate and apart will have no effect on debtor-creditor relations except that the post-separation earnings of each spouse are separate rather than community property (*see supra,* §§43-47). This could come as an unpleasant surprise to a pre-separation creditor of one

spouse who was relying on earnings of the other spouse as a source of repayment, but that risk is assumed by any creditor who fails to make both spouses contractual obligors.

    a. **Effect of future obligations:** [§296] Since the rights of a contract creditor do not depend on whether the debt is community or separate, separation of the spouses has no effect on *post-separation* creditors other than to convert post-separation earnings into separate property. Post-separation torts are likely to be separate torts, so that the tort creditor can be compelled to levy first on the tortfeasor's separate property. However, a separation that makes subsequent earnings separate under California Family Code section 771 does not alter the nature of community property already acquired; and a separated spouse could still commit a community tort—*e.g.,* while maintaining pre-separation community real estate. Tort liability incurred in operating a community business after separation should be considered at least partly community for "pecking order" purposes, since the reverse *Pereira-Van Camp* formulas make part of the earnings of the business after separation community property (*see supra,* §75).

    b. **Contrary dictum:** [§297] One court has said that after a couple formally separates, debts incurred are separate so that only the debtor's separate property is liable. [American Olean Title Co. v. Schultze, 169 Cal. App. 3d 359 (1985)] This dictum is wrong. Pre-separation community property would also be liable.

2. **Divorce:** [§298] Before 1985, divorce did not eliminate the liability of community property for a debt even if the asset at issue was awarded by the divorce court to the nondebtor spouse. Under present law, all property owned by the obligor-spouse after division at divorce ***still is liable*** on the debt that spouse incurred, even if the divorce court orders the ***other spouse to pay*** the debt. [Cal. Fam. Code §916] However, other provisions in this statute eliminate liability of some community property that existed before the divorce.

    a. **Effect of assignment of debt:** [§299] Whether property is liable for payment of the debt depends on the assignment of the debt by the divorce court.

        (1) **Debt assigned to obligor spouse:** [§300] If the obligor spouse is ordered to pay the debt, community property awarded to the nonobligor spouse is ***not*** liable, absent a lien in favor of the creditor. (*And note:* The same is true for a separate debt of the obligor spouse that the court had no power to assign to the nonobligor spouse. [Cal. Fam. Code §916(a)(2)])

        (2) **Debt assigned to nonobligor spouse:** [§301] If the nonobligor spouse is ordered to pay the debt, the pre-divorce separate property of the nonobligor spouse becomes liable for payment of the debt—property that seldom was liable prior to such an assignment.

        (3) **Reimbursement:** [§302] If the court orders the nonobligor spouse to pay the creditor, but the creditor proceeds (as he can) against the obligor spouse instead, the obligor spouse is entitled to reimbursement from the spouse who was ordered to pay the debt. [Cal. Fam. Code §916(b)]

b. **Post-divorce judgment:** [§303] No property of the ex-spouse who is ordered to pay a debt that he did not incur is liable on a post-divorce judgment obtained by the creditor unless the ex-spouse was a party to the proceeding. [Cal. Fam. Code §916(a)(3)]

E. **ALIMONY PENDENTE LITE AND LUMP SUM ALIMONY**

1. **In General:** [§304] California Family Code section 4338 provides that in enforcing a decree against a spouse to support the other, the court shall order payment first from earnings and accumulations that are separate property of the debtor spouse under section 771 (the "living separate and apart" doctrine) but that would otherwise have been community assets. Payments may then be compelled (in the following order) from community property, the debtor's quasi-community property, and the debtor's ordinary separate property.

2. **Scope of Statute:** [§305] Section 4338 applies to support payable during marriage and to lump sum alimony ordered at divorce. However, it should *not apply* to alimony in periodic payments after divorce, since at that juncture the assets owned by the debtor can no longer be classified as "separate," "community," or "quasi-community."

IV. DISSOLUTION OF THE COMMUNITY

chapter approach

This chapter discusses the division of property at dissolution of the community by divorce or death. General guidelines for you to follow are:

1. **Divorce:** At divorce, there is a winding up of the community partnership much like that of a 50-50 business partnership. There are numerous rules of law for you to keep in mind, and as you apply these rules to the facts of your question, remember that the purpose of the rules is to assure that a division of property is truly *equal*. Another important policy at work is the "*clean break*," which favors an item-by-item division of the property so that the divorcing spouses do not remain co-owners. Use these policies to structure your answer.

    Also, exam questions asking what a divorce court should do with marital property will almost always raise one of the classification issues covered in Chapter I; therefore, you should be familiar with those rules as well. Additionally, the divorce court must assign outstanding debts to one spouse after classifying the debts under rules that sometimes are illogical. Keep in mind that a spouse's creditor can be harmed by a divorce because half of the community property may cease to be liable to the creditor.

    Finally, remember that although a California divorce is "no fault," wrongdoing by a spouse can become a factor if the other spouse asserts a reimbursement claim.

2. **Death of Spouse:** When the community ends at death, focus on the implications of the use of the "*item theory*" of ownership, such as the possibility that a will puts the surviving spouse to an election. Also, a death dissolution can affect the rights of creditors and may alter the liability of various properties; thus, exam questions involving a death should alert you to consider the position of *third parties*.

A. **DIVISION OF PROPERTY AT DIVORCE**

   1. **Separate Property:** [§306] California courts cannot award any portion of a spouse's *solely owned separate property* to the other spouse.

      a. **Compare—joint tenancy and tenancy in common:** [§307] California Family Code section 2650 authorizes a California divorce to divide assets owned by the spouses in joint tenancy or tenancy in common in making an equal division of divisible property. This removes the primary significance of the statute presuming at divorce a community characterization notwithstanding use of a joint tenancy form deed (section 2581).

   2. **Community Property:** [§308] The general rule is that community property must be divided equally at divorce. [Cal. Fam. Code §2550] However, the "item theory" of community ownership, applicable where the community is dissolved by death (*see infra*, §348), does not apply at dissolution by divorce. Accordingly, a spouse is merely entitled to receive community assets with a *value equal to half* the community estate and has no right to a half interest in any particular asset. This is referred to as the "aggregate theory" of community ownership.

Community Property—69

a. **"Tenancy in common" division disfavored:** [§309] A divorce court may divide the community by declaring the spouses to be tenants in common of all (or of particular) community assets, but this type of division is an abuse of discretion when it is reasonably possible to award entire assets to one spouse and other entire assets of equal value to the other. [Marriage of Knickerbocker, 43 Cal. App. 3d 1039 (1974)] *Rationale:* Since the spouses have been unable to arrive at a property settlement agreement, they will likely be at loggerheads as post-divorce tenants in common of former community assets. Recognizing this problem, courts frequently apply the aggregate theory of division by awarding the community home to W and the community business to H (with other assets distributed so as to equalize value).

(1) **Co-ownership of community pension interests:** [§310] Tenancy in common divisions are *not*, however, at all disfavored when the divorce court deals with pensions because of the difficulty in valuing the community interest in pension interests where there are numerous conditions to enjoyment of the benefits (*e.g.*, the employee spouse must work nine more years on the job). If the court can fairly value the contract rights, it can award the pension to the participant spouse and community property of offsetting value to the other spouse at divorce. Where valuation is too difficult (or where the court prefers an alternative approach), each spouse can be awarded a fractional interest of future pension benefits if and when received. [Marriage of Brown, *supra*, §208]

(a) **Diminishing community fraction of benefits:** [§311] If the participant spouse continues on the job after divorce, this subsequent labor is taken into account in determining the separate and former community interests. Thus, the fractional share of the former community decreases over time (although the *value* almost certainly increases because the total benefits are usually increasing and, in the case of a defined contribution plan, the plan operator can invest (and reinvest) the community contributions until benefits are finally paid). The formula for calculating the interest of the nonparticipant spouse (say, W) on a "time" apportionment would be as follows:

X = number of months on job while H is married to W and living with her

Y = number of all other months on the job calculated at time benefits are received

$$\text{W receives } \frac{1}{2} \times \frac{X}{X+Y}$$

Note that it is the Y figure that increases after divorce due to H's continued labor.

(b) **Management and control over benefits:** [§312] If the divorce court uses the fractional share approach to division of property pension benefits, the former spouses technically own the contract rights against the employer as tenants in common. Ordinarily, a tenant in common has management and control over his or her fractional interest, but in the case of pension plans, the employer has contracted with only one of the spouses (the participant). Thus, the nonparticipant spouse takes tenancy in common ownership rights subject to the exclusive power of the participant spouse to deal with the employer regarding the plan. [*See* Marriage of Brown, *supra*]

1) **Participant's obligations to nonparticipant:** [§313] California property law provides that one cotenant cannot deal with the cotenancy property to the prejudice of the other. [Tompkins v. Superior Court, 59 Cal. 2d 65 (1963)] Under this rule, a nonparticipant W can enjoin H from selecting pension plan options that are more favorable to him than her after a fractional sharing award at divorce. [Marriage of Lionberger, 97 Cal. App. 3d 56 (1979)] For example, if H has the option of receiving lifetime benefits at a high level payable to him or a lower level of benefits plus post-death benefits payable to his widow, H's choice of the latter option would prejudice W-1 if H remarried because the terminable interest rule imposed by E.R.I.S.A., the federal statute that governs most pensions (*see infra*, §503), would bar W-1 from any share of widow's benefits (*supra*, §198). ***State*** law will not permit H to diminish the former community interest of W-1 in this manner.

2) **Result where participant does not retire at maturity:** [§314] Suppose H reaches the age at which he could retire and begin receiving benefits, but instead he elects to stay on the job. It is now settled that he can be compelled to begin making payments to the ex-wife under the decree recognizing her as owning a fractional interest of future retirement benefits. The theory is that H cannot manage the co-owned asset just to carry out his own plans as to when he would like the flow of money to begin. The periodic payments unretired H must make are discounted to take into account the fact he may die before he receives any payment (as well as other factors that would reduce the present value of the flow of money that will begin at H's actual retirement). [Marriage of Shattuck, 134 Cal. App. 3d 683 (1982)]

    a) **Segregating shares in account:** [§315] In the case of many state employee spouses, at the request of the nonparticipant spouse, the dissolution court must order the pension plan to divide the account into two parts, one of which consists of the requesting spouse's community and quasi-community interest. [*See, e.g.*, Cal. Gov. Code §21215] The nonmember may then ask the pension plan operator to treat her as "retired" (even though the participant has not retired or is not even eligible to retire) and to begin paying her appropriate benefits based on the size of the segregated share of the total pension package.

b. **"Equalizing" by promissory note:** [§316] The community estate at divorce may contain one asset whose value is greater than that of all other community property. May the court award this asset to one spouse and order her to give the other spouse a promissory note for the difference, so as to "equalize" the division of property?

(1) **Impaired value test:** [§317] California Family Code section 2601 provides that "where economic circumstances warrant, the court may award any asset to one party on such conditions as it deems proper to effect a substantially equal division." This has been interpreted by some courts to mean that the divorce court may order an equalizing promissory note only when a true equal division would impair the value of community assets. [Marriage of Brigden, 80 Cal. App. 3d 380 (1978)] In the case of land, it is hard to imagine how converting from community property to tenancy in common ownership would reduce the value of the asset. With a controlling block of corporate stock, however, converting to tenancy in common could eliminate control—so that the aggregate value of the two cotenancy shares would be less than the value of the controlling community share before divorce.

 (a) **Small promissory note:** [§318] In any event, no abuse of discretion will be found when a divorce court orders a relatively small promissory note (compared to the total value of the community) to effect an equal division and avoid a tenancy in common—even if creation of a cotenancy technically would not impair the value of the property.

 (b) **Discharge:** [§319] The obligor on a divorce court's property award, like the debtor on a promissory note, can have it discharged in whole or in part in bankruptcy if: (i) the debtor is unable to pay it from income because of obligations to support himself and/or his dependents; or (ii) if the benefit of discharge of the obligor outweighs the detriment to the obligee. [11 U.S.C. §523(a)(15)] *Note:* If discharge is obtained before the divorce decree is final, the divorce court may *not* restructure the property division to make it equal (*e.g.,* by awarding more property to the spouse who cannot collect on her note).

c. **"Equalizing" by assignment of debts:** [§320] What must be "equal" in the division of property at divorce is the net value received by the spouses after deducting *community* debts that the spouses are ordered to pay. [Marriage of Eastis, 47 Cal. App. 3d 459 (1975)] Assignment of debts to one spouse or the other can therefore equalize the aggregate division between the parties.

(1) **Where debts exceed assets:** [§321] California Family Code section 2622(b) provides that "to the extent that community debts exceed total community and quasi-community assets, the excess of debt shall be assigned as the court deems just and equitable, taking into account such factors as the parties' relative ability to pay."

(2) **Effect of one spouse's bankruptcy:** [§322] If one spouse, say H, has obtained a discharge in bankruptcy of certain community debts, the divorce court obviously cannot assign the debts to H but must assign them to W. By force of federal law, they must be treated as W's *separate debts* and not taken into account in determining whether her net share of community properties after division at divorce is equal to H's. If this approach

were not taken, H would in effect be charged anew with a debt for which he has been discharged by a federal bankruptcy court. [Marriage of Williams, 157 Cal. App. 3d 1215 (1984)]

(a) **Post-divorce discharge:** [§323]   If the divorce court in making an equal division of the community orders H to pay W's separate debt, W remains liable on her contract to the creditor. Thus, the creditor can collect from her, but she has a cause of action for reimbursement against H (to restore the equality of the property division).

(3) **Debt payment as alimony:** [§324]   A few divorce courts have effectuated an unequal division of property by labeling an order to pay community debts as an order to pay alimony (spousal support). [*See In re* Hendricks, 5 Cal. App. 3d 793 (1970)] Since alimony terminates at the death of the spouse or (usually) upon remarriage, such an order to one spouse with respect to *future* community debts (such as time payment on a loan) might not succeed in shifting the entire debt to the spouse ordered to pay it.

(a) **Limitation:** More recent cases have limited this approach by holding that an order to pay an existing community debt cannot be disguised as alimony unless the debt is related to support needs of the benefited spouse—as where removing the debt enables the spouse to occupy a residence, get a job, etc. [Marriage of Chala, 92 Cal. App. 3d 996 (1979)]

(4) **Treatment of separate debts:** [§325]   At divorce each spouse is liable for his or her own separate debts, and such debts are not considered when dividing community property. California Family Code section 2627 provides that the benefit test of section 1000(b) (*see supra,* §286) is used to classify tort debts owed by H or W. According to sections 2621-2625, nontort debts are classified according to the following rules: (i) debts incurred before marriage by one spouse are the separate debts of that spouse; (ii) debts incurred during separation and before divorce are the separate debt of the incurring spouse except that those incurred for the "common necessaries of life" for either spouse or the minor children of the marriage are community; and (iii) debts incurred during marriage but before separation are characterized as separate or community based on whether they were incurred "for the benefit of the community." [Cal. Fam. Code §2625]

(a) **Example:** In one case, attorney's fees incurred by W defending an embezzlement charge were classified as her separate debts because it was not shown that the embezzlement benefited the community. [Marriage of Stitt, *supra,* §291] Funds illegally obtained by labor would have been community, but still there would be no actual benefit because of the obligation to return them. Note that *Stitt* would not classify debts incurred in a *lawful* business venture as separate just because it failed and the community came out a loser.

(b) **Criticism:** Suppose after separation H hires X to repair a community-owned apartment building that is generating community rents.

By all logic, X's unpaid wage should be a community debt at divorce, but California Family Code section 2623 (rule (ii), above) compels classifying it as H's separate debt because it was incurred after separation.

(c) **Educational loans:** [§326] By statute, an educational loan is *presumptively* a separate debt of the spouse so educated. However, a portion or even all of the amount of the loan unpaid at divorce may be classified as a community debt on the basis of a finding of community benefit from the education (*e.g.,* a large community income). [Cal. Fam. Code §2641] The presumption is *against* such benefit to the extent that the loan proceeds were expended for education *less than 10 years* before the divorce action was filed and in favor of the community benefit if expended more than 10 years before filing.

d. **Valuing assets and debts:** [§327] For purposes of equalizing the division of property, community assets are assessed at *market value* rather than at face value. For example, if a debtor owes $10,000 in repayment of community funds lent to him, the debtor's solvency at the time of the divorce might make the cause of action against him—the community asset—worth far less than $10,000.

(1) **Same rule for promissory note:** [§328] Where the divorce court obtains an equal division by ordering one spouse to execute a promissory note in favor of the other, it is likewise the market value rather than the face value of the note that determines whether equality has been achieved. [Marriage of Tammen, 63 Cal. App. 3d 927 (1976)] If the note is unsecured, or the interest rate is low, its market value will not be as high as face value.

(2) **Impact of tax liability:** [§329] The tax cost of converting an asset to cash is disregarded in determining the value of community assets for purposes of division. The theory is that such tax liability is speculative, since it is not known when (if ever) the taxable event will occur or how the spouse assigned the asset in question may be able to reduce the tax cost (by offsetting gain with capital losses, etc.). [Marriage of Dennis, 143 Cal. App. 3d 851 (1983)]

(a) **Example:** Assume that Blackacre and Whiteacre are parcels of community realty, each having a market value of $100,000. Depreciation taken for structures on Blackacre leaves that parcel with a present tax basis of $10,000, whereas Whiteacre—which was purchased for $100,000 and has not been depreciated—has a basis of $100,000. Clearly each spouse would prefer to receive an assignment of Whiteacre, since it can be converted to cash without incurring income tax liability. However, case law holds the two parcels are equal in value for purposes of division.

(b) **Exception:** If an asset is sold as part of the division of the community property at divorce, each spouse is responsible for taxes on half the gain as his or her separate (tax) obligation. This rule applies even when one spouse is able to postpone tax liability on his half of the gain on sale of a community residence by "rolling over" the proceeds through quick purchase of a new residence, while the other divorcing spouse is, for economic reasons, unable to buy a new residence and incurs at once a capital gains tax liability. [Marriage of Harrington, 6 Cal. App. 4th 1847 (1992)]

    (c) **Treatment of pension plans:** [§330] Almost all pension plans are structured so as to avoid income taxes on annual gain; *i.e.,* no tax is owed until benefits are received after retirement. Since this tax benefit is not speculative but a known attribute of pensions, it probably *should* be considered in valuing the community interest in a retirement plan. [*See* 5 Pepp. L. Rev. 191]

(3) **Time of valuing assets—general rule:** [§331] The basic rule is that community assets are to be valued, for purposes of making the equal division, at the *time of trial*. [Cal. Fam. Code §2552(a)]

    (a) **Exception for post-division catastrophes:** [§332] In one case, after the divorce court had awarded a community house to W but before the judgment was final, the house was lost on foreclosure when mortgage payments were not made. It was held that the court had to *reformulate an equal division*, taking into account the loss of the equity in the house awarded W. [Marriage of Olson, 27 Cal. 3d 414 (1980)] This seems fair where a loss is due to an earthquake for which insurance coverage was not reasonably available, but in *Olson,* W was in possession of the house and was the spouse who could reasonably be charged with the primary obligation to make the missed mortgage payment.

e. **Exceptions to equal division rule**

(1) **Tort recoveries:** [§333] Recall that certain portions of community property recovered for the personal injury of a spouse are in effect converted to separate property at divorce and are awarded entirely to the victim-spouse. (*See supra,* §§136-148.) Thus, community personal injury damages should not be considered in assessing whether an equal division has been made. [Cal. Fam. Code §2603]

(2) **Default divorce:** [§334] If the net value of the community and quasi-community assets is less than $5,000 and the defendant-spouse cannot be located despite diligent effort, the divorce court may award up to all of the property to plaintiff. [Cal. Fam. Code §2604] (Technically, there is no plaintiff or defendant in a California dissolution, but these terms usefully describe the parties involved.)

f. **Treatment of out-of-state land:** [§335] A divorce court is encouraged to divide property so as not to disturb any interests in out-of-state realty. [Cal. Fam. Code §2660] If it is not practicable to do so, and the land would have been divisible had it been located in California (*i.e.,* would not have been separate property as defined in California), the divorce court may: (i) order a party to convey to the other such interest in the out-of-state land as is necessary to make an equal division, or (ii) award the other party the cash value of the interest that would have been conveyed under the first alternative.

3. **Adjustment for Monies Owed One Spouse by the Other:** [§336] Although section 2550 calls for an equal division of community property in most instances, the divorce court has the power to order one spouse to pay the other sums owed on reimbursement claims. The court may effectuate the payment of such claims by ordering an unequal division of the community. (For example, if the community assets at divorce total $40,000 and the community has a $4,000 reimbursement claim against H's separate estate, an appropriate division of the community would be $22,000 to W and $18,000 to H.) Moreover, since reimbursement claims are really creditor claims, the divorce court can hold the debtor spouse's separate property liable and award appropriate portions thereof to the claimant. [Provost v. Provost, 102 Cal. App. 775 (1929)]

   a. **Claimant may be general creditor:** [§337] If the spouse is seeking reimbursement or other adjustment claims as a creditor, is the spouse on a par with other unsecured creditors of the debtor? If so, the adjustment might render the debtor spouse insolvent and be overturned in bankruptcy as well as giving "regular" creditors cause to intervene.

   b. **Types of offsets permitted:** [§338] A claimant spouse, say W, may press claims at divorce for half of the community's right to reimbursement for improvements made to H's separate property with community funds, for gifts of community property not consented to in writing by W, or for H's failure to account for missing property under his exclusive management. The divorce court can also award damages or make offsets for violation by a spouse of the good faith standard of California Family Code sections 721(b) and 1100(e) (*see supra*, §261).

   c. **Reimbursement for payment of separate debts:** [§339] A spouse can also obtain reimbursement (apparently without interest) of half of the community's right to reimbursement for payments of "separate debts" by the other spouse with community funds. For purposes of reimbursement, a debt can be partly community and partly separate, so that only a portion of the community funds paid need be reimbursed. [*See* Weinberg v. Weinberg, 67 Cal. 2d 557 (1967)] (*But see supra*, §282, for limitations on the right of reimbursement when community funds are used to pay separate alimony and child support debts.)

   d. **Reimbursement for separate use of community assets:** [§340] At dissolution, one spouse may also be awarded half of the community's reimbursement claim arising out of the other's separate use of community assets. For example, a separated H's use of community-owned business properties (*e.g.*, the office building where he works) to generate separate income is such a use, as is the separated H's occupancy of a community residence. For both uses, H owes the community fair rental value (unless the business usage is compensated in a different manner under "reverse" *Pereira* and *Van Camp* apportionments; *see supra*, §75). [Marriage of Watts, 171 Cal. App. 3d 366 (1985)]

   e. **Statute of limitations for reimbursement claims:** [§341] The following reimbursement claims must be brought no later than three years after the claimant spouse has knowledge of the expenditure creating the right of reimbursement, or must be asserted in divorce proceedings for division of property or in administration proceedings following the death of a spouse if either occurs *before* the three-year period expires:

(i) A claim under Family Code section 914(b) that separate properties of the claimant were applied to pay a *necessaries debt* when community or separate assets of the benefited spouse were available (*see supra*, §280);

(ii) A claim under section 915(b) that community assets were used to pay *child support or alimony obligations* when separate property of the obligor spouse was available (*see supra*, §282).

[Cal. Fam. Code §920]

(1) **Post-divorce reimbursement:** [§342]   Section 920 also requires a spouse to bring an action for reimbursement within three years after she paid a debt she incurred but that was assigned by the divorce court to the other spouse (*see supra*, §§298-303). The right of reimbursement is to effectuate an equal division of the community.

4. **Treatment of "Nondistributable" Community Assets:** [§343]   Some community assets are not subject to distribution, in that they can be owned by only one spouse (*e.g.*, community-owned goodwill of W's sole business). Likewise, federal law prohibits awarding any community interest in National Service Life Insurance to the spouse of the insured. [Wissner v. Wissner, 338 U.S. 655 (1950); *and see infra*, §§482-485] In these situations, the divorce court must value the community interest in the asset, order it distributed to one spouse, and award the other spouse community assets of equal value or (if necessary) a promissory note.

    a. **Inalienable assets:** [§344]   One decision states that if a benefit acquired by community labor or money cannot be sold for cash, its value must also be zero. [*See* Lorenz v. Lorenz, *supra*, §94] This is inconsistent with the treatment given inalienable professional goodwill of a spouse (*see supra*, §204). Thus, although memberships in a social club may not be assignable, they do have value that the court must estimate. (If the club membership was recently acquired, the initiation fee should be a good measure of value.)

5. **Effect of Failure to Distribute Asset or Assign Debt:** [§345]   The divorcing spouses may agree in their own property settlement on how community assets will be distributed. If neither a spousal agreement nor a divorce court judgment deals with a particular item of community property, the effect of an entry of divorce is to convert it into tenancy in common property. [McBride v. McBride, *supra*, §92] This has frequently happened with respect to community interests in spouses' retirement plans. California Family Code section 2556 gives the divorce court continuing jurisdiction to make a belated division of such omitted property as well as to assign a community debt not previously assigned. The statute states that an equal division is presumptively proper but it allows unequal division in the "interests of justice." (No such flexibility exists where the asset or debt are timely dealt with by the divorce court.)

    a. **Effect of divorce on debts:** [§346]   If any community debts (*supra*, §§320-326) are not assigned by contract or decree to a particular spouse, each is apparently ultimately responsible for payment of one-half thereof. If this were not the case, equal division of the community would not occur. Thus when either former spouse voluntarily or involuntarily pays such a community creditor, a right of reimbursement arises as to half the sum taken by the creditor.

B. **DEVOLUTION OF PROPERTY AT DEATH**

1. **Separate Property:** [§347]   A decedent spouse may by will dispose of his or her separate estate (excluding quasi-community property) as desired, subject to liability to creditors and to statutory protections for the surviving spouse (*e.g.*, family allowances). (*See* Wills Summary.) At least one-third of the separate property passing *intestate* goes to the surviving spouse. [Cal. Prob. Code §6401(c)]

2. **Community Property:** [§348]   The decedent spouse has testamentary power over his or her *half interest* in the community property. [Cal. Prob. Code §6101(b)] Whereas an aggregate theory is used in dividing the community at divorce, the "item theory" determines rights of the surviving spouse and the scope of decedent's testamentary powers when dissolution is by death. This approach recognizes the surviving spouse as owner of an undivided half interest *in every item* of community property—a right that the decedent cannot defeat by will even if the latter disposes of no more than half the community estate by value.

    a. **Possible exception to use of item formula:** [§349]   California courts have not considered how the item theory may apply to community assets incapable of transmission by will to a third party. For example, suppose W is a lawyer and H dies. H's will can probably bequeath to his son his half interest in W's community-owned law books, desk, accounts receivable, expectant interests in contingent fee contracts where litigation is pending, etc.; but H *cannot* bequeath W's goodwill, which is also a community asset.

        (1) *One solution* would be to allow H to invoke the aggregate theory to the extent of half the value of W's goodwill—*e.g.*, "I bequeath to W my half interest in her professional goodwill worth $20,000 and to Son the entire community interest in Blackacre, which is worth $40,000." If the aggregate theory were accepted, W could not elect against the devise of Blackacre (*see* below).

        (2) *Alternatively*, a court might hold that the interest in goodwill can only pass intestate (as an exception to California Probate Code provisions on testamentary power) or it might create a form of the terminable interest doctrine (use of which is perhaps barred by statute only at divorce; *see supra*, §198) so that H's half interest in the goodwill ended at his death.

    b. **"Election" by surviving spouse:** [§350]   Use of the item theory means that a will attempting to dispose of the interest in a community asset owned by the *survivor* gives the survivor an election. Unless the will states otherwise, all dispositions to the survivor are deemed to be made on condition that the survivor permits the will to dispose of the property interest owned by the survivor. In essence, the will is an offer to contract: The estate of decedent offers various bequests or devises to the surviving spouse if the surviving spouse will permit the will to dispose of property not owned by decedent.

        (1) **Example:** Suppose the community owns Blackacre and Whiteacre, each worth $100,000. H dies and his will devises "all of the community interests in Whiteacre to my son and in Blackacre to my wife." The devise to W of H's half interest in Blackacre is assumed to be conditioned upon W's not asserting her ownership of half of Whiteacre. [Estate of Murphy, 15 Cal. 3d 907 (1976)]

(2) **Wills construed to avoid election where possible:** [§351] The law presumes that a decedent intends to devise or bequeath only what he owns, and all ambiguities will be resolved against a construction that the survivor's interest is included. [Estate of Moore, 62 Cal. App. 265 (1923)] In the previous hypothetical, for example, a statement in H's will that "I leave Whiteacre to my son" would be construed as devising only H's community half interest. Similarly, a bequest of "all my property" will be confined to decedent's own community half interest plus his separate estate.

   (a) **Declarations of separate ownership:** [§352] If a will states directly or indirectly that an asset that is actually community is decedent's *separate* property and disposes of it, the surviving spouse is required to make an election. [Estate of Wolfe, 48 Cal. 2d 570 (1957)] Under this approach, a devise of "my ranch in Fresno County" would probably be construed as including the half interest of the surviving spouse.

   (b) **Mistaken declarations:** [§353] Even where the evidence shows that the testator made a mistake in declaring an item of property to be separate and devising it entirely to a third party, courts have held that the bequests and devises to the surviving spouse must be construed as conditional upon the surviving spouse allowing the mistaken devise to take effect. [Estate of Moore, *supra*] This position seems misguided. Insofar as the will poses an election for the surviving spouse, it is an offer to contract with the decedent's estate, and it is reasonable to assume that the decedent would not have made such an offer had decedent known the true facts.

(3) **Applies to separate property:** [§354] The election doctrine also applies where decedent's will purports to dispose of separate property of the surviving spouse. For example, suppose H's will states, "I devise Blackacre, which my wife and I own as joint tenants, to my son; Whiteacre to my wife; residue to ABC Church." If the survivor W wishes to take the devise of H's half interest in Whiteacre (which is community property), she will have to give up her survivorship claim to Blackacre (as joint tenant) and let Son inherit it.

(4) **No forfeiture of rights to intestate succession:** [§355] If the surviving spouse, say W, elects against the will to claim her share of any community assets or her separate property, the bequests and devises made to her in the will lapse and property will pass to any designated alternate legatee—often a legatee named for the situation where W has predeceased H. (*Example:* "If W predeceases me, property I have left to her goes to Sister." W's electing against this will should be treated as the equivalent of her predeceasing H.) If no alternative taker is named, the property will pass under the residuary clause—so that if W is residuary legatee she can freely elect against the will in such a case. Technically, W's residuary legacy will be forfeited; but this means that the assets would pass intestate, and the surviving spouse is the intestate heir of any portion of decedent's community property estate not disposed of by the will. [Cal. Prob. Code §6401(a)] The right to take intestate is *not* forfeited by an election against the will. [Estate of King, 19 Cal. 2d 354 (1942)]

(5) **Applies to will substitutes:** [§356] Property can be passed outside a will by designating a beneficiary in a document recognized by statute or common law as not being subject to the formalities of a will. These "will substitutes" or "nonprobate transfers" include pension benefits accruing at an employee's death, bank account or Totten trusts, life insurance, etc. The election doctrine also applies to these will substitutes. [Tyre v. Aetna Life Insurance Co., 54 Cal. 2d 399 (1960)] Thus, if H uses community funds to buy two life insurance policies on his life and names Son beneficiary of one policy and W beneficiary of the other, H may condition the designation of W as recipient of his half community interest in the latter policy upon her not electing to void as to one half the designation of Son on the other policy.

(a) **Note—limited scope of forfeiture:** [§357] In the example above, if H had not specifically put W to an election, she would have forfeited nothing in claiming her half share in the policy in which H named Son beneficiary. This is so because the courts treat the will and each will substitute as distinct units for election purposes. Thus, the surviving spouse asserting community property claims forfeits only benefits she receives within the particular unit where the election is made.

(6) **Method of election:** [§358] A surviving spouse who accepts distribution of bequests or devises that were implicitly or expressly conditioned on agreeing to disposition of property owned by the survivor elects by her actions to accept the will. Alternatively, the survivor can file a formal document with the probate court either electing to take under the will or renouncing its bequests and asserting ownership of property the will attempts to dispose of.

(a) **Election after survivor's death:** [§359] If the surviving spouse dies without making an election, it can be made by the personal representative of the spouse. [Estate of Kelley, 122 Cal. App. 2d 42 (1953)]

c. **Restrictions on interest of surviving spouse:** [§360] As noted, the decedent spouse may not bequeath to a third party any community property interest of the surviving spouse (unless the survivor elects to permit this result). Similarly, the decedent may not by any type of instrument or transaction restrict the management power the survivor has over half of the community property after dissolution by death, unless the instrument or transaction has a substantial inter vivos purpose. [Tyre v. Aetna Life Insurance Co., *supra*]

(1) **Contract having business purpose permissible:** [§361] If W and X are business partners, they may contract that at the death of one the survivor may purchase the entire community interest in the partnership according to a specified formula. This contract is an estate planning instrument of a semi-testamentary nature, in that it extends W's community management powers beyond her death; but it has a valid business purpose (*i.e.,* X might not otherwise have become W's partner). Thus the restrictions imposed upon the rights of H as a surviving spouse are permissible under *Tyre, supra.*

(2) **Long-term investments permissible:** [§362] Bona fide investments that would restrict the liquidity of community funds beyond the death of a managing spouse are permissible, since they have the legitimate inter vivos purpose of making a gain for the community. Thus, for example, a surviving W may not void a certificate of deposit contract made by H under which the deposited funds cannot be withdrawn for a period extending beyond his death without heavy penalty, since the deposit of funds was an inter vivos management decision by H. [Beemer v. Roher, 137 Cal. App. 293 (1934)]

(3) **Life insurance provisions may be voided by survivor:** [§363] Suppose H uses community funds to purchase insurance on his life with an option to have benefits paid as a cash lump sum or as an annuity for the life of the beneficiary, W. H then selects the annuity form of payment. Since the designation regarding payment has no inter vivos implications but is simply H's decision as to what should happen to W's half interest in the policy after he dies, W can void selection of the annuity option. [Tyre v. Aetna Life Insurance Co., *supra*] However, the court in *Tyre* implied an election provision for the survivor (W)—*i.e.*, in order to get **her** half interest in cash, W had to give up her claim as beneficiary of H's half interest in the policy (in favor of alternate beneficiaries named by H).

(a) **Scope of rule unclear:** Suppose instead that H, using community funds, simply purchases from XYZ Insurance Co. an annuity for W's life to commence upon H's death. The action has no inter vivos implications, but what is W's remedy at H's death (*e.g.*, to compel the return of half the cash paid to XYZ)? XYZ would be well advised to obtain W's written consent to such a contract, which would bar her from attacking it later.

(b) **Note:** If the annuity calls for payment of benefits to W to begin at age 60 (rather than on H's death) and H dies when W is 58, the inter vivos effects of the investment—*i.e.*, the potential for supplying support owed by H to W during marriage had he lived longer—would probably make the contract valid under *Tyre*.

3. **Property Passing by Will Substitute:** [§364] For a spouse to pass to a beneficiary both community halves of property by a will substitute (*e.g.*, a life insurance policy), the other spouse must consent. But what if after that consent the designating spouse alters the designation (*e.g.*, by changing the beneficiary or the mode of payment to the original beneficiary)? Where this happens, if the consenting spouse is alive, the alteration revokes the consent and the beneficiary cannot take both halves of the property. If the consenting spouse has died before the modification, the alteration is effective only as to the half interest in community of the modifying party; the consenting spouse's half interest passes, on the survivor's death, according to the original designation consented to, unless the survivor had the consenting spouse's written authorization to make modifications affecting all interests in the funds. [Cal. Prob. Code §5023]

4. **Ancestral Property Rules:** [§365] All assets owned by a surviving spouse are of course his or her separate property, but the pre-death characterization of such

property may significantly affect succession when the survivor dies intestate. Special provisions in California Probate Code section 6402.5 (referred to as the ancestral property rules) provide that *former in-laws of the surviving spouse* may be entitled to inherit certain property in the survivor's estate; *i.e.*, the property is returned to the predeceased spouse's family line.

a. **Scope of doctrine:** [§366]   California Probate Code section 6402.5 restricts the scope of the ancestral property doctrine.

   (1) **Intestate survivor leaving no descendants or spouse:** [§367]   The doctrine applies only when the surviving spouse dies *intestate without lineal descendants or a surviving spouse* (from a remarriage).

   (2) **Property attributable to predeceased spouse:** [§368]   The ancestral property rules apply only to property (not disposed of by will or will substitute) which is attributable to the predeceased spouse:

   (i) *One-half* of property that was *community* when the predeceased spouse died;

   (ii) *One-half* of property that was the separate property of the survivor when the predeceased spouse died but which *had been community* before the predeceased spouse gave her interest in it to the survivor;

   (iii) *One-half* of property that was held in *joint tenancy* between the spouses when the predeceased spouse died; and

   (iv) *All separate property of the predeceased spouse* that the survivor received by devise, intestate succession, or inter vivos gift.

   Note that for purposes of section 6402.5, quasi-community property is treated as community property.

   (a) **Time limitations:** [§369]   Despite the above rules, the ancestral property rules do not apply if the surviving spouse survives the predeceased spouse by:

   1) *Five years* for property that was *personalty* when the predeceased spouse died.

   2) *Fifteen years* for *real property*.

b. **Devolution of property:** [§370]   Property subject to the ancestral property rules passes as follows:

   (1) *To lineal descendants of the predeceased spouse.* (These would have to be children from another marriage or born outside of marriage, since the rules do not apply if the surviving spouse leaves lineal descendants.)

   (2) *If there are no such lineal descendants*, to the parent(s) of the predeceased spouse, or if none, to the issue of the parents by right of representation (*i.e.*, the predeceased's siblings or their issue).

(3) ***If there are no surviving parents, siblings, or issue of siblings*** of the predeceased spouse, to the heirs of the intestate surviving spouse (as determined by ordinary intestate succession rules).

c. **Determining source of title:** [§371]   Former in-laws claiming under the ancestral property statutes have the burden of establishing that particular assets in the survivor's estate were former community property, former separate property of the predeceased spouse, former joint tenancy property of the spouses, or former quasi-community property. [Estate of Abdale, 28 Cal. 2d 587 (1946); Estate of Baxter, 96 Cal. App. 2d 493 (1950)] If assets subject to the ancestral property rule are commingled by the survivor with other assets, and withdrawals at least equal in amount to the former assets are then made, the former in-laws would probably be unable to establish a right to inherit under section 6402.5. [Estate of Adams, *supra,* §14]

   (1) **When source will be inferred:** [§372]   If the surviving spouse dies intestate shortly after the predeceased spouse while owning approximately the same amount of property she had at her spouse's death, it can be inferred that the survivor still has on hand property received from the predeceased spouse's estate.

   (2) **Treatment of increases in value:** [§373]   Enhanced value of the assets arising after the survivor obtained separate title will have the same source as the asset where such increases are due to natural causes (such as inflation). However, increases in value attributable to subsequent ***labor*** of the survivor should not be inherited by former in-laws. Interest and dividends accrued after the predeceased spouse's death without labor by the survivor have the same character (*e.g.,* former community property, former separate property of the predeceased spouse) as the capital that produces the profits.

   (3) **Tracing through change of form permitted:** [§374]   Former in-laws usually can trace former community property or separate property of the predeceased spouse through any changes of form that it undergoes after dissolution of the marriage. [Simonton v. Los Angeles Trust & Savings Bank, 205 Cal. 252 (1928)] This tracing rule should apply where one item of realty subject to section 6402.5 is traded for another within 15 years. Wholly unsettled is whether tracing is allowed when the original realty is sold for cash or traded for personalty more than five years after the death of the predeceased spouse. If the survivor gives the property away before death and the donee (in an unrelated transaction) gives it back to the survivor, the latter gift is the new source of the property; *i.e.,* the in-laws may not trace beyond the survivor's unrestricted gift of the property. [Estate of Westerman, 68 Cal. 2d 267 (1968)]

C. ADMINISTRATION OF PROPERTY AND CREDITORS' CLAIMS AT DEATH

1. **Property Required to Be Administered:** [§375]   Property of a decedent passing to someone other than her spouse is subject to administration in a probate court proceeding; decedent's separate property and her half of the community property passing to her spouse by testate or intestate succession are not required to be administered in such a proceeding unless the asset at issue will be held in trust or unless the surviving spouse receives less than a fee simple absolute interest (*e.g.,* the survivor gets only a life estate under the will). [Cal. Prob. Code §13501]

a. **Election by surviving spouse:** [§376]   Even where no administration of the property is necessary, the surviving spouse still may elect to have the decedent's share passing to him (or even his own half of the community property) subjected to administration by decedent's personal representative. [Cal. Prob. Code §13502] The advantage is that the assets ultimately distributed to the surviving spouse by the personal representative will generally be free of creditors' claims for community debts, and the surviving spouse will not be personally liable for community debts. This election may also be made by the survivor's estate (if the survivor dies within the four-month election period), or by his conservator or guardian.

b. **Election to pay to trustee:** [§377]   The survivor (or the guardian, conservator, or estate if the survivor dies during the election period) may elect to have the survivor's share of community and quasi-community property or portions thereof paid directly to the trustee of a testamentary trust created by the decedent spouse's will or to an inter vivos trust created by the decedent into which community assets are "poured."

(1) **Purpose:** This procedure accommodates "election wills" (*supra*, §§350-359), which usually bequeath the survivor's community interest to a trustee.

2. **Confirmation Proceedings for Community Property Passing to Surviving Spouse:** [§378]   When probate administration is not used for community and quasi-community property passing to the surviving spouse, the survivor will benefit from some official documentation of ownership when subsequently dealing with third parties (title companies, stock transfer agents, etc.). Such documentation can be obtained through confirmation proceedings under California Probate Code sections 13650 through 13658.

a. **Procedure:** [§379]   The surviving spouse must file a petition alleging that specified assets were community and quasi-community property and that the survivor now owns decedent's interest therein under a will or by intestate succession. After notice to decedent's personal representative (if someone other than the surviving spouse) and the legatees, and in the absence of proof to the contrary, the court will issue a judgment confirming the surviving spouse as owner of the assets in question. [Cal. Prob. Code §§13655-13656]

b. **Advantages of confirmation proceedings:** [§380]   Confirmation proceedings are an alternative to full-scale probate administration and are less costly than such administration. Among other things, the personal representative receives no statutory compensation based on the value of assets subjected to confirmation proceedings; and attorneys are compensated on the basis of services rendered rather than on a percentage of the property value (as in full-scale probate).

3. **Post-Death Management and Control of Community Assets:** [§381]   A survivor spouse retains management over all community property that passes to the survivor free of trust or in a form other than a qualified interest (*e.g.*, life estate), unless the survivor elects to subject the property to administration or to pay it to a trustee-legatee.

a. **Community realty:** [§382]   Forty days after the death of one spouse, the survivor spouse (or her guardian, conservator, or personal representative) obtains full power to sell, lease, mortgage, or otherwise deal with and dispose of community and quasi-community *realty* subject to administration unless notice of a claim is filed by a devisee under decedent's will. These management rights may be exercised by the survivor without regard to the form of "title" to the community realty (*i.e.,* even if it was held in decedent's name). [Cal. Prob. Code §13540] The effect of the devisee's filing notice of a claim of interest is that the surviving spouse does not get the management power provided for by the 40-day statute.

b. **Compare—personal property:** [§383]   Generally, the surviving spouse cannot seize management of community personalty (unlike realty; *see* above) from the decedent's personal representative. *Exception:* The survivor may deal with community securities registered in the name of the survivor alone. [Cal. Prob. Code §13545] Creditors of the estate and a legatee bequeathed decedent's half interest in such securities apparently have a claim on the proceeds of sales by the surviving spouse and probably in new securities bought with sales proceeds.

4. **Liability for Debts at Dissolution by Death:** [§384]   Unlike the situation at divorce (*see supra,* §§298-301), dissolution of the community by death does *not*—absent failure of a creditor to assert his rights—relieve any community property from liability for a debt imposed upon it prior to the death. [Dawes v. Rich, 60 Cal. App. 4th 24 (1997)]

   a. **Where no probate proceedings over community property occur:** [§385]   Unless both halves of the community property are subjected to probate administration, the surviving spouse will be personally liable to most creditors on obligations incurred by the decedent. [Cal. Prob. Code §§13550-13351] However, personal liability at the date of death cannot exceed the value of the survivor's half interest in community and quasi-community property and so much of the decedent's half interest in such property as passes to the survivor less any liens or encumbrances thereon.

      (1) **Certain creditors barred:** [§386]   If *any* of the decedent's property is subject to probate administration, creditors who do not file claims thereby lose the right to proceed against the surviving spouse (and the property he keeps or obtains) unless such creditors:

         (i) Obtain the survivor's acknowledgment of liability; or

         (ii) Commence judicial proceedings against the survivor during the time for filing claims with decedent's personal representative.

         [Cal. Prob. Code §13552]

      (2) **Offsets and defenses available to survivor:** [§387]   A surviving spouse personally liable for decedent's debts may raise the same offsets and defenses that the decedent could have asserted against the creditor if she were living.

b. **Where probate proceedings are conducted and claims are filed:** [§388] When creditors' claims are received by decedent's personal representative, the estate must determine which assets will be used to pay them—*i.e.,* separate property or community. Where community property is liable, there is the additional problem of how much the decedent's half interest should pay. Moreover, the decedent's share of community property is probably liable for debts of the surviving spouse; and the Probate Code permits the survivor to bring such debts into the probate proceedings. [Cal. Prob. Code §11440]

   (1) **Classification of debts:** [§389] The decedent's personal representative and the surviving spouse may make an agreement classifying decedent's debts (and the debts of the survivor for which property being administered is allegedly liable) as community and separate and provide for the payment of those debts from appropriate sources. Such an agreement is binding if approved by the probate court as substantially protecting the rights of all affected parties. Absent an agreement, "each debt of the decedent shall be apportioned based on all of the property of the spouses liable for the debt at the date of death that is not exempt from enforcement of a money judgment, in the proportion determined by the value of the property less any liens and encumbrances, adjusted to take into account any right of reimbursement that would have been available if the property were applied to the debt at the date of death, and the debt shall be allocated accordingly." [Cal. Prob. Code §11444]

   (2) **Effect of "adjustment" clause:** [§390] The effect of the final clause of section 11444 calling for an adjustment based on reference to reimbursement law is that the decedent's separate debts are to be paid solely from decedent's separate property (if sufficient) and community debts are to be paid 50% from the decedent's half of the community and 50% from the survivor's half (again, if sufficient). Proration based on the relative values of separate and community property directed in the first part of the statute occurs only for debts that are neither separate nor community. The best examples are the costs of administration (executor's fee, attorney's fee).

5. **Effect on Ex-Spouse of Decedent of Failure to File Claim:** [§391] Suppose a divorce court orders H to pay a community debt that W had incurred. Later, one of them dies. Since the effect of the divorce court order made each party liable to the creditor, the creditor's failure to file a creditor's claim against the decedent's estate should not bar him from pursuing a remedy against the survivor.

   a. **Remedy for surviving ex-spouse:** [§392] When a former spouse dies with community debts unpaid (although assigned by the divorce court to that spouse, or owed 50-50 by the former spouses as unassigned debts), the surviving ex-spouse can protect herself by filing a contingent creditor's claim against the decedent's estate based on her potential right of reimbursement if she is held liable in such a manner as to render the property division at divorce unequal.

[§§393-396]

V. RELATIONSHIPS SHORT OF VALID MARRIAGE

chapter approach

On your exam, you may encounter a question concerning a couple not lawfully married. The superior answer to such a question will explore *all possible remedies*. For example, just because the woman may qualify as a putative spouse is no reason not to discuss other claims that she can assert under the *Marvin* case. Thus, before you stop writing, consider all the possibilities.

Also recall that the law here distinguishes between parties who had a *good faith belief* in the existence of a marriage and those who just knowingly cohabit. And don't overlook the public policy considerations—especially if analysis indicates a "Marvinizer" is going to be treated better (or even the same as) a lawful or putative spouse.

Finally, if a lawful spouse is inserted into the problem as a third party, you probably should discuss the *living apart doctrine* (covered in chapter I) before leaping into a discussion of what an equitable result would be.

A. PUTATIVE MARRIAGES

1. **In General:** [§393] Rules of law somewhat similar to the community property system apply to couples domiciled in California who have attempted to marry but whose marriage was void or voidable due to some legal impediment. These rules apply, however, only if *at least one* of the "spouses" believed *in good faith* that the marriage was valid. (If both partners knew of the legal impediment at the time of the attempted marriage, their relationship is usually governed by the *Marvin* decision (*infra*, §§430 *et seq.*) rather than by the law of invalid marriage.)

    a. **"Putative marriage" used to describe relationship:** [§394] An invalid marriage wherein one or both parties acted in good faith has been referred to as a "putative marriage" in many cases, and California Family Code section 2251 refers to the good faith partners to such a union as "putative spouses." Under a pure putative marriage system (such as that in Louisiana), *all* of the property rights of a lawful marriage flow to the good faith spouse.

    b. **Good faith presumed:** [§395] At civil law (and probably in California as well), good faith is presumed, so that a party who contends that California putative marriage rules are inapplicable has the burden of establishing lack of good faith.

    c. **Test for lack of good faith:** [§396] In deciding whether good faith in the validity of marriage is lacking, the courts first look to the *subjective* belief of the would-be spouse—*i.e.,* what his or her belief actually was (not what someone from a different background might believe). If that belief was that the marriage was valid, the courts then ask if such a belief is *objectively reasonable*. This reasonableness requirement severely undercuts prior decisions [*see, e.g.,*

Estate of Foy, 109 Cal. App. 2d 329 (1952)] that found good faith despite a mistake of law, and probably most mistakes of *fact* will not be held objectively unreasonable.

(1) **Example:** An Iranian woman visiting in California secretly conducted for herself and her would-be husband a wedding ceremony appropriate for her Islamic sect. No wedding license was obtained; the couple did not cohabit. It was held that the requisite belief for her to obtain putative spouse status was that *California law* would recognize a valid marriage; it was not sufficient that she believed that she was married under her religion. [Marriage of Vryonis, 202 Cal. App. 3d 712 (1988)]

(2) **No common law marriage in California:** [§397] Unlike several states, California does not recognize nonceremonial common law marriages attempted in California. Before *Vryonis* added the ***objectively reasonable*** test, courts held that a subjective belief that California did recognize common law marriages, coupled with the appropriate acts for such a marriage at common law, produced putative spouse status. [Wagner v. County of Imperial, 145 Cal. App. 3d 980 (1983)] Now such a belief about the nature of California marriage law is held objectively unreasonable. [Centinela Hospital v. Superior Court, 215 Cal. App. 3d 971 (1989)]

(3) **Treatment of out-of-state marriages:** [§398] California courts generally test the validity of marriages according to the law of the place of celebration. [Cal. Fam. Code §308] Accordingly, a couple domiciled in California might contract a common law marriage in a state where such marriages are lawful and have it recognized as lawful (rather than merely putative) in California.

(4) **Marriage by estoppel:** [§399] In one case, where H-2 and W, at H-2's suggestion, went through a formal marriage ceremony, both knowing W was married to H-1, H-2 was estopped from denying they were "married." [Marriage of Recknor, 138 Cal. App. 3d 539 (1982)] Likewise, where H, not yet divorced from W-1, "married" W-2, stating in the marriage license application that he was single, on W-1's death he was estopped to claim rights as W-1's husband. [Estate of Anderson, 60 Cal. App. 4th 436 (1997)] As explained in *Anderson,* the theory of these cases is not estoppel *in pais,* which requires the party claiming estoppel to have relied, to her detriment, in good faith, on a misrepresentation by the estopped party, but instead it is quasi-estoppel. Under quasi-estoppel, a party invoking the benefits of a status cannot repudiate it to avoid its burdens.

(5) **Effect of one party's lack of good faith:** [§400] Insofar as the California version of the putative marriage doctrine is the product of case law, a "spouse" aware of the invalidity of the marriage probably could *not* invoke the rules applicable to putative marriage (although the other "spouse" in good faith would be able to do so). [*See* Flanagan v. Capital National Bank, 213 Cal. 664 (1931)]

(a) **Rule at annulment unclear:** [§401] California Family Code section 2251(a), governing division of property at annulment, provides that if the court should find "either party or both parties believed in good faith that the marriage was valid, the court shall . . . [d]eclare *such party* or parties to have the status of a putative spouse." This would clearly indicate that the "spouse" lacking good faith does not have such status (since it would otherwise be impossible for only one "party" to be a putative spouse). However, section 2251 also provides that when this determination is made, the court "shall divide, in accordance with section 2550 [the equal division statute], that property acquired during the union which would have been community property or quasi-community property" had the marriage been lawful. This latter directive to divide is not limited to acquisitions of the spouse lacking good faith but—read literally—also directs a 50-50 division of acquisitions by the good faith "spouse." Thus interpreted, section 2251 gives the benefits of the putative marriage doctrine at annulment to the bad faith mate of a good faith party.

1) **Case law:** *Marriage of Cary,* 34 Cal. App. 3d 345 (1973), interpreted section 2251 to give the bad faith "spouse" the benefits of the putative marriage doctrine. *Marvin v. Marvin,* 18 Cal. 3d 660 (1976), overruled other aspects of *Cary* but specifically held that this question is an open one.

2) **Commentaries:** Most commentators consider it wrong to accord the "spouse" lacking good faith the benefits of section 2251 at annulment. Under their view, acquisitions of the good faith spouse should be treated at annulment as separate property.

(b) **Unique nomenclature in statute:** [§402]   Section 2251 provides that the property subject to a 50-50 division at annulment shall be called "quasi-marital" property. The term "quasi-marital" property has not been used outside the context of annulment cases and is quite different from quasi-community property (*infra,* §455).

2. **Status During Putative Marriage of Acquisitions by Labor:** [§403]   The status *before annulment* of "quasi-marital" property—*i.e.,* property that would have been community had the marriage been valid—is still unsettled in California. There appear to be four possible approaches:

a. **Property is community:** [§404]   Under this approach, the property would be treated for all purposes (management and control, creditors' rights, etc.) as community. However, if one "spouse" lacked good faith, this rule would probably apply only to his or her acquisitions; those of the other "spouse" would be treated as separate property.

(1) **Approach rejected:** [§405]   While this approach seems most fair to all parties affected and obtains the benefits of equal management for the bona fide "spouse," it has been rejected by the courts on the ground that there must be a valid marriage for community property to exist. [*See, e.g.,* Wilkinson v. Wilkinson, 12 Cal. App. 3d 1164 (1970)]

(2) **Possible distinction:** [§406]   If California makes marriage a prerequisite to community property status, a distinction could be made between *void* marriages (*i.e.,* incestuous or knowingly bigamous under the Family Code section 2200) and marriages that are merely *voidable*. Voidable marriages include marriages where a party is underage or insane, where consent was obtained by fraud or force, where a party is incurably impotent, or where (although the marriage was in fact bigamous) a former spouse was believed to be dead or had not been heard of for five years. [Cal. Fam. Code §2210] Such marriages must have *some* effect in law until they are annulled (to distinguish them from void marriages); and property acquired therein should be, prior to annulment, community.

(a) **Note:**   Some cases involving voidable marriages have said that such marriages cannot produce true community property. [Coats v. Coats, 160 Cal. 671 (1911)] However, such decisions can be limited to situations in which an annulment retroactively eliminates community property. No decision has held that community assets cannot exist in a voidable marriage that has not been voided by annulment.

b. **Property is tenancy in common:** [§407]   According to another view, the putative spouses are tenants in common of acquisitions that would otherwise have been community property. [Sousa v. Freitas, 10 Cal. App. 3d 660 (1970)] Under this theory, each party would have management power over only one-half of the property.

c. **Property arises from partnership:** [§408]   A few courts have indicated that a good faith putative spouse has an interest only in those acquisitions (other than his or her own) to which that "spouse" contributed a joint effort. [*See* Goff v. Goff, 52 Cal. App. 2d 23 (1942)] This suggests a sort of business partnership relationship, with acquisitions outside the scope of the "partnership"—even by labor of a "spouse"—being his or her *separate* property. Under such an approach, laws applicable to business partnerships rather than tenancy in common property would seem to govern the co-owned acquisitions.

d. **Property is separate property of acquiring spouse:** [§409]   The fourth approach would be to find that all property rights in an acquisition that would have been community in a lawful marriage are *separate* property of the acquiring party until annulment or death unless "title" is taken in some other form (*e.g.,* joint tenancy), in which case the form of title would control ownership. The cases stating that at annulment or death of a party the nonacquiring spouse has a mere claim for an equitable division of quasi-marital property [*see, e.g.,* Oakley v. Oakley, 82 Cal. App. 2d 188 (1947)] are consistent only with this fourth theory—since community property, tenancy in common, and partnership law theories would confer a property right. [*See also* Menchaca v. Farmers Insurance Exchange, 59 Cal. App. 3d 117 (1976)—dictum that an insurance policy purchased by one party with earnings during a putative marriage and that covered the insured's "spouse if a resident of the same household" would not apply to the putative wife]

e. **Treatment of Social Security benefits:** [§410]   An individual who is a putative spouse under California law is a "wife," "husband," "widow," or "widower" for purposes of receiving benefits under the Social Security Act, at least if there is no lawful spouse making a claim. [*See* 42 U.S.C. §§402(b)(1), 416(h)(1)(A); Aubrey v. Folsom, 151 F. Supp. 836 (N.D. Cal. 1957)]

3. **Remedies at Annulment of Putative Marriage:** [§411]   As indicated above, California Family Code section 2251 provides for division at annulment of all quasi-marital property—(*i.e.,* property that would have been community and quasi-community in a valid marriage) at least in favor of a good faith putative spouse. If there is no such divisible property, or if the amount is insignificant, some older cases have allowed a good faith spouse to assert quasi-contractual claims against the other party for the value of services rendered in excess of consideration received. [Sanguinetti v. Sanguinetti, 9 Cal. 2d 95 (1937)] Of course, the fact that no divisible quasi-marital property is on hand suggests that it has been spent for the benefit of the couple and that the services of either party (*e.g.,* household chores, mowing the lawn, etc.) may not be worth more than the monetary benefits received.

   a. **Remedy should be neutral as to sex:** [§412]   In reported cases to date, only a putative wife has received relief in quasi-contract (quantum meruit); but under present law, a putative husband should have as much right to seek compensation for services rendered during a putative marriage. In many cases, there would likely be an offset.

   b. **Defendant need not be in bad faith:** [§413]   The defendant in an annulment proceeding (usually the male) may be liable in quasi-contract even though he entered into the "marriage" in good faith. [Lazzarevich v. Lazzarevich, 88 Cal. App. 2d 708 (1948)] As yet, there is no authority that a bad faith "spouse" can recover in quasi-contract from a good faith "spouse," but the tenor of the *Marvin* decision (*see infra,* §430) is that such a party could recover.

   c. **Alimony available:** [§414]   Alimony pendente lite and post-annulment alimony may be ordered for a putative spouse under California Family Code section 2254. However, the statute is clear that the recipient must have had a good faith belief in the marriage (presumably at the time of marriage).

      (1) **Effect of knowledge of the impediment:** [§415]   One case has said that the good faith or putative status of a spouse ends the moment she learns of the impediment to the marriage. [Lazzarevich v. Lazzarevich, *supra*] On this theory, all rights for the period following the obtaining of such knowledge would have to be based on the *Marvin* doctrine rather than the putative spouse doctrine. The rule seems very harsh on a party who believed in good faith that the marriage was valid but does not abandon the other "spouse" (perhaps because they have children) once she learns of the impediment. One Louisiana case said in dictum that putative status originally attaching should continue until annulment even though, of course, the "spouses" must at some time before annulment is adjudged learn of the impediment to the marriage. [Jackson v. Swift & Co., 151 So. 816 (La. 1934)]

4. **Termination of Putative Marriage by Death of a "Spouse":** [§416]   No statute controls the rights of parties to an invalid marriage when the union is terminated by death. Cases thus far have generally concerned claims of a surviving "wife," and where that party has had a good faith belief in the validity of the marriage and no

lawful wife has made a claim, the courts have given the putative spouse the same half interest in quasi-marital property that section 2251 would have given her at annulment. Thus, the surviving putative spouse has the same right as a lawful spouse to elect against the decedent's will in order to claim half of what would have been community property had there been a lawful marriage.

    a. **Surviving "spouse" has full intestate rights at mate's death:** [§417] Where there is no lawful widow or widower, a surviving putative spouse inherits intestate all assets that a lawful spouse would have received and also has the priority status for appointment as administrator conferred by statute on a lawful surviving spouse. [Estate of Leslie, 37 Cal. 3d 186 (1984)]

    b. **Other death benefits for surviving "spouse"**

        (1) **Action for wrongful death:** [§418] When one party to an invalid marriage is tortiously killed, the survivor may bring a wrongful death suit under California Civil Procedure Code section 377.60 if the survivor had a good faith belief in the validity of the marriage. The statute does not state whether good faith must exist at the time of the death or only at the time of the marriage. The fact that a lawful surviving spouse may also have a wrongful death action does *not* deprive the putative spouse of a claim.

        (2) **Workers' compensation benefits:** [§419] A surviving putative spouse has also been treated as a surviving spouse under workers' compensation statutes. [Brennfleck v. Workmen's Compensation Appeals Board, 265 Cal. App. 2d 738 (1968)] It is not clear, however, whether the putative spouse would be entitled to benefits if a claim had also been made by a lawful surviving spouse.

        (3) **Pension and retirement benefits:** [§420] Finally, a putative spouse has been treated as a surviving spouse under statutes providing for annuity and death benefits for dependents of public employees. [Adduddell v. Board of Administration, 8 Cal. App. 3d 243 (1970)] In awarding such benefits, the court in *Adduddell* stressed the good faith of the survivor and the fact that no lawful surviving spouse existed to make a claim.

            (a) **Note:** *Adduddell* merely establishes that the term "widow" or "surviving spouse" in death benefit *legislation* includes putative spouses. With respect to pension plans privately contracted for, the rights of a putative spouse would be determined by the intent of the parties to the contract. [Allen v. Western Conference of Teamsters, 788 F.2d 648 (9th Cir. 1986)]

B. COEXISTING BIGAMOUS MARRIAGES

1. **In General:** [§421] If a putative marriage is invalid because it is bigamous, there may be a lawful spouse of one (or both) of the parties who can also lay claim to acquisitions of the bigamist spouse. The issue can arise at annulment of the invalid marriage, at dissolution of the valid marriage by divorce, upon the death of any of the parties involved, or when a creditor seeks to seize property.

2. **"Living Apart" Doctrine Usually Determines Result:** [§422] In most bigamous marriages, the twice-married person, say H, will have separated from W-1 before "marrying" W-2. Under the living separate and apart doctrine, W-1 has no

claims to H's post-separation acquisitions by labor (except on his death intestate, as heir to part of his separate property); and W-2 could have no claims on pre-second-"marriage" acquisitions. [Patillo v. Norris, 65 Cal. App. 3d 209 (1976)]

3. **Equity Governs When Spouse Keeps Two Households:** [§423]   In one case, H "married" good faith W-2 and began living with her *without* separating from W-1 (spending about half the week in each home). [Estate of Vargas, 36 Cal. App. 3d 714 (1974)] No statutes address this situation, and the courts apparently will apply equitable principles to sort out the property tangles arising from the simultaneous relationships.

   a. **Earnings of W-1:** [§424]   The earnings of W-1 would appear to be community property of H and W-1, so that creditors of either spouse could reach all and so that H at dissolution would receive half the earnings notwithstanding his misconduct. W-2 could persuasively claim that *she* has a right to one-half of H's half on the theory that it is an acquisition by H other than purely separate property that he obtained during the "marriage" of H and W-2. However, there is no authority on point.

   b. **Earnings of W-2:** [§425]   The earnings of W-2 are probably her purely separate property as to which H has no claim (*see supra,* §401). Even if section 2251 were interpreted to make a putative spouse's earnings quasi-marital in *some* cases, the statute does not seem to be directed to the two-wife situation where H is cohabiting with both. Under equitable principles (*e.g.,* "unclean hands"), H would seem barred from claiming half of W-2's earnings. *If* he were to receive half, W-1 has a logical claim to one-half of this half, since the acquisition occurred during the lawful marriage while the spouse cohabited and was not by gift, will, or inheritance.

   c. **Earnings of H:** [§426]   Under the applicable statutes, H's earnings in this situation are community property *and* quasi-marital property at the same time. In *Vargas, supra,* H died intestate and the court was able to give effect to full *property right* claims (*i.e.,* to one half) of both W-1 and W-2 in such earnings. Neither W-1 nor W-2 took anything as intestate heir.

      (1) **Result where H dies testate:** [§427]   In a case that was legally similar to *Vargas* (*i.e.,* under the law then in effect, H's earnings while living separate and apart from W-1 when he set up his household with W-2 were nonetheless community), H died testate. The court awarded *one-fourth* of H's acquisitions after the second "marriage," taken from W-1's half share, to H's legatee. [Sousa v. Freitas, *supra,* §407] The court was undoubtedly seeking an equitable result and was influenced by the fact that W-1 was not assisting H in any way when he earned the property at issue.

         (a) **Application to *Vargas* facts:** [§428]   If H in *Vargas* (where H cohabited with both lawful W and putative W) had died testate, there appear to be four possible solutions for dividing up his earnings during the time he kept two marital households:

            1) *50% to W-1, 50% to W-2, and none to the legatees*, who would be tainted with H's inequitable conduct. This could work an unfair result if, for example, H's legatees were children of yet another marriage, lawfully dissolved before H married W-1.

2) *25% percent to W-1, 25% to W-2, and 50% to the legatees.* This approach does not penalize H's legatees for his misconduct, and has been used outside California. [*See, e.g.,* Prince v. Hopson, 89 So. 2d 128 (La. 1956)]

3) *One-third to W-1, one-third to W-2, one-third to legatees.* This approach simply treats all interested parties equally (viewing the legatees as one claimant group).

4) *Three-eighths to W-1, three-eighths to W-2, one-fourth to legatees.* Here, the result is based on the theory that H's testamentary power should be halved because he was a husband in two households.

(2) **Where intestate H had separated from W-1:** [§429] In *Estate of Hafner,* 184 Cal. App. 3d 1371 (1986), after separating from W-1, H "married" W-2, who had putative spouse status. His earnings while living with her were simultaneously quasi-marital property as to W-2 and separate property (under California Family Code section 771) as to W-1. The majority gave W-2 half these acquisitions as *owner* and half to W-1 and H's children as intestate heirs. A credible dissent argued that denying good faith W-2 any status as heir was contrary to her rights as a putative spouse and to *Estate of Leslie, supra,* §417. The dissent considered W-2 entitled to half as owner plus half of what the majority accorded to W-1 as heir to H's separate property. (Since W-2 claimed as heir to H's half of his acquisitions during the "marriage" that would have been *community property* and is treated as such for W-2's benefit, her claim to this half was stronger than W-1's, because a wife, as intestate heir of *separate property*, shares it with her husband's children but is sole heir of his half of community property. Thus, W-2's claim to three-fourths of H's acquisitions during the "marriage" in *Hafner* was equitably based.)

C. NO PUTATIVE MARRIAGE ("*MARVIN*" RELATIONSHIPS)

1. **Introduction:** [§430] Older case law applied the term "meretricious relationship" to situations in which a male (M) and female (F) simply lived together with ***both parties aware that they were not married.*** Since the word "meretricious" connotes some sort of moral or legal opprobrium, it seems inappropriate today when the law gives considerable legal recognition to such unions. In view of the nationwide attention given to the leading case in this area involving Lee and Michele Marvin [Marvin v. Marvin, *supra,* §401], the living-together arrangement can be referred to conveniently as a *Marvin* relationship.

    a. **Note:** M and F are used throughout the text for convenience since most cases have dealt with male and female cohabitants. However, the rules set forth below, including the invocation of *Marvin,* are also applicable to same-sex cohabitants.

2. **All Property Presumed Separately Owned:** [§431] All property in a *Marvin* relationship is presumed to be the *separate* property of the parties involved. Absent an agreement to the contrary, "title" presumptively controls; *i.e.,* if an instrument of title names M and F as co-owners, they are tenants in common. (However, parol evidence would be admissible that one party supplied all or more than half of the

consideration and did not make a gift of a half interest to the other.) Where there is no document of title, the party making the acquisition would presumptively be considered the sole owner.

    a. **Result if parties agree to live in community:** [§432] If M and F expressly contract that the community property laws applicable to lawful marriages shall apply to their acquisitions while living together, the contract is not necessarily void. Since there can be no true community of property between putative spouses in an invalid marriage (*see supra,* §405), there is almost certainly no true community between M and F, and their acquisitions may perhaps be owned in tenancy in common (*see supra,* §407). However, a good argument can be made that if M and F contracted to live in community and represented to the public that they were married, they would be estopped to invoke the rule that only married persons can own community property where a creditor would benefit if a community did exist. For example, if M purchases items on credit (and is not acting as F's agent in so doing), F could be estopped from claiming that her earnings are held in tenancy in common—so that M's creditor can reach all such earnings.

    b. **Result if parties agree simply to share ownership:** [§433] The parties to a *Marvin* relationship may agree to share ownership of the acquisitions of each while living together without specifying just how such property will be owned. (Indeed, the *Marvin* decision holds that such a general sharing agreement can be implied from the conduct of M and F.) Under such an agreement, acquisitions that would be the community property of the parties if lawfully married apparently will be owned in ***tenancy in common***, each party having ownership of and management power over only a half interest (unless an agency is proved to expand management power over the whole). Alternatively, if M and F work together in a business or profession, their acquisitions therein may be subject to the law of business partnerships.

        (1) **Caution:** A *Marvin*-style pooling agreement may not be self-executing. In a case where M and F agreed to share earnings 50-50 and F had brought suit some years after the couple split up, the court (apparently because of F's pleadings) viewed her claim as one for damages (for M's failing to pay over to her half of his income) rather than a suit as cotenant owner of a half interest to obtain partition. The result was a statute of limitations bar. [Estate of Fincher, 119 Cal. App. 3d 343 (1981)]

        (2) **Note:** It is conceivable, of course, that the express or implied contract of the parties was for a sharing of ownership only at a breakup of the relationship, with each party owning his or her acquisitions prior to that time as separate property. *Marvin* suggests that the courts will not imply a contract to share what would be separate property in a lawful marriage (*e.g.,* an inheritance). However, a ***specific contract*** by M and F to share even such "separate" acquisitions would be enforced unless it was contrary to public policy on other grounds.

3. **Public Policy Limitations:** [§434] A contract between the parties will be unenforceable "if sexual acts form an inseparable part of the consideration for the agreement"—*i.e.,* if the monetary sharing is conditioned on the sharing of sexual favors. [Marvin v. Marvin, *supra*] However, the court in *Marvin* noted the mere fact that sex is "involved" does not automatically invalidate the contract.

4. **Duration of Contract:** [§435] In an *express Marvin* contract, the parties may agree to mutually support each other financially so long as both live or only so long as they live together. In the latter case, neither party would owe the other anything comparable to alimony after their breakup. No case has addressed whether the mere conduct of M and F could imply a promise to provide support that would survive their breakup.

5. **Legal Status of Cohabitant:** [§436] For many purposes, the case law holds M and F to be legal strangers to each other rather than the equivalent of husband and wife, notwithstanding their agreement to pool gains. Thus, F cannot sue for M's wrongful death, as could his widow. [Harrod v. Pacific Southwest Airlines, 118 Cal. App. 3d 155 (1981)] And if the pair have no children, F's quitting work to follow M's move out of state is not good cause for loss of her job that would entitle F to unemployment compensation. [Norman v. Unemployment Insurance Appeals Board, 34 Cal. 3d 1 (1984); *but see* MacGregor v. Unemployment Insurance Appeals Board, 37 Cal. 3d 205 (1984)—awarding F unemployment benefits, relying on the existence of a stable family with children rather than her *Marvin* agreement with M]

   a. **Damages for emotional distress, loss of consortium:** [§437] A *Marvin* relationship seems to create no status for purposes of tort law. Thus, if M is injured so that he is incapable of having sex, F gets no recovery. Similarly, if M observes a negligent tortfeasor grievously injure F and suffers severe emotional distress, he can collect no damages as could a lawful husband. [Eldon v. Sheldon, 46 Cal. 3d 267 (1988)]

6. **Alternative Remedies for Cohabitant:** [§438] The statutes governing community property and quasi-marital property do not apply to parties in a *Marvin* relationship. However, remedies not based on express or implied-in-fact contract may be available.

   a. **Quantum meruit:** [§439] A nonmarital partner may recover in quantum meruit for the reasonable value of household services rendered (less the reasonable value of support received) if it can be shown that he or she rendered services with the expectation of a monetary reward. [Marvin v. Marvin, *supra*] Such a showing is likely to be very difficult to make; and if it is made, the defendant may be able to claim a refund (reimbursement) for overpayment for the value of the services—since the plaintiff (by suing for recovery) has shown that the relationship did not involve gifts.

      (1) **Caution:** Quantum meruit is probably *unavailable* for household services rendered with expectation of monetary reward if supplying sex was an "inseparable part" of the arrangement. (*See supra*, §434.)

      (2) **Advantages of noncontractual remedies:** [§440] In seeking quantum meruit, the nonmarital partner claims as a *creditor* rather than as a co-owner of property. Therefore, the plaintiff can reach purely separate property (*e.g.*, an inheritance owned by the other partner before they began living together). A defendant sued in quantum meruit could defend on the ground that quantum meruit is not available because the express or implied-in-fact agreement for the pooling of gains made suit to enforce such a contract the sole remedy available to the plaintiff.

b. **Constructive or resulting trust:** [§441]   The equitable remedies of constructive trust and resulting trust, by which a person may obtain a share of ownership where title to property is in another, were also held available in *Marvin*, but the court gave no indication of the type of wrongdoing by the titleholder that would make these remedies appropriate. A noncontractual, fraudulent promise to hold in co-ownership would support the constructive trust remedy if fraudulent when made (*i.e.*, the promisor at the time had no intention of keeping it). (*See* Remedies Summary.)

7. **Treatment of *Marvin* Companion vs. Lawful Wife:** [§442]   Suppose H begins living with F in a *Marvin* relationship while still maintaining a household with his lawful wife, W. If an express sharing contract between H and F is established, half of H's earnings would be owned by F (unless such contracts are against public policy when H is cohabiting at the same time with lawful W). If there is no agreement and quantum meruit is owed, F would proceed like any other creditor against the community. W in turn may have a suit as creditor against H for bad faith management of the community in entering into an express or implied contract with F (*see supra*, §261).

    a. **Lawful wife may benefit financially:** [§443]   The half of F's earnings that would go to H under any sharing contract between H and F will be community property of H and W (if he has not separated from her during the living arrangement with F). If F earns more than H, W might thereby benefit monetarily from the *Marvin* sharing contract to the extent that this income is not consumed.

VI. CONFLICT OF LAWS PROBLEMS

chapter approach

In dealing with change of domicile problems keep in mind the following:

1. Different rules of law apply when the issue arises **during marriage** as opposed to at termination of the community (and even then there are minor differences in the way quasi-community property principles apply at death and at divorce); and

2. The policy at work here is to treat quasi-community property the same as actual community property except when doing so raises **constitutional** problems (such as a taking of property, discussed in chapter VII).

A. SELECTION OF APPLICABLE LAW [§444]

California analyzes conflict of laws problems so as to make a separate choice of law on *each issue raised*. (*See* Conflict of Laws Summary.) Thus, in determining what interest a spouse may have in a given piece of property, the court will select a particular state as the most appropriate to supply the governing law for that issue, even though a different state or states may be chosen for other issues in the case.

1. **Acquisitions by Nondomiciliaries:** [§445] Suppose H acquires personal property by his labors while living in Oregon and married to W. The spouses then move to California, and W contracts a debt with Creditor, a Californian, on which she defaults. In deciding if (and to what extent) Creditor can levy on the property at issue, a California court would probably select Oregon law to determine the property rights of H and W in the asset but apply California law to determine the extent to which the property right is liable on the contract with Creditor. This mixture of Oregon and California law results from applying two established choice of law rules: First, the rights of the spouses in personal property are governed by the law of their domicile at the time of acquisition. (If they had different domiciles, the domicile of the acquiring spouse would govern.) Thus even if an acquisition took place in California, its laws would not apply to Oregon domiciliaries. Second, the law governing liabilities of Californians to one another arising from transactions occurring in California is California law, and at the time of contracting with Creditor, H and W were domiciled in California.

    a. **Problems with nomenclature:** [§446] The term "separate property" is used in various states to define quite different classes of acquisitions. Thus, it is important to remember that because an acquisition is labeled "separate" by another state does not necessarily mean that California law relating to "separate property" as defined in California Family Code section 770 will apply.

        (1) **Example:** In the previous hypothetical, Oregon would label H's acquisition his "separate" property, but one should not therefore immediately apply the California rule that "separate" property of H is not liable for W's contractual debt. The preliminary question is what rule of California law on creditors' rights applies to a spouse's earnings during marriage while domiciled in another state, and there are three possible solutions:

(a) *Treat the Oregon earnings as community property in California*—since they were *earnings* acquired during marriage—and make them liable for W's debt;

(b) *Treat as critical the fact that Oregon recognized no property right* of W in the earnings, so that—being more like California separate property than community property—H's earnings should not be liable for W's debt;

(c) *Conclude that California law has no answer* to the question of whether H's earnings during marriage in which W has no property interest are liable for W's debt (since no such property exists under California law) and decide the liability issue under Oregon law, while applying California law on such issues as whether a contract existed, whether W breached the contract, etc.

b. **Approach in California to date:** [§447] In the *absence of a statute* governing the issue, California case law has thus far allowed solution (b) above, treating property denominated "separate" by the law of another state as separate in the California sense and ignoring inconsistencies (such as the fact that it was property acquired by a spouse's labor during marriage). [Estate of Burrows, 136 Cal. 113 (1902)—homestead rights; Estate of Bruggemeyer, 115 Cal. App. 525 (1931)—post-death liability of property]

c. **Change of form will not alter label:** [§448] A married couple moving to California from another state may bring with them money acquired by labor during marriage and invest it in California assets (*e.g.,* land) while domiciled in California. Under the case law, a "separate" label attached by the former domicile to the cash would not (during marriage with respect to almost all issues) be lost but could be traced through the changes in form and invoked during marriage to apply California rules applicable to separate property. [*See, e.g.,* Melvin v. Carl, 118 Cal. App. 249 (1931)]

2. **Out-of-State Acquisitions by California Domiciliaries:** [§449] If either spouse acquires personal property out of state while domiciled in California, California law clearly will be used to classify the property as separate or community.

   a. **Out-of-state contracts:** [§450] If H or W (or both), while domiciled in California, makes a contract out of state with non-Californians, the law of the other state *may* govern such issues as validity of the contract, what constitutes breach, measure of damages, etc., but California law would be used to characterize funds acquired under the contract as separate or community.

   b. **Out-of-state torts:** [§451] Recovery of tort damages by H or W for an out-of-state accident suffered while domiciled in California (even if obtained in out-of-state litigation) will be characterized in accordance with California law.

   c. **Out-of-state land:** [§452] California law is applied in *California* courts to determine the rights of spouses in out-of-state land acquired by one spouse during marriage and while domiciled in California. [Ford v. Ford, *supra,* §96] Thus, if community funds were used to buy land out of state, a California court will treat the land as community. [Tomaier v. Tomaier, *supra,* §185]

(1) **Caution:** Another forum—*i.e.,* the state where the land is situated—might well reject California law in determining the rights of the spouses in the acquisition and instead apply the law of the situs. Indeed, this is a more common choice-of-law approach in situations concerning realty than California's use of the law of domicile.

(2) **Judgment may not be enforced:** [§453] Moreover, where California applies the law of the domicile (rather than the law of the situs) to adjudicate rights of spouses in out-of-state land, the courts of the situs state may decline to enforce the California judgment. [*See, e.g.,* Rozan v. Rozan, 129 N.W.2d 694 (N.D. 1964)] It is an open question whether the Full Faith and Credit Clause of the United States Constitution permits the situs state to follow this course. (*See* Conflict of Laws Summary.)

B. STATUTORY CHANGES—QUASI-COMMUNITY PROPERTY [§454]

In situations where a married couple moves to California after acquiring assets in a former domicile, quasi-community property legislation alters in most cases the judge-made rule that the property label attached by the former domicile will control treatment of the asset in California. These statutes, which create the category of ***quasi-community*** property, provide instead that the source of the property is controlling.

1. **Quasi-Community Property Defined:** [§455] California Family Code section 125 defines quasi-community property as any realty or personalty acquired by a spouse while domiciled elsewhere that would have been community property had the acquiring spouse been domiciled in California. The statute also specifically calls for tracing quasi-community property through changes of form (*e.g.,* cash invested in land) so that the characteristic is not lost. This definition applies at divorce and in creditors' rights cases during marriage. (For devolution at death, a more restricted definition applies; *see infra,* §460.) California rules of law are applied to the source of acquisition (*e.g.,* inheritance, earnings during marriage, etc.) to classify the property.

    a. **Treatment of out-of-state community property:** [§456] California accepts the domiciliary state's definition of community property—to the extent that it is broader than California's definition—and treats as community property assets acquired while domiciled in a state that would so classify them at the time of acquisition. [Cal. Prob. Code §28(b)] For example, rents and profits of separate property acquired by spouses while domiciled in Texas would be community (as they are in Texas) in a post-acquisition California dispute involving a former Texan now living in California—even though they would have been considered separate under California Family Code section 770(a)(3).

2. **When Characterization Is Significant:** [§457] The characterization of an asset as quasi-community property is mainly significant at dissolution of the community by death or divorce. (Recall that at death the quasi-community property concept is employed in the ancestral property statute; *see supra,* §368.) Effective 1985, quasi-community property is to be treated during marriage like community property for purposes of liability for debts. (*See supra,* §273.)

    a. **Treatment of quasi-community property at divorce:** [§458] At divorce, quasi-community property is treated like community property for the purpose of dividing assets; *i.e.,* the general rule is an equal division under an aggregate theory approach.

- (1) **Limitation:** [§459] To avoid constitutional problems, the statute calling for an equal division of quasi-community property at divorce has been construed not to apply where California has a "minimal" interest in the marriage and marital property.

    - (a) **Example:** Where spouses domiciled in Pennsylvania separated and H then moved to California, the California divorce court could not apply the quasi-community property doctrine to H's Pennsylvania acquisitions. Pennsylvania law applied to determine the extent to which the California court could award part of this property to W. [Marriage of Roesch, 83 Cal. App. 3d 96 (1978)]

    - (b) **But note:** Subsequent to *Roesch,* the United States Supreme Court substantially broadened the power of a court to apply the law of a state on slim factual connections of the state to the action. [Hague v. Allstate Insurance Co., 449 U.S. 301 (1981)] As a matter of federal constitutional law, probably California can apply the quasi-community property law when the spouse making a bona fide change of domicile brings property to California or the other spouse owns property situated there.

b. **Treatment of quasi-community property at dissolution by death:** [§460] A restricted definition of quasi-community property applies when the community is dissolved by death of a spouse so that *out-of-state land is excluded*. [Cal. Prob. Code §66] In this situation, a California court will not assert jurisdiction over the land, or, if it does, will apply the law of the situs. Moreover, property acquired by the *surviving* spouse that would be quasi-community at divorce is not so treated at dissolution by death. Thus, the decedent (nonowner) cannot dispose of half of it by will.

- (1) **Death of spouse who owns property acquired under out-of-state law (quasi-community property):** [§461] Upon the death of an owner-spouse while domiciled in California, the surviving spouse is a forced heir of one-half of the quasi-community property; *i.e.,* the survivor's share cannot be defeated by will. [Cal. Prob. Code §101] The other half of such property is subject to decedent's testamentary disposition, but the surviving spouse is the intestate heir of any part not so disposed of.

    - (a) **No mandatory election:** [§462] The survivor may claim half of the quasi-community property *without* forfeiting bequests under the will unless the will specifically imposes such a condition on the devise.

    - (b) **Power to void gifts as to half of property:** [§463] If the owner of quasi-community property dies domiciled in California, the surviving spouse also has a right under California Probate Code section 102 to set aside inter vivos transfers made without the survivor's consent and for less than fair consideration, to the extent of the half-interest the surviving spouse would take had there been no transfer.

Two other conditions must be met in order to exercise this right: (i) the decedent must have retained a substantial quantum of ownership or control over the property (*e.g.*, as trustee); and (ii) the survivor must have had an expectant interest under section 101 at the time of the transfer—which means that the spouses must have moved their domicile to California by the time of the transfer and that gifts made while domiciled in the former jurisdiction cannot be set aside at all.

VII. CONSTITUTIONAL LAW ISSUES

chapter approach

Constitutional issues include the scope of "separate property" under the state constitution, plus equal protection and due process considerations. However, the constitutional issue you are most likely to encounter in an exam question is preemption of state law by a federal rule under the Supremacy Clause of the United States Constitution. In recent years there has been increasing interference by the federal government into family law, especially at divorce. From a policy standpoint this intrusion is regrettable because the federal rules do not treat spouses as equal partners but generally favor men over women (*e.g.,* the *McCarty* decision concerning a soldier's pension benefits). From an exam standpoint, be sure you are familiar with the statutes and cases dealing with preemption.

A. SCOPE OF "SEPARATE PROPERTY" UNDER CALIFORNIA CONSTITUTION [§464]

The California Constitution presently provides that "property **owned before marriage** or acquired during marriage by **gift, will, or inheritance** is separate property." [Cal. Const. art. 1, §21] A similar predecessor provision was construed as also mandating that **rents and profits** of such property likewise be classified as separate. [George v. Ransom, 15 Cal. 322 (1860)]

1. **Effect:** [§465] The constitutional definition of separate property means that the legislature cannot narrow the present statutory definitions of such property. However, it could **expand** the scope of separate classes of property—*i.e.,* narrow the statutory definition of **community** property by making separate classes of property not covered by the constitutional definition. [Woodall v. Commissioner, 105 F.2d 474 (9th Cir. 1939)]

2. **Transmutations Not Restricted:** [§466] Note that the constitutional limitation concerns only legislative or judicial restrictions on separate property. Thus, California spouses may contract between themselves to make community various assets that would be separate under the state constitution.

B. EQUAL PROTECTION STANDARDS UNDER CALIFORNIA CONSTITUTION [§467]

Under the Equal Protection Clause of the California Constitution [art. I, §7], sex discrimination is subject to the same "strict scrutiny" test applied to racial discrimination. [Sail'er Inn, Inc. v. Kirby, *supra,* §31] Sex discrimination in the area of community property would therefore seem to be almost impossible to defend.

1. **Statutes Possibly Invalid:** [§468] Retention of the pro-female presumptions in California Family Code section 803 (*supra,* §22) may be unconstitutional since there appears to be no legitimate justification for such discrimination where no reliance interests are defeated by applying a gender-neutral rule of law.

C. DUE PROCESS ISSUES UNDER CALIFORNIA CONSTITUTION—RETROACTIVITY OF CHANGES IN COMMUNITY PROPERTY LAW

1. **Old Rule:** [§469] Earlier California cases held that legislative changes in community property laws could not apply to preenactment acquisitions [McKay v. Lauriston, 204 Cal. 577 (1928)] nor to the rents and profits of such acquisitions received after the change in law [Boyd v. Oser, 23 Cal. 2d 613 (1944)]. Also, preenactment law was held to apply to assets traced back to preenactment acquisitions that had been sold and the proceeds reinvested.

   a. **Example:** In 1917, the California legislature passed a statute requiring W's joinder in conveyances of community realty by H. If H bought land in 1925 with community money he earned in 1916, and sought to sell the realty in 1930, to require W's joinder would have been unconstitutional, since the asset could be traced back to an acquisition prior to enactment of the new law. [Roberts v. Wehmeyer, 191 Cal. 601 (1923)]

   b. **Exception:** [§470] Despite the general restriction on retroactivity, the courts held that *inheritance rights* (involving mere expectancies) could be changed and that the new laws would apply retroactively to preenactment acquisitions (although not to estates of persons dying before enactment). [Estate of Phillips, 203 Cal. 106 (1928)] Also, testamentary power could be withdrawn from preenactment acquisitions.

2. **Rejection of Old Rule**

   a. **Legislative changes taking effect before dissolution:** [§471] Where applying a new law to preenactment acquisitions would not take any *property right* away from a spouse, California courts have held that the legislature may constitutionally apply the new statute to such preenactment property. [*See* Robertson v. Willis, 77 Cal. App. 3d 358 (1978)]

      (1) **Example:** Prior to 1975, W's post-1951 uncommingled community earnings were not liable for H's debts. A 1975 statute specifically directed at preenactment acquisitions removed this exemption. The court in *Robertson, supra,* held that the new rule could apply to preenactment acquisitions of W and preenactment debts of H because no property right was taken— *i.e.,* W would stand to lose as much "property" if the creditor took H's community earnings and she would still have a reimbursement claim if H's "separate" debt were involved. The court also found that W could not have any reliance interest in the old law that would outweigh the social utility of applying the new rule to all community property.

      (2) **"Equal management" legislation is retroactive:** [§472] Although *Robertson* dealt with liability of property and not per se with the 1975 change from male management to equal management of most community assets, the court's approach in that case leaves no doubt that it viewed the legislative directive to apply the new management rules to pre-1975 acquisitions to be constitutional.

   b. **"Taking" property at divorce:** [§473] The California Supreme Court has also held that the strong police-power interest of the state in a fair property division between the spouses at divorce will permit the divorce court to order a "taking" of one spouse's property by awarding it to the other. [Marriage of Bouquet, 16 Cal. 3d 583 (1976)]

(1) **Example—quasi-community property:** [§474] Suppose a spouse, say H, acquired an asset while domiciled outside California and the law of H's domicile would not permit dividing that asset at divorce. Applying the California quasi-community property statute (*see supra*, §§455, 459) to the asset when H and W move to California and are then divorced results in a "taking"; but the courts have held that it would *not* violate due process. [*See* Addison v. Addison, 62 Cal. 2d 558 (1965)]

(2) **Example—living apart doctrine:** [§475] Prior to 1971, what is now California Family Code section 771 made W's earnings separate property while the spouses lived separate and apart, but H's were community. The 1971 "sex-neutralizing" amendment has been held to apply, at least at divorce, to H's preenactment acquisitions, changing them from community to H's separate property and thus "taking" W's half-interest. [Marriage of Bouquet, *supra*] The retroactive change was applied to exempt the earnings from 50-50 division at divorce; and the court in *Bouquet* stressed "the state's paramount interest in the equitable distribution of marital property upon dissolution."

c. **"Taking" at dissolution by death:** [§476] As noted above, a change in intestate succession law or a change expanding or restricting an owner's testamentary power can apply retroactively. However, a statute providing that on the death of nonowner W she has testamentary power over half of H's property that was acquired by his labor during marriage in a common law state (quasi-community property) would probably be unconstitutional. [Paley v. Bank of America, 159 Cal. App. 2d 500 (1958)] This situation is distinguishable from the divorce setting in *Bouquet, supra*, because W is now dead and not in need of support.

d. **"Taking" having effect during marriage:** [§477] The court in *Bouquet* did not hold that the 1971 change in what is now section 771 ***immediately*** converted H's preenactment earnings from community to his separate property. Assuming the former law was constitutional despite its sex discrimination, an immediate conversion would create the problem of a "taking" before the state's police-power interest in fair division at divorce arose, and would probably violate W's due process rights.

(1) **And note:** California Family Code section 910, which makes a spouse's quasi-community property liable for debts in situations where community property would be liable, arguably results in an unconstitutional taking of the nondebtor spouse's property. The statute makes the nondebtor's separate property that meets the definition of quasi-community property liable on the debt. It is doubtful whether the state has a strong police-power interest in providing such a windfall for a creditor who contracted only with the other spouse to justify this taking. (*See supra*, §273.)

e. **Retreat from permissive approach—rank injustice test developed:** [§478] Most recently, the California Supreme Court has said that retroactive application of a change in law was allowed in *Addison* and *Bouquet* only because the preenactment law that was changed was causing a "rank injustice." In two recent cases, the preenactment law was found to be not rankly unjust; thus the court held that retroactive application of the new law *would be unconstitutional*.

 (1) **Overturning oral agreement:** Where W had an oral agreement with H that her separate property contributions to acquire land under a joint tenancy title would "buy in" to title—an agreement valid under the then-controlling *Lucas* case (*see supra,* §123), due process would be violated by applying at divorce the subsequently enacted California Family Code section 2581, which required a written agreement to reserve W's right to buy in to title rather than just obtain reimbursement. [Marriage of Buol, 39 Cal. 3d 751 (1985)]

 (2) **Creating reimbursement cause of action:** In the other case where pre-reform law was not found to be rankly unjust H had made separate property contributions to acquire an asset under a community property title without getting any agreement from W as to his rights based on such contribution. Under *Lucas,* he thus had no rights. To allow the subsequently enacted Family Code section 2640 to create an automatic right of reimbursement for him, to the detriment of W, would deny due process. [Marriage of Fabian, 41 Cal. 3d 440 (1986)]

f. **Unique "rank injustice" test still applied:** [§479] The California Supreme Court as recently as 1995 held that only if a prior law on distribution of property at divorce was rankly unjust could the new statute replacing it be constitutionally applied to preenactment property. [Marriage of Heikes, 10 Cal. 4th 1211 (1995)] This means that the legislature could not adopt a uniformly applicable law shifting from equal to equitable division of community property at divorce, since equal division is not unjust. Under the *federal* Due Process Clause there is no such restriction on legislative change of the law concerning property rights at divorce.

 (1) **Application of current rule:** [§480] Under the "rank injustice" test, the court of appeals' decision in *Robertson* expanding creditors' rights (*see supra,* §471) is erroneous. The prior law there exempted W's uncommingled community earnings that were managed solely by her from liability for H's debts—hardly a "rankly unjust" rule. Moreover, even if somehow California Family Code section 910, declaring quasi-community property of one spouse liable for the debts of the nonowner spouse (*see supra,* §§273, 477), can be constitutionally applied to quasi-community property acquired after its enactment, the preenactment nonliability is not rankly unjust, and hence the new liability rule at least cannot be applied to preenactment acquisitions.

D. FEDERAL PREEMPTION UNDER UNITED STATES CONSTITUTION (SUPREMACY CLAUSE) [§481]

In a number of situations, the rights of the spouses, creditors, or others must be determined under law mandated by *federal courts* rather than by state law which California courts would apply, because of federal preemption under the Supremacy Clause of the United States Constitution.

1. **Test for Preemption:** [§482]   State law regularly applicable will govern unless Congress has spoken with "*force and clarity*" to declare that a different rule should apply instead. Absent a congressional expression of such "force and clarity," preemption is found only if state law, if applied, will substantially impair a significant federal interest. [Wissner v. Wissner, *supra*, §343] Congress cannot simply preempt state law at its whim. It must act under some source of federal power (*e.g.,* the commerce power).

   a. **Note:** In some cases where federal courts have held preemption bars California from treating an asset as community, the courts seem to order state judges to apply instead not some federal marital property law but the California rule applicable to separate property.

2. **Examples of Federal Preemption**

   a. **Armed services insurance:** [§483]   In *Wissner, supra,* H acquired National Service Life Insurance ("NSLI") during marriage, by labor or by paying premiums with community funds. The Supreme Court held that the California law allowing W to assert a community half-interest in the proceeds against a claim by H's designated beneficiary was preempted by a federal statute authorizing H to name a beneficiary for such insurance and immunizing the beneficiary from suit by creditors or others. The Court said the federal statute "forestalled" California's rule that would vest an interest in W; thus no taking of her property occurred. The Court relied on the federal war and defense power as the source for preemption of California law.

      (1) **Extent of preemption:** [§484]   Lower federal courts and the IRS have construed *Wissner* as preempting state law to the extent that the policy and proceeds are H's separate property. However, California courts, ignoring the "forestalling" holding of the United States Supreme Court, have held that it was California's anti-gift statute (*see supra,* §248) that was preempted in *Wissner*—*i.e.,* that H could give away all the proceeds, but that the proceeds and the policy were still community. Under the California view, the policy at divorce is valued and awarded to H as community property, while W receives other community property of equal value. [Marriage of Milhan, 13 Cal. 3d 129 (1974)]

         (a) **Note:** While the Court in *Wissner* held that W had no recourse against the beneficiary of H's policy, it did not consider whether she was barred from seeking ***reimbursement*** against H's estate (from assets other than the proceeds) on the theory H had "improved" his separate estate with community funds, or even from suing H's estate for an unlawful gift of community assets (*see supra,* §259).

      (2) **Scope of Supreme Court ruling:** [§485]   *Wissner* has been held ***not*** to apply to life insurance available under act of Congress to federal civil service employees ("EGLI"). To the extent that these benefits are acquired by community funds or labor during marriage and cohabitation, they are therefore community property in all respects. [*See* Carlson v. Carlson, 11 Cal. 3d 474 (1974)]

   b. **United States government land grants:** [§486]   Many federal statutes providing for homesteads and other grants of federal lands have been interpreted

Community Property—107

as requiring that record "title" (rather than source of funds used or nature of labor applied to make necessary improvements) must control ownership of the property in question. [Harris v. Harris, 71 Cal. 314 (1886)] Other statutes are viewed as preempting the pro rata sharing approach to title when ownership is acquired over time and substituting for it a federally-fashioned inception of title approach [McCune v. Essig, 199 U.S. 382 (1905)] or even a federally-created rule whereby marital status at the time a deed is granted governs community versus separate ownership. [Ellis v. Ellis, 97 Cal. App. 2d 808 (1950)]

(1) **Constitutionality:** When a federal statute is on the books before labor of a spouse is expended to acquire federal land, the federal law should preempt California law that would consider the labor as creating a community interest. To the extent community *money* is spent to obtain a separate title, there is no suggestion that reimbursement will be denied; so any "taking" is only of the right of the party getting reimbursement to instead share fractionally in the gain in value enjoyed by the asset.

c. **Federal retirement plans**

(1) **Social Security benefits:** [§487] The right to receive future Social Security Act benefits has been held to be *separate property* of the worker. [Marriage of Nizenkoff, 65 Cal. App. 3d 136 (1976)]

(a) **Constitutionality of federal provisions:** [§488] Although technically it is labor during marriage that earns the right to receive Social Security and Railroad Retirement Act benefits, these programs are in fact funded by "taxes" paid by employees and employers. The power to tax and spend for the general welfare allows Congress to collect community funds owned by a married couple but pay benefits only to the laborer spouse. And so long as the federal law is in effect when the labor that earns the benefits is performed, it can operate to prevent California from vesting any property right in the laborer's spouse. The rule that there is no community interest in the right to receive these welfare-plan benefits is therefore constitutional, and could constitutionally be extended to sums paid out before dissolution as well as expectant benefits. [*See* 25 U.C.L.A. L. Rev. 417 (1978)]

(2) **Railroad Retirement benefits:** [§489] To the extent that they parallel Social Security benefits, benefits payable in the future under the Federal Railroad Retirement Act are the separate property of the worker. [Hisquierdo v. Hisquierdo, 439 U.S. 572 (1979)] However, the Railroad Retirement Act provides for benefits *beyond* those available to participants in the Social Security system, and 1983 federal legislation reversed so much of *Hisquierdo* as required states to treat those additional benefits as separate property even though acquired by community labor or payroll deductions during marriage. [45 U.S.C. §231(a)] *State law* now can apply to these *additional* ("Tier II") benefits.

(a) **Basis for preemption of state law:** [§490] *Hisquierdo* found the "language of force and clarity" needed to preempt California law in (i) the Act's "spendthrift" clause protecting the payee of benefits from attachment "or other legal process"; (ii) a provision in the Act for a wife's or widow's annuity that would terminate on divorce (but that under the Social Security Act would not be terminated but converted into a divorced wife's benefit); and (iii) a statute creating an exception to the spendthrift clause to allow benefits to be seized to pay alimony but specifically excluding any "community property settlement." (Only point (iii) even approaches the requisite language of "force and clarity.")

1) **Note:** The California Supreme Court has repeatedly held that a federal spendthrift clause alone does *not* preempt state law conferring an ownership interest on the spouse of a payee receiving benefits pursuant to an act of Congress—on the ground that the clause operates against creditors rather than co-owners. [*See, e.g.,* Carlson v. Carlson, *supra*]

(3) **Military retirement pay:** [§491] The Supreme Court extended the *Hisquierdo* preemption rule to future military retirement pay [McCarty v. McCarty, 453 U.S. 210 (1981)], but Congress responded with legislation overturning almost all aspects of the decision. Where jurisdiction is based on the armed service member's domicile, residence other than by reason of military assignment, or consent, the divorce court can treat the future military retired benefits as community property under state law and order the service member to pay to his spouse fractional amounts in the future, not to exceed one half.

(a) **Direct payments by plan operator:** [§492] Where the marriage lasted 10 years, during which one spouse was in the service, the court may order the operator of the military pension to make direct payments to the ex-spouse of up to 50% of net benefits payable to the service member. [10 U.S.C. §1408]

(b) **Military disability pay not divisible:** [§493] The United States Supreme Court has held that (i) California must treat military ***disability*** pay as separate property (no matter what it was received in lieu of), and (ii) the state cannot apply its law (*see supra,* §158) classifying as community the portion of disability pay equal in value to the "regular" retirement pay (longevity pay) waived by the disabled spouse in order to get the maximum amount of disability pay. [Mansell v. Mansell, 490 U.S. 581 (1989)]

1) **Approach unchanged:** *Mansell* and the 1997 *Boggs* case (*see infra,* §503) continue the approach of *Hisquierdo* and *McCarty,* which readily infers preemption from ambiguous statutory language without any legislative history suggesting that Congress intended preemption or even knew what the preempted state law was. They thereby repudiate a California Supreme Court decision holding that Congress's statutory restoration of most of the spousal rights eliminated by *McCarty* also restored the historical approach to preemption that permitted state law to apply absent a congressional mandate enacted "with force and clarity" [Casas v. Thompson, 42 Cal. 3d 131 (1986)] or a major impairment of federal interests via application of state law.

(4) **Preemption of remedies:** [§494] The Supreme Court in both *Hisquierdo* and *McCarty* stated that California could not correct any unfairness at divorce from treating H's interest in retirement benefits as his separate property by awarding W a greater share of the community property than H. The Court said that such unequal division would indirectly penalize H for participation in the federal plan, a result the Court found contrary to the intent of Congress. However in *Marriage of Milhan, supra,* §484, the state supreme court did order such an offsetting award when it felt compelled by federal law to confirm to H at divorce military fringe benefits that California law considered community.

(a) **Reimbursement barred?** [§495] *Hisquierdo* did **not** hold that W was barred from claiming reimbursement for half of the amount of "taxes" paid with community funds by H as a participant in the federal benefit plan, or for half of the value of labor during marriage that qualifed H for separately owned benefits. However, such reimbursement would probably "penalize" H as effectively as an offsetting award of community property. [*See* 6 Com. Prop. J. 5 (1979)]

(b) **Constitutionality:** [§496] *Hisquierdo* did not consider the constitutionality of a federal statute barring California from making, through an offsetting award (*see supra,* §494) what it considers a fair and just division of community property (*i.e.,* an offsetting award) at divorce. The only possible source of such federal power in *Hisquierdo* would be the Commerce Clause and a federal interest in seeing that railroad employees receive more benefits than their spouses at divorce in order to encourage married persons to work for railroads. (In *McCarty,* the war and defense power provides a clearer basis for preempting state law.) Whatever the merits of the Commerce Clause argument, it is not relevant when California seeks an offsetting award when forced by preemption to treat the expectant *Social Security* benefits of H or W as separate property. It is questionable whether the federal power to tax and spend the tax proceeds (Social Security taxes) empowers Congress to dictate to the state as to what constitutes a fair division of property at divorce where one or both spouses is a Social Security participant.

d. **Federal bonds:** [§497] If one spouse, say W, invests community property in United States Savings Bonds and takes "title" in the names of both spouses as joint tenants, California law would permit H (unless he agreed in writing to the joint tenancy) to bequeath a half interest therein upon his death before W. However, federal law has preempted this testamentary right and has made the surviving spouse in effect a forced intestate heir of the decedent's half interest. [Free v. Bland, 369 U.S. 663 (1962)] Such preemption is constitutional, since Congress has the power to raise funds by selling bonds, and the taking of a testamentary power is not considered a taking of property under the Fifth Amendment.

(1) **No taking of property allowed:** [§498] In *Yiatchos v. Yiatchos,* 376 U.S. 306 (1964), H invested community funds in federal bonds, designating in the title (pursuant to federal regulations) that his brother would own the bonds at H's death. The Washington State Supreme Court held this

designation void and awarded all of the bonds to W at H's death. On appeal, the United States Supreme Court held that state law was preempted insofar as it prevented the brother from taking H's half interest. (California law would have let the brother take that anyway.) At the same time, however, the Court held that federal law would not allow H to "defraud" W of her half interest.

(2) **Federal test for fraud used:** [§499] *Yiatchos* held that a federal rather than state law test for fraud on W must be used. It would seem, however, that if the federal test allowed H to transfer W's interest to H's brother in circumstances where state law would not allow it, due process would be violated.

(3) **Federal procedure used:** [§500] *Yiatchos* also held that federal law required W to prove that she had not consented to H's designation, even though state law placed on the brother the burden of showing that she had. Presumably the assignment of burdens of proof is so procedural a matter that no "property" rights of W are taken by this preemption of state law by the federal rule. However, there was nothing at all in the statute involved or in its legislative history that implied that Congress wanted to change state law concerning burden of proof. That part of *Yiatchos* is erroneous.

e. **Pensions governed by E.R.I.S.A.:** [§501] The federal Employee Retirement Income Security Act ("E.R.I.S.A.") does not *totally* preempt state law recognizing a community interest in private-sector pension plan rights that a laborer spouse acquires during marriage. [Marriage of Campa, 89 Cal. App. 3d 113 (1979), *appeal dismissed,* 444 U.S. 1028 (1980)]

(1) **Management by laborer spouse:** [§502] In dictum, one court has said that E.R.I.S.A. preempts state law [*see* Marriage of Lionberger, *supra,* §313] that allows a divorce court to enjoin ex-H from electing a form of pension payment that might be unfavorable to ex-W, who is after divorce his tenant in common. [Roebling v. Office of Personnel Management, 788 F.2d 1544 (Fed. Cir. 1986)] By similar logic, federal law might give the laborer spouse sole management over his pension during marriage as well.

(2) **Terminable interest doctrine:** [§503] Although Family Code section 2610 (*see supra,* §198) purports to abolish the terminable interest doctrine, federal law overrides this statute and engrafts both aspects of the doctrine onto E.R.I.S.A.-governed pensions (and most pensions are governed by E.R.I.S.A.). First, when the nonlaboring spouse (or ex-spouse following a divorce) dies, he or she cannot bequeath a community half interest in *future* pension benefits earned by the other spouse (who survives). Second, even though a pension plan participant earned the pension by his labors during marriage to his first spouse whom he divorced, there is no community interest in a widow's pension payable to his second spouse. [Boggs v. Boggs, 117 S. Ct. 1754 (1997)]

(a) **Offsetting award barred:** [§504] Like prior Supreme Court decisions (*see supra,* §494), *Boggs* holds that state courts *cannot* correct the unfairness to a spouse caused by federal tampering with principles of equality by an offsetting award, *e.g.,* giving W testamentary power over whole assets of community property, not just her half, because of her loss of testamentary power over what would have been her half of future pension benefits under state law. (Recall that under *state* law, where a special statute imposes the terminable interest doctrine as *Boggs* does, courts will make an offsetting award; *see supra,* §199.)

gilbert LAW SUMMARIES — CHARACTERIZATION OF PROPERTY WITH FEDERAL ASPECTS

Type	Characterization
Armed Services Life Insurance Proceeds	SP
Social Security Benefits	SP
Railroad Retirement Benefits	Social Security-type are SP; supplemental are apportioned CP
Military Retirement Benefits	Apportioned CP/SP at divorce if statutory requirements met
Disability Benefits	SP
U.S. Savings Bonds	SP (unless fraud involved)

f. **Federally created causes of action:** [§505] In creating federal tort causes of action (F.E.L.A., Jones Act, etc.), Congress has the power to extend or withhold rights to sue with respect to the spouse of an injured or deceased person. Moreover, Congress may define "spouse" as it wishes—*e.g.,* to exclude or include a putative spouse. [Beebe v. Moormack Gulf Lines, 59 F.2d 319 (5th Cir. 1932)] Usually, however, such federal statutes referring to a "wife" or "spouse" are construed as incorporating state law on the subject.

g. **Debtor's exemptions:** [§506] If a spouse is indebted to the United States for nonpayment of taxes, state law exempting certain classes of property from the reach of creditors will be preempted; any exemption must be found in federal law. [*See* United States v. Overman, 424 F.2d 1142 (9th Cir. 1970)] Thus if H incurred a federal tax obligation before marriage, W's earnings during marriage kept in her own bank account would not be liable therefor under state law [Cal. Fam. Code §911; *see supra,* §281], but the United States could seize H's half interest in such earnings due to federal preemption. (If the government did so, the remaining half should probably become W's separate property.)

h. **Indian law:** [§507] Many acts of Congress restrain states from interfering with the self-government of Indian tribes. If a Native American acquires certain "trust" lands with community funds, federal law may prevent a divorce court from awarding his spouse any share of that land (especially if she is not a tribe member), but it has been held that this form of federal preemption does not bar an award reimbursing the community for funds spent to acquire and improve trust land that had to be awarded to the "titled" Native American spouse at divorce. [Sheppard v. Sheppard, 655 P.2d 895 (Idaho 1983)—presumably good law in California]

REVIEW QUESTIONS

FILL IN ANSWER

1. Before marriage, W wrote a novel that became a best seller. Shortly thereafter, she married H. Are the royalties received during marriage her separate property or community property? _____

2. H and W have been married for 30 years; divorce is now pending. Stocks and bonds worth $100,000 are held in H's name. At time of trial, W proves that the stocks and bonds were acquired by H during marriage. In the absence of other evidence, will the court find the securities to be community property? _____

3. H and W have been divorced for five years. H dies. W files suit against H's estate claiming that he concealed community assets at the time of their divorce. She proves that $50,000 worth of the securities in H's estate (not mentioned in the divorce decree dividing marital property) were acquired during his marriage to W. In the absence of other evidence, will the court find that W has an interest in the securities? _____

4. During marriage, W receives $10,000 as a beneficiary under a testamentary trust. Is the money separate or community property? _____

5. During marriage, W receives $10,000 as winnings on a television quiz show. Is the money separate or community? _____

6. During marriage, H and W purchase a house with community funds. Shortly thereafter, H and W permanently separate. W remains in the house and uses the support payments that she receives from H to pay for a needed roofing of the house. At divorce, does W have a reimbursement claim? _____

7. During marriage, H writes a screenplay but is unable to find a producer willing to buy it. Several years after H and W are divorced, H finally sells the screenplay for $100,000. Is W entitled to any interest in the money received by H? _____

   a. Would W be entitled to any interest in the money if H had written the screenplay while *living separate and apart* from W? _____

8. During marriage, H invested $10,000 of his separate funds and $30,000 of community funds in stock of Goldfields, Inc., which he held in his own name. Later, the stock increased in value to $100,000, and H sold the stock and invested the proceeds in rare coins. Later, H separated from W and sold the coins for $250,000, which he deposited in a bank account in his own name. Is the bank account separate or community property, or both? _____

9. Before marriage, W accumulated $10,000 in savings that she invested in a laundromat business. During marriage, she operated this business part-time and it increased in value to $50,000 due to its excellent location. However, the business produced very little net income. H and W are now separated and seek dissolution of their marriage. Is the community entitled to any interest in the laundromat business or its increased value? _____

10. During marriage, H had income totaling $100,000 from labor and $50,000 as rents from a separately owned apartment house. All of this income was deposited in a checking account from which he paid all expenses (including both family living expenses and the expenses attributable to the separately owned apartment house). He also withdrew $5,000 from this account to purchase stock in Goldfields, Inc., in his own name. At the end of the marriage, there is no balance left in the checking account and the Goldfields stock is worth $150,000.

   a. In the absence of other evidence, is the Goldfields stock community property or H's separate property?

   b. Assume that shortly before H purchased the Goldfields stock, he had deposited into the checking account (which then had a $70,000 balance) $5,000 as rental income from his separate property. In the absence of other evidence, is the Goldfields stock separate or community property?

   c. Assume that as of the date H purchased the Goldfields stock, his total earnings during marriage were $300,000, which was $10,000 less than he had already spent (drawing on the commingled account) for family living expenses to that date. In the absence of other evidence, is the Goldfields stock separate or community?

11. During marriage W used $40,000 of community funds to purchase a laundry business. Immediately thereafter she and H separated permanently. For two years before divorce, W operated the business and made $20,000 net profits each year, half of which she retained in the business, which is now worth $110,000 (due in great measure to growth in the area of the city where it is located). Does W's interest in the business exceed H's?

12. Before marriage, H signed a five-year contract to coach a professional football team at $280,000 per year. Shortly thereafter, H married W. Are the payments received after marriage separate or community property, or both?

13. Before marriage, H purchased an insurance policy on his life, naming his mother beneficiary. After marriage, he continued the policy in effect, paying the premiums with his earnings, but never changing the beneficiary. On his death, does W have any right to the insurance proceeds?

14. Before marriage, H purchased furniture and furnishings for the house in which he and W planned to live after marriage. H paid for these by borrowing money from Bank. He repaid the bank loan from his earnings during marriage.

   a. Are the furniture and furnishings separate or community property?

   b. In the event the marriage was dissolved, would the community be entitled to reimbursement for the amounts paid to Bank?

15. During marriage, H and W lived in H's separately owned house. The house needed considerable repairs, and H spent almost every weekend working on the house. W now sues for dissolution and claims there is a community interest in the house because it is now worth substantially more due to H's repair work. In the absence of other evidence, is the house separate or community, or both?

16. During marriage, H borrows $10,000 from Bank and invests these funds in stocks and bonds which are now worth $50,000 due to general economic conditions.

   a. If W never signed the bank loan, and the stocks and bonds are held in H's name alone, is this sufficient to establish that they are H's separate property? _____

   b. If Bank made the loan *primarily* on the basis of H's separate credit, yet in part on the basis of existing community assets, would the stocks and bonds be H's separate property or community property, or a mix of both? _____

   c. If H failed to repay the loan, could Bank reach W's earnings to satisfy the debt? _____

   d. Suppose W's earnings were used to satisfy the loan in b. above. Would this affect ownership of the stocks and bonds? _____

17. Before marriage in 1970, H purchased a house in which he and W lived after their 1973 marriage. The recorded deed named H as sole grantee.

   a. Do the facts that the house was purchased before marriage and that title stands of record in H's name alone preclude a finding that the house is community property? _____

   b. If, during marriage, H used community funds to make the monthly payments on the trust deed (mortgage) on the house, is the community entitled to an ownership interest in the house? _____

   c. If, during marriage, H used community funds to pay the property taxes, insurance, and household repairs, would such expenditures entitle the community to an ownership interest in the house? _____

18. During marriage real property was acquired in the names of "John and Mary Jones, husband and wife." A down payment of $20,000 was made using $10,000 of community earnings of H and $10,000 W had inherited from her mother during the marriage. Subsequent mortgage payments on an $80,000 note were paid half with H's earnings and half with interest paid on money W inherited. The mortgage has been reduced to $50,000 and the house is worth $180,000. How is it owned? _____

19. Before marriage, H was injured in an auto accident. Suit was filed and a judgment was obtained in H's favor. Just before the judgment was paid, H married W. Are the funds received by H in satisfaction of the judgment separate or community, or both? _____

20. During marriage, H takes W for a drive in the community owned car. An auto accident occurs due to the combined negligence of H and D, the driver of the other car. W sustains serious injuries in the collision.

   a. If W sues D for lost earnings, can D reduce the damages for which he is liable by showing that H was also at fault in causing the accident? _____

Community Property—117

b. If W while living with H obtains a recovery against D for pain and suffering, is it separate or community property?

c. Would it make any difference if H and W had *separated* by the time W *received* the recovery for her injuries?

d. Could a divorce court award W more than half of the funds received by W for her injuries?

e. Change the facts: Assume that W filed suit *against* H for her injuries instead of suing D. Would the settlement paid by H's insurance company be separate or community property? (Assume that H and W are still living together.)

21. Assume that Betty, H and W's minor child, was killed in the auto accident referred to in the previous question. W now sues D for the wrongful death of Betty.

    a. Would any recovery in the suit be community property?

    b. Could D reduce liability on the ground that H was also at fault in causing the accident?

22. The day before their marriage in 1989, H and W orally agree that earnings or property acquired by either during marriage will be their respective separate property *and* that neither would ever make any claim for support against the other. Is the oral agreement enforceable after marriage?

23. During marriage in 1974, H and W purchase a home with community funds, taking title in both names "as joint tenants with right of survivorship." In 1980, H says to W, "I give you my interest in the house," W dies and her will leaves "all my separate property to Sister." Who is entitled to the house—H, Sister, or both?

24. Before his marriage in 1989, H owned a house outright. The day *after* marriage to W, H orally told her, "This house is our home, our community property," and they treated it as such during the balance of their marriage. If H dies leaving his separate property to Brother, and his share of the community property to W, who is entitled to the house—W, Brother, or both?

25. During marriage in 1970, H and W used community cash to buy land under a deed naming the grantees as "H and W, as tenants in common." Neither spouse had any idea what a tenancy in common was. In 1994, W's post-marriage contract creditor levies on the land. Disregarding exemptions, how much can the creditor reach?

26. During marriage in 1994, H used community property funds to purchase a new car for W's use, title to which was registered in her name alone. In the absence of other evidence as to the parties' intent regarding status, is the car separate or community property?

27. After their 1997 marriage, H uses $10,000 of community funds to renovate a yacht, which is his separate property. W is aware of H's use of the community

118—Community Property

funds and has encouraged such use because the yacht is H's favorite hobby. Two years later, W sues for dissolution of the marriage and demands that H reimburse her for $5,000. Who wins?

28. During marriage in 1998, H and W purchased a house. The deed, which neither of them signed, recited that they took "as joint tenants with right of survivorship." How is this property now classified?

    a. Would your analysis be different if the purchase took place in 1980?

29. H and W had been married for a number of years and had accumulated $10,000 in a joint savings account. On February 2, 1975, W withdrew the entire balance and loaned it to a friend. The loan appeared well-secured at the time, but the friend went bankrupt. Now at divorce, H seeks relief on the ground that W had no right to loan funds accumulated prior to 1975 without his consent. Who wins?

30. During marriage, W operates a beauty shop. Although W does her best, the shop loses money each month. H complains and demands that W cease operation in order to avoid running up debts. However, W persists in trying to make a go of it. Ultimately, however, the shop fails, leaving debts of $10,000 that have to be paid out of community funds. At divorce H seeks relief on the ground that he did not want to continue operation of the business. Who wins?

31. During marriage, H uses his earnings to purchase a mountain cabin, title to which is taken in his name alone. In 1989, H separates from W and lives by himself in the mountain cabin. In 1997, he sells the cabin to a neighbor, Ned, for a fair price. Ned at once records his deed. H squanders the proceeds.

    a. W finds out about the transaction later in 1997 and immediately sues Ned to set aside the sale. Can she prevail?

    b. If the sale were to be set aside, would W have to reimburse Ned for all of the money paid to H?

    c. Assume H died by the time W's suit against Ned came to trial. Would this change the result?

32. During marriage, and after 1975, W uses savings from her salary to buy a mountain cabin. Unbeknownst to H, title is taken in W's name alone. W sells the cabin to BFP, a purchaser for value who takes without knowledge that W is married.

    a. Can H have the sale set aside because he did not consent thereto?

    b. Would your analysis be different if W purchased the cabin in 1950 with her community earnings?

33. During marriage, H made a gift of a valuable community owned yacht to his mother. W *orally* approved the gift at the time it was made, but within a few months she changed her mind and sued Mother to have the yacht returned. Who wins?

34. During marriage, W in 1998 withdraws $5,000 of community funds from a savings account and gives it to her mother. After H and W are divorced, H finds out

Community Property—119

and promptly sues Mother to repay the $5,000. Is H entitled to recover $5,000, $2,500, or nothing at all? (Assume no statute of limitations bars H's suit.)

35. Before marriage, H borrowed $10,000 from Bank for a business venture that failed. H is now married and the loan remains unpaid. W has $10,000 in a bank account in her name, $5,000 of which was received by her as an inheritance and $5,000 as savings from her earnings during marriage. What part, if any, of the bank account is subject to be taken in satisfaction of the debt owed by H to Bank—$10,000, $5,000, or none?

36. During marriage in 1997, W was injured, and her mother contracted for hospital care for W. Is property H inherited from his father liable for the hospital bill if W possesses property inherited from her aunt?

37. During marriage in 1997, H makes child support payments to his former wife out of his weekly paycheck, which is his only property. When his present wife sues for dissolution, she demands that H reimburse the community for the amount paid to his former wife. Who wins?

   a. Would your analysis differ if during the time H paid alimony to his ex-wife from his earnings, he possessed about as much separate property as there was community property on hand?

38. On their anniversary, H presented W with a diamond necklace purchased with his earnings during marriage. The card with it said, "To Wilma, with love from Hal." Shortly thereafter a victim of a tort committed before marriage obtained a judgment against H. May the victim levy execution on the necklace (assuming it is not exempt and that H is not insolvent)?

39. Before marriage, W borrowed money from Finance Co. to cover her living expenses. After marriage, she pays off Finance Co. out of her paycheck. At the time of dissolution, H demands that W reimburse the community for the amount paid. Who wins?

40. W files suit for divorce. The couple has always lived in California.

   a. If there are no community assets, can the court award W a share of separate property solely owned by H?

   b. Must the court make an equal division of *all* community assets?

41. H and W are boating on Clear Lake in a rented power cruiser. H carelessly loses control of the boat and causes it to strike a piling, which collapses a dock and results in serious injury to W. H's separate estate is worth $20,000; W's separate estate is worth $100,000; and there are community assets worth $10,000. There is also a personal liability insurance policy, purchased with community funds, covering H up to a limit of $20,000.

   a. The owner of the dock recovers a judgment against H for $23,000 for damages done to the dock. What assets can be reached, and in what order, to satisfy this judgment?

- b. W recovers a judgment against H for $70,000 for her injuries. What assets can be reached, and in what order, to satisfy this judgment?

- c. Assume H and W are later divorced. Does the court have power to award H *any* portion of the recovery obtained by W under b. above?

- d. Does the divorce court have the power to order H to **reimburse** the community for the community property taken in satisfaction of either tort claim?

42. On his death, H's will provides: "I hereby convey the entire community assets of myself and my wife to Trust, to be held for my wife for her lifetime, and on her death to my children."

    - a. Can W elect to retain her share of the community assets free of the trust?

    - b. If W does elect to retain her share outside the trust, does she get the income from H's share as provided in the will?

43. Blackacre and Whiteacre are community owned farms of equal value. If H's will devises one to W and one to their daughter, is the will free from attack?

44. During marriage, H takes out a $100,000 insurance policy on his life. He names W as the sole beneficiary of the insurance but provides that the death benefits shall be payable only in the form of an annuity for the balance of her life. H's mother is the alternate beneficiary. All premiums are paid from H's earnings.

    - a. In the event of divorce, if the policy has a cash value of $50,000, is W entitled to any interest in the policy?

    - b. In the event of H's death, if W insists on asserting her community property rights in the policy, is she entitled to the $100,000 outright (as opposed to the annuity form of payment)?

45. W's will devised half of community owned Blackacre to her son and named Bank executor of her will. May H, over Bank's objection, sell the entire interest in Blackacre to a third party?

46. Al and Betty lived together as husband and wife in Texas, although they never went through a wedding ceremony. Such living together constitutes a common law marriage under Texas law. If Al and Betty move to California, will their subsequent property acquisitions be community property?

47. H and W went through a wedding ceremony. H believed that a prior divorce he had obtained was valid, but actually it was void for lack of jurisdiction. W also believed that she and H were lawfully married.

    - a. Prior to annulment, does W have equal management power over H's earnings?

    - b. At H's death intestate prior to annulment, will W be the owner of all property purchased with H's earnings during their union?

Community Property—121

c. If H inherited a ranch and died intestate before annulment, survived by W and nephew N, his nearest blood kin, would W inherit half the ranch and N half?

48. Sam and Nancy lived together in California, although both knew they were never validly married. After seven years, Nancy files suit asking for one-half property accumulated during the seven years.

   a. In the absence of other evidence, is Nancy entitled to one-half of all the property?

   b. Assume that Nancy alleges she did all of Sam's housekeeping for seven years in the expectation that she would share in his earnings. If Sam proves that he and Nancy never spoke about property at all, will this preclude a recovery by Nancy of a share of property titled in H's name but acquired during their union?

49. H and W lived all their lives in Oregon; they recently separated and H moved to California. There is land in Oregon in H's name which he bought during marriage with his earnings. H sues W for divorce in California and obtains jurisdiction over W while she was visiting in California. May the court, under California law, order H to deed to W half of that land?

50. H and W lived most of their lives in Virginia but are now retired and have established their domicile in California. H's sole asset is a large farm in Virginia which he acquired during marriage with his earnings prior to moving to California; he now receives rental income from the farm which he uses to support himself and W.

   a. In the event of divorce, can the court divide the farm between H and W?

   b. In the event H died and left a will devising the farm to his brother, B, could W claim an interest therein as "quasi-community property"?

51. When H and W moved to California from a common law state, H owned 1,000 shares of General Motors stock which he had accumulated from earnings during marriage. Shortly before his death, he donated the stock to the University of California subject to a retained life estate. W is independently wealthy.

   a. Can W recover the stock from the University of California?

   b. Assume instead that W had sued **during H's lifetime** to set aside the transfer to the University of California. Would she have prevailed?

52. At divorce, the court values H's future benefits under the Federal Railroad Retirement Act at $100,000, and W's future benefits under Social Security at $50,000. The spouses married before going to work and separated only a few days before the divorce. May the court order H to pay W a portion of Railroad Retirement Act benefits he receives after divorce?

53. At divorce the only assets before the court are H's future Social Security benefits earned by labor and payroll deductions during marriage and a house bought with community funds. The court values the future Social Security benefits at $60,000, and the equity in the house at $60,000. Can the court award the Social Security benefits to H and the house to W?

122—Community Property

ANSWERS TO REVIEW QUESTIONS

1. **SEPARATE** Although received during marriage, the right to payment was acquired prior to marriage, hence on tracing principles, W's separate property. [§§2, 50]

2. **YES** There is no presumption that property held in H's name is his separate property. Rather, the general presumption of community ownership applies. [§§1, 5-6]

3. **NO** There is no presumption of community ownership of assets owned by a decedent where the marriage was dissolved more than four years prior to death. [Cal. Fam. Code §802] [§19]

4. **SEPARATE** Monies received by gift or inheritance are separate no matter when received. [§33]

5. **COMMUNITY** The TV show had no donative intent so the prize could be viewed as W's earnings for labor. Moreover, the money would fall under the general presumption of community because it was received during marriage. [§§4-6, 36, 39]

6. **YES** "Accumulations" of W after separation are her separate property. [§43] California Family Code section 2640(b) assures her of reimbursement (the new roof seems to be an "improvement"). But this claim may possibly be reduced or even offset by a community claim for half of the fair rental value of the house occupied by W while separated from H. [§340]

7. **YES** As "proceeds" of a former community asset. The screenplay was written with community labor and took the status of a community asset. (Normally, however, it would be expected that the court in the dissolution proceeding would divide the community assets and award this asset to one party or the other. In the absence of such award, it would become an asset held in tenancy in common.) [§345]

    a. **NO** H's labors while separated from W would generate separate property if the separation was "final" and hence anything created by his services would also be his separate property. [Cal. Fam. Code §771] [§§43-45]

8. **BOTH** Commingling of separate and community funds does *not* alter status as long as each fund is *identifiable*. The stock took the status of funds used to purchase the same (*i.e.,* 75% community); and the bank account can be traced back through changes in form to the original cash used. Hence the account is 75% community, 25% separate. "Title" to the account is irrelevant; nor does the separation affect a then existing community interest. [§§43, 50, 77]

9. **NO** The capital grew solely because of natural occurrences and not because of any labor by W. There are no retained earnings in the business to apportion. Thus this is a case of identifying an asset W owned before marriage not altered by community labor. [§50]

10.a. **COMMUNITY** The question provides no evidence that H intended to use separate funds to buy the stock. [§54] Therefore the pro-community presumption attaching to acquisitions during marriage cannot be overcome.

    b. **COMMUNITY**   *See* above. There is still no evidence of drawer intent and ample community funds were available here to have been used in the purchase.

    c. **UNCLEAR**   Under "total recapitulation," all the community funds are exhausted and the stock is separate property. The *See* case prohibited that approach, but it is now unclear if *See* is good law. Under *See*, H would have to prove, in order to rebut the community presumption, that there was always at least $5,000 in the account prior to the purchase of the stock and that whenever a family expense draw was made there were sufficient community funds in the account to cover it. [§57]

11. **PROBABLY**   After separation W applied separate labor to make a community asset productive. The doubling in value is caused primarily by the nature of the capital rather than W's labor. Hence, the formula for apportionment more favorable to the community should be selected. If a fair salary for W is $15,000 or less, the formula would be "reverse" *Van Camp*. A fair salary for W surely exceeds $10,000 per year so that her separate estate has a share in the business. [§§74-76]

12. **COMMUNITY**   Although the contract was entered into before marriage, it was for services *to be rendered*—hence, no fixed right to payment. Consequently, the status of payments depends on H's marital status when the consideration was given by H. [§§81-82]

13. **YES**   The proceeds are traced to the *last* premium paid, which is presumptively community. Thus, W can elect to claim her half of any community interest. [§§77, 92-94]

14.a. **SEPARATE**   Because obtained with funds borrowed on H's separate credit (before marriage). The fact that community funds were used to repay the loan does *not* alter the status of assets purchased outright before marriage. [§§96-101]

    b. **PROBABLY NOT**   If a spouse uses community funds to pay his own separate debt (as a loan taken out to buy separate property), reimbursement is available at dissolution. When reimbursement is sought, however, the amount may be reduced because of benefits enjoyed by the estate making the claim. The furniture was used by the community and might have been repossessed had H not paid off his loan. Substantial offset is likely. [§§116, 339]

15. **SEPARATE**   There can be no presumption of gift here, but the improvements become part of the property itself (fixtures doctrine) and hence assume its status—*i.e.*, separate. However, the community is entitled to **reimbursement** for the **value of H's services**, subject to offset based on the community benefit in occupying the house. [§§103-106]

16.a. **NO**   The stocks and bonds are proceeds of the bank loan. Status of the bank loan depends on the **lender's intent**—*i.e.*, whether Bank was looking to H's separate assets or community assets for repayment. [§96] The pro-community presumption cannot be overcome here since there is no evidence that H had separate credit on which Bank relied.

    b. **SEPARATE**   So far courts refuse to apportion loan proceeds into part separate and part community where the lender relied primarily on separate credit yet secondarily on community credit. [§96] But one case would hold the proceeds community unless the lender relied *solely* on separate property for repayment. [§97]

c. **YES** All community assets (including W's earnings) are liable for contract debts of either spouse incurred *during* marriage. [§273]

d. **NO** At most, this would give the community a reimbursement claim if Bank relied on H's separate credit. [§101]

17.a. **NO** Record "title" is seldom conclusive as to actual ownership, at least in litigation between the spouses themselves. There could be a pre-1985 oral transmutation of what was H's separate property at marriage. [§166] Even after the enactment of a Statute of Frauds for transmutation [§174], there could be a signed but *unrecorded* transmutation document.

b. **YES** California Family Code section 2640(b) makes reimbursement the remedy when the issue arises *at divorce* (not the case here) and when *separate* funds are applied but the property is community or titled in the names of H and W. However, in other situations (as here, where community funds are used for the mortgage payment), recent cases recognize the amount of a payment that reduces principal owing as acquiring a pro rata share of ownership. These cases impliedly overrule older cases that made reimbursement the remedy. [§§111-112]

c. **NO** Expenditure of community funds for purposes of *improving* H's separate property (as opposed to acquiring title) entitles community to *reimbursement*, but does not entitle community to interest in ownership. [§§103-106]

18. **COMMUNITY** Case law imposed a presumption of gift in this situation where W used separate funds but knew title was in the community. By statute applicable only at divorce there is no gift [Cal. Fam. Code §2640], but since the statutory remedy is reimbursement for W, the title must be as it was under the pre-statutory case law: all community. [§114]

19. **PROBABLY SEPARATE** Present law *traces* the recovery during marriage back to the time the cause of action arose (when H was single). This makes the entire recovery separate. [§133] An argument can be made, however, that H's marriage converted to community property damages awarded for post-marriage lost earnings. [§135]

20.a. **NO** Under modern California law, there is no imputed negligence in a suit where a spouse seeks recovery for personal injuries. [§154]

b. **COMMUNITY (POSSIBLE CHANGE IN LAW HERE)** Even though W's body (her separate property owned before marriage) was damaged, California cases so far refuse to trace any tort recovery to such a separate property source. Some cases recognize this to be illogical, so change in the law is possible. [§§140-143]

c. **UNCLEAR** The statutes say that the time of accident, not time of receipt, governs classification, indicating all recovery would be community. Logically, however, so much of the recovery as compensates W for lost earnings after the separation (which would have been separate property) should be W's separate property. [§§133, 140]

Community Property—125

    d. **YES** — California Family Code section 2603 allows award of ***all*** personal injury damages to the victim spouse even though they are community. However, H could receive up to half the award if the "interests of justice" would be served. [§144]

    e. **SEPARATE** — Recoveries for interspousal torts are the injured spouse's ***separate*** property. [§151]

21.a. **YES (POSSIBLE CHANGE IN LAW HERE)** — The cases so far simply say the cause of action was acquired during marriage and is community without realizing that much of the recovery may be an award to W for gifts Betty might have given her and therefore logically separate property to the extent the gifts would not be to both spouses. [§162]

    b. **DEPENDS** — If any of the recovery consists of economic damages, D is jointly and severally liable. For these damages, D can have H's negligence imputed to W thereby reducing what he owes based on D's share of the fault under comparative negligence law. [§164]

22. **NO** — Although previously a prenuptial ***oral*** agreement as to property status was enforceable as long as "ratified" or "executed" by conduct consistent therewith during marriage, in 1985, a Statute of Frauds applicable to premarital agreements was enacted, requiring a written agreement. Most likely the courts will not employ ratification or execution gimmicks as a means of validating an oral agreement. [§167] Moreover, although an antenuptial waiver of post-divorce alimony is now permitted, a waiver of support ***during*** marriage could still be contra to public policy. [§170]

23. **PROBABLY SISTER** — The community funds were presumptively transmuted to joint tenancy by the pre-1985 deed. The oral transmutation by H was thus from his separate property to W's. Before 1985, no writing was needed for community-to-separate transmutations even of realty [§172]; thus H's intent can be given effect if his joint tenancy interest becomes momentarily community before it becomes W's separate property, even if a separate-to-separate transmutation requires a writing. If this gift had been made in 1985 (or later), it would be void if not evidenced by a writing. [§174]

24. **BROTHER** — Beginning in 1985, a post-marriage oral agreement is ineffective to change the status of property from separate to community; to be effective, the agreement would have to be in writing. [§174]

25. **ALL** — The statute presuming community property ownership in the face of a contrary co-ownership title applies only at divorce. Since H and W accepted a writing referring to tenancy in common, a pre-1984 transmutation is possible. But a transmutation is a contract, and here the spouses did not intend tenancy in common ownership. W's creditor has standing to establish that because of their ignorance the apparent transmutation never occurred. [§§193, 185-186]

26. **PROBABLY SEPARATE** — While in most gift situations donative intent is not presumed and the trier of fact can draw what inference it wishes, when a spouse causes ***title*** to be placed in the name of the other the donative intent is often presumed. The cases do seem inconsistent. Here, H "consented to" the written title so the Statute of Frauds for immodest gifts [Cal. Fam. Code §852] can be satisfied although there is a problem with whether the document is sufficiently "express" to satisfy the 1985 statute. [§§179, 181, 176]

27. **UNCLEAR** W has not here put *title* in H's name, but she has apparently approved his improving an asset to which he has separate title. Probably the "pure" gift cases involving no title control here and the trier of fact must determine if W had the intent to make a gift to H of her community interest in the funds used. If not, she has a right of reimbursement for $5,000. [§§103, 179] This "improvement" case involves a "mix" of community and separate funds so is not subject to the transmutation Statute of Frauds, section 852. [§177]

28. **COMMUNITY** The mere acceptance of a deed reciting a joint tenancy probably does not equate to acceptance of an "express" declaration of transmutation as required since 1985 by California Family Code section 852. The funds used to pay for the property are presumed community. [§189]

    a. **PROBABLY** If the attempted transmutation occurred pre-1985, it is valid. It is *presumed* that both spouses agreed to the change of ownership. Therefore, the property would be treated as joint tenancy property. However, if it can be shown that in fact the spouses (or just one of them) did not read the deed or know of the joint tenancy recital, the presumption of transmutation is rebutted. [§185]

29. **W** The spouses have equal rights as to management and control, and hence W would have had the right to loan community funds, subject only to her duty to act in good faith. By statute, this applies retroactively—even as to assets acquired prior to 1975. In an analogous context retroactive application has been held constitutional. [§§217, 472]

30. **W** Under California Family Code section 1100(d), the spouse operating a community business has the *sole right* to make such decisions. Hence, as long as she was acting in good faith, the fact that she lost money would not constitute a breach of any duty owed to H required of a fiduciary. [§218]

31.a. **YES** Since W's suit was filed *within one year* from the date the deed was recorded, she will win by proving that the property was in fact acquired with community funds (H's earnings). Although the sale to Ned is presumed valid (because title held in H's name alone), the presumption is rebutted by proof of the source in community earnings. W's joinder in the deed was required. [§§229, 231-232]

    b. **YES** *Mark v. Title Guarantee & Trust Co.* [§245]

    c. **PROBABLY** Apparently, W would be entitled to have the sale set aside only as to a half interest in the property; the rest would be upheld as tantamount to testamentary distribution of H's half. W must reimburse Ned for half of what he paid H. [§242]

32.a. **YES** Since W acquired title after 1975, there is no presumption in favor of bona fide purchasers that property held in her name alone is her separate property, and H could have the sale set aside by showing the acquisition date during marriage and his nonjoinder in the instrument of sale. [§§22-23, 229, 243]

    b. **YES** A pre-1975 deed naming W grantee raised in favor of a bona fide purchaser from her a conclusive presumption that the property was her separate property; thus, joinder by H would not be needed. The exception arising when W uses property under her management and control could not apply here, as W did not control her own earnings until 1951. [§§22-23, 26]

33. **PROBABLY W** — Section 1100(b) requires W's written consent to the gift if H is the donor; if W is viewed as co-donor, no writing is required. Something more than oral consent apparently is required to give W co-donor status; otherwise there would never be need for a writing. [§249]

34. **$2,500** — The cause of action against Mother ceased to be community property at divorce. H could not now recover W's half interest in the money, only his own. It became a tenancy in common asset. [§§257, 345]

35. **NONE** — A premarriage debt could not trigger the "necessaries" doctrine. Hence, W's separate property cannot be liable. Since W's name alone is on the bank account and since she has not commingled with her earnings other types of community property, the earnings are not liable for H's premarital obligation. [§§274, 276, 281]

36. **YES** — The treatment was a necessary of life provided W during marriage. It is not essential that W herself made the contract for necessaries if she received the benefit. [§§276, 279] It is irrelevant that W owns property that also is liable.

37. **H** — Under present law the child support obligation is a separate debt, but a statute provides reimbursement is available only if community property was used to pay it at a time when H's separate property was also available. [§282]

   a. **YES** — If separate funds are available to pay the separate debt, reimbursement is owed. [§282]

38. **DEPENDS** — This is the pure gift situation where the trier of fact is free to infer donative intent or find none. [§179] If there is none, the community property is secondarily liable for H's separate tort (no community benefit being suggested in his premarriage conduct causing the injury). W can compel the creditor to first exhaust H's separate property. [§§283-288] If the necklace was not substantial in value in view of the wealth of the parties, no writing is required to change ownership. [§176] Note that the writing here is not sufficiently "express" to transmute if the exception to the transmutation Statute of Frauds for modest gifts is inapplicable. [§174]

39. **DEPENDS** — A debtor spouse's own earnings are liable for his or her premarital obligations. [§273] But where community assets are so used, the community is entitled to reimbursement at dissolution. [§339] However, there is a three-year statute of limitations for such claim. [§341]

40.a. **NO** — A court has no power to award separate assets of either spouse to the other except for a spouse's separate interest in joint tenancy or tenancy in common property. [§§306-307]

   b. **NO** — Personal injury damages are not subject to equal division, the 50-50 rule does not apply to default divorces involving less than $5,000, and there may be offsets for various reimbursement claims. [§§333-334, 336-340]

41.a. **INSURANCE AND COMMUNITY FIRST; THEN SEPARATE** — W's separate assets are not liable for H's torts. H's separate estate is liable, but community assets ($20,000 insurance and $10,000 other) must be taken first because this tort apparently was committed while H engaged in a "community activity" (family recreation). [§284]

b. **INSURANCE FIRST, THEN SEPARATE, THEN COMMUNITY** Recovery for interspousal torts comes first out of any available insurance ($20,000), then out of the tortfeasor's separate assets ($20,000), and then out of the community assets ($10,000); probably only H's half of the latter $10,000 is credited to paying off the judgment, leaving $25,000 unsatisfied. [§§292-293]

c. **NO** Recovery for interspousal torts is the injured spouse's separate property [§151], and the court has no power to award separate property to the other spouse. [§306]

d. **NO** Since no "separate" obligation is involved, reimbursement is apparently not available. Negligence in piloting a boat does not seem to be a violation of fiduciary duties that H owes W. [§339]

42.a. **YES** Neither spouse has testamentary power over the other spouse's share. The value of the life estate W gets under the will cannot bar her from asserting "item theory" rights. [§348]

b. **NO** By electing against the will, she is disqualified from taking thereunder. [§350]

43. **NO** Under the "item theory" applied at death, W can insist on keeping her half interest in both properties. [§348]

44.a. **YES** The policy was acquired during marriage and is presumptively community. W is co-owner of it. [§§5-6] (Since the policy has a cash surrender value it cannot be wholly a "term" policy, which one court has held to have no value at divorce as a community asset.)

b. **NO, ONLY $50,000** The annuity option does not take effect until H dies; it is a testamentary act that H could make only with respect to his half interest. However, to assert the right to take her half interest free of H's testamentary act, W must elect to give up her right in H's half. Mother would get that half. [§§360, 363]

45. **DEPENDS** Forty days after W dies, H may sell community realty unless the devisee (Son) files notice of his claim. After such filing, the buyer would take subject to the devise. [§382]

46. **YES** A marriage valid *where entered into* is valid in California. [§398]

47.a. **PROBABLY NOT** The cases have said that acquisitions in a putative marriage that would be community if the marriage were lawful are held in tenancy in common or are the acquiring spouse's separate property subject to equitable division at annulment. It has not been decided whether the quasi-marital property statute changes this result. Moreover, it is unclear if the spouse's beliefs were "objectively reasonable." [§§403-409]

b. **PROBABLY** W would be a good faith putative spouse and hence H's intestate heir of what would be community property in a lawful marriage, assuming H's first wife makes no claim. Additional facts could overcome the presumption of W's good faith by showing her belief to be "objectively unreasonable." [§§416-417]

c. **PROBABLY** *Estate of Leslie* makes a putative wife heir of her "husband's" separate property in the same manner as a lawful wife, again assuming H's lawful wife makes no claim. [Cal. Prob. Code §6401(c)(2)][§417]

48.a. **NO** The law of community property does not govern termination of a nonmarital relationship since there is no "marriage" to dissolve; nor does it require equal division of property acquired during a nonmarital relationship. [§433]

b. **NO** The court may examine the relationship of the parties and enforce an implied agreement or tacit understanding as to their rights in property acquisitions. Alternatively, Nancy could probably recover in quantum meruit for the value of her services (minus support received from Sam). [§§438-439]

49. **PROBABLY NOT** Under the 1978 *Roesch* case [§458], the court could not apply California law because of lack of contacts of California to the marriage. A subsequent Supreme Court decision casts some doubt on *Roesch,* but California's contact to the marriage is especially weak where the major asset of marital property is located in W's domicile and the state that was the last marital domicile. [§459]

50a. **YES (QUALIFIED)** Out-of-state land is "quasi-community property" for purposes of dissolution proceedings. [§§455, 458] The court "if practicable" should avoid altering title to out-of-state land [§452] but cannot avoid doing so here.

b. **NO** Out-of-state land is *not* "quasi-community" for inheritance purposes, but W would still have whatever marital rights (*e.g.,* dower) are recognized under the law of Virginia. [§460]

51a. **YES AS TO HALF** The stock is quasi-community property; at death the survivor spouse may void as to half gifts made by the decedent of such property if decedent kept quantum of ownership (here the reserved life estate). [§463]

b. **NO** Although a wife can sue to set aside a gift of community property without her consent during the marriage, no such right is recognized with respect to quasi-community property. **During marriage** such property is treated as the acquiring spouse's property for purposes of management and control. [§457]

52. **IN PART** With respect to Railroad Retirement Act and Social Security Act benefits, federal law preempts state law. Social Security benefits must be treated as separate property and so much of the Railroad Retirement Act benefits as H would be paid if he participated solely in the Social Security program must also be treated as separate. But the excess ("Tier II") Railroad Retirement benefits can be treated as community property. [§§487-490]

53. **NO (QUALIFIED)** The Supreme Court has held that the unfairness caused by federal preemption may not be corrected by an unequal division of community property. [§495] The constitutionality of such federal interference in California's policy of making an equal division has not been tested, however. [§496]

SAMPLE EXAM QUESTION I

In 1989, H, a California-domiciled attorney lawfully married to W, found a diamond ring on the street. Without reporting this to authorities as he should have if he wished to obtain title as a finder, H pocketed the ring. Two days later, he sold it for $20,000. With half of this sum, he purchased insurance on his own life, naming his mother, M, as the beneficiary. With the other $10,000, H purchased federal bonds and, pursuant to federal regulations, had them registered in the names of H and W as joint tenants with right of survivorship. W was unaware of these investments.

In 1997, W died survived by H and Sam, a son by W's prior marriage. W's will stated:

> I wish to divide my estate between my husband and Sam. Therefore I devise the entire interest in Greenacre to Sam. I bequeath my interest in my husband's law practice—including its goodwill and accounts receivable—to my husband. The residue of my estate goes to Sam.

H had started his unincorporated law practice after marrying W and built up its clientele and other assets through his labor. Greenacre had been purchased with profits from H's practice.

Shortly after W died and before distribution of her estate, H died intestate and without issue. M and Sam are alive and lay claim to as much of the above-described assets as they can. (H's father predeceased him.)

What are the rights of M and Sam in the assets on hand?

SAMPLE EXAM QUESTION II

In 1958, H and W married, and just before the ceremony, executed an unrecorded agreement stating that all their subsequent acquisitions would be community property and that in the event of divorce neither would owe the other any alimony. At that time W had just graduated from law school; H was an unknown poet. In 1959, with her earnings as a lawyer, W bought $10,000 worth of diamonds without any document of title. She had the seller of the diamonds make out a bill of sale reciting W had used her separate funds to make the purchase and held the diamonds as her separate property. In 1960, W sold the diamonds and, without telling H, used the proceeds to purchase in her own name Blackacre, a 20-acre parcel of land. Later that year, W leased the east half of Blackacre to farmer F for 50 years by written instrument. H was also ignorant of this transaction. W collected rents from F and spent them on family expenses.

In 1983, W asked H if it was all right with him if she made a gift of some land to her sister. H replied, "You do as you wish—you handle all the finances." W then executed a deed of gift of the west half of Blackacre to Sis, who began renting it out to F. Sis has earned $5,000 per year in rentals from Blackacre.

In late 1997, W became mentally ill and was confined to an institution. H was now a widely published poet making a sizeable income. However, H and W had spent their earnings lavishly for food, travel, entertainment, etc. There were few assets of value on hand. H began dating other women. His investigation of the H-W financial status disclosed W's 1960 purchase and her lease to F and deed to Sis. H entered onto the east half of Blackacre and ordered F off, asserting that F had no right to be there. A fistfight ensued, during which H injured F.

Shortly thereafter the following actions were brought:

1. F vs. H for trespass to land.

2. H vs. F to quiet title and void any instruments under which F claims a right to possession to the farm.

3. H vs. Sis to have the deed of gift declared void and to recover the rentals collected by Sis.

4. H vs. W for divorce, in which W's conservator seeks a support (alimony) award for the mentally ill W.

Analyze the legal issues presented in these actions by the above facts. If F obtains a tort judgment against H for battery during their fistfight, may F levy execution on Blackacre?

SAMPLE EXAM QUESTION III

H and W were married in 1961 and H went to work for Acme Co., which offered employees an unusual employment option. After 30 years on the job and before retirement at age 65, Acme employees could opt to work half time yet receive 100% of the salary at the level paid at the 30-year work anniversary, or the employee could work full time and receive double that salary until retirement age.

In January 1989, H and W separated and ceased contact between each other. H went to live in a community-owned cottage that the couple had purchased in January of 1981. The purchase price for the cottage was $40,000, of which $10,000 was paid in community cash and $30,000 by promissory note to the vendor secured by a purchase money mortgage. The repayment plan called for amortized monthly payments to vendor of $400 for 10 years. The 1981 deed named H alone as grantee. When H and W separated, eight years of monthly payments had been made using H's earnings at Acme. While occupying the cottage after separation, H continued making payments from his Acme earnings.

After the separation, W lived in a community-owned city residence. She did not work. H sent her each month a check for $300 from his earnings. She deposited that in a checking account along with $300 each month of interest paid on bonds she inherited from her mother and $300 each month of dividends on stock purchased with her earnings during 1967-1972 when she was employed. The only sums she withdrew from this account, opened in January 1989 when she and H separated, were spent for her upkeep.

W sent the bill for real property taxes on the city residence to H, who paid $2,000 ($1,000 for 1989 and $1,000 for 1990) in taxes from his post-separation earnings.

In December 1991, H and W were divorced. The trial court made determinations on the issues described below. You are a law clerk in the California court where the case is now on appeal. Your Justice says the lower court may have erred in dealing with all four issues below and asks for the correct analysis.

A. A few days before the divorce, H, aged 50, was able to opt for half-time employment at full pay or full-time employment at double pay. Did W have any community interest in the future pay? If so, how should it be calculated?

B. While the divorce suit was pending, the vendor of the cottage marked the $30,000 note "paid" and canceled the mortgage on the cottage. What community rights were there in this acquisition?

C. W had lived frugally, spending two-thirds of the $900 per month deposited into her account. Thus she had saved $10,800 in three years in the bank account in her name. Did H have any community interest in this?

D. H asserted a right of reimbursement from W's half of the community assets or from her separately owned bonds for taxes paid on the residence whether the divorce court awarded it to H or W. Was this claim sound? If so, how much should H have obtained?

SAMPLE EXAM QUESTION IV

In 1982, unmarried H bought Blackacre for $100,000 cash, taking a deed naming himself as grantee. In 1983, he proposed to W. They orally agreed (before many witnesses) that during marriage all properties in which either had an interest would be community property. Five days later, they married. H did not change the title to Blackacre, and six months later, he conveyed it to his father for $50,000 without asking W's consent. With this sum H purchased a house in 1984 that he and W moved into. He had the vendor deed the property to H and W "as joint tenants with right of survivorship." W never saw this deed and never discussed with H the manner in which the house would be owned. In 1997, C obtained a judgment of $40,000 against W for nonpayment of a promissory note she had executed in 1982. (W had squandered the borrowed money before meeting H. She was supposed to repay C in 1993.) A few days after C's judgment was filed, H and W separated. Then W's father died and she inherited $20,000.

A. What assets are liable on C's judgment? (Give particular attention to ownership interests in or rights concerning the house.)

B. Assume that before C is paid, H and W are divorced. The spouses neglect to inform the court about C's claim but do provide information concerning all community and separate assets. How will the property be divided? In addition to the house (still worth $50,000) and W's $20,000 inheritance, there is on hand $10,000 of H's pre-separation earnings.

C. After the property is distributed as in Part B, what remedies does C have against H? Against W?

SAMPLE EXAM QUESTION V

In 1996, H and W, then engaged to marry each other, lived in Oregon. Shortly before their wedding, W embezzled funds from her employer, X. After marriage, the couple lived in Oregon for a few months and then moved to California. In 1997, as cohabiting California domiciliaries, H and W held property consisting of the following assets located in California: (1) Blackacre, worth $100,000—W's separate property inherited from her father; (2) Whiteacre, worth $99,000—H's separate property inherited from his mother; (3) $3,000 cash placed in a bank account in W's name only—earnings of H after moving to California; (4) an oil painting worth $1,000 purchased with W's earnings when she and H were married and domiciled in Oregon (a common law state); (5) a community-owned car, of nominal value due to a chattel mortgage on it; (6) a policy of liability insurance covering all tort liability incurred by H or W after its issuance in 1993—all premiums having been paid with H's California earnings. The policy would pay up to $100,000 to any person injured in any one accident, maximum $300,000 per accident.

One day late in 1997, H—with his friend D as a passenger—was driving the community-owned car home from bowling. W and her neighbor N were standing on N's lawn chatting. D negligently distracted H, and H negligently took his eyes off the road. The car struck a dog, left the street, and plowed into W and N, injuring them both. W was rushed to Peace Hospital, which supplied blood for transfusions and rendered other care. Lawsuits in California have resulted in judgments that:

(a) W owes X $40,000 in restitution for the funds she embezzled in 1996.

(b) H and D, equally negligent and both the cause of W's injuries, are liable to W for $75,000 each, for W's pain and suffering and are jointly and severally liable to W for $50,000 in lost earnings.

(c) H and D are each liable to N for $20,000.

(d) Peace Hospital has obtained a judgment for $15,000, the value of services provided to W.

In answering the following questions assume that there are no applicable special exemptions such as homestead exemptions.

A. What assets can X levy execution on? If more than one asset, can H or W require X to proceed first against a particular asset or assets?

B. If D is judgment proof, so that W can collect on her judgment only against H, what properties can she levy on, and how much can she obtain? Can H require her to first exhaust any assets?

C. If D is wealthy and W collects $125,000 from him, what assets can D reach in seeking contribution from H?

D. Disregarding the availability of insurance, what assets can N levy on? If more than one, can H or W require N to proceed first against particular assets?

E. Again disregarding the insurance proceeds, what assets can Peace Hospital reach? If more than one, can H or W require it to proceed first against particular asset(s)?

SAMPLE EXAM QUESTION VI

Hal and Wanda, Ohio domiciliaries, lawfully married in Ohio in 1993. Hal deserted Wanda a month later. During the next year Hal lived alone and made a lot of money as a singer in a rock band. He invested $50,000 of these earnings in an Ohio farm, Blackacre, and another $50,000 in a vacant city lot in Cleveland.

Then Hal met Paula. They dated and Hal proposed marriage. Knowing full well that he was lying, Hal told Paula that he and Wanda were divorced. Paula believed this, and in 1995 she and Hal went through a marriage ceremony in Ohio, where they both were domiciled and where bigamous marriages are void.

Hal and Paula rented an apartment in Ohio and set out to make a living growing exotic herbs on Blackacre. Because of Hal's "green thumb," the operation was a success. After deducting business and household expenses, the profit in 1996 was $30,000, which they invested in corporate stock.

Early in 1997, Hal sold Blackacre for $100,000 and the stock for $30,000. Hal and Paula moved to California and spent the $130,000 cash to buy a motel, taking title in Hal's name. But shortly thereafter, Hal deserted Paula, leaving her to manage the motel. Due to Paula's inexperience, she was lucky to make any profit, yet by the end of 1998 she had saved, after deducting business and household expenses, $6,000, which she placed in a bank account in her name.

A. If Paula and Hal's "marriage" is annulled in a California court, how will the lot in Cleveland (still worth $50,000), the motel (still worth $130,000) and the $6,000 in Paula's bank account be divided? (Assume that Wanda makes any claims she can.)

B. If Hal died intestate before Paula sought an annulment, how would the properties have been distributed? (Again, assume that Wanda makes all colorable claims that she has.)

SAMPLE EXAM QUESTION VII

In 1997, H and W, lawfully married and cohabiting in California, owned: (1) Blackacre, worth $3,000, community property bought with H's earnings but with title taken in H's name alone; (2) Whiteacre, worth $8,000, W's separate property; (3) Greenacre, worth $100,000, H's separate property; and (4) $5,000 in cash, community property in a checking account in H's name. H wanted to buy Redacre for $15,000, which Bank X agreed to loan. H signed a promissory note for $15,000. For security, X demanded and received a mortgage on Blackacre executed by H alone and a mortgage on Whiteacre executed by W.

H paid the $15,000 to the vendor of Redacre and had the vendor execute a deed naming H grantee and reciting that H would own Redacre as his separate property.

Shortly thereafter, a magazine published grisly details about a childhood disease H had suffered. H filed suit for invasion of privacy. He settled for $16,000, which he paid to X, which canceled the note and mortgages. ($1,000 was interest owed X.)

Next, H borrowed $5,000 from Z. H gave Z security consisting of a mortgage on Greenacre. H deposited the $5,000 loan proceeds in the checking account in his name along with the $5,000 of community funds already there. Shortly thereafter, H withdrew $5,000, which he spent to have a water well dug on Redacre. The loan from Z remains unpaid.

H then died with a will leaving "Greenacre to W and the rest of my property to my secretary S."

1. What are the rights of S and W with respect to:

    a. Redacre?

    b. The $5,000 left in the checking account?

2. On the above facts, do W and H's estate have any claims or causes of action against each other? Discuss.

ANSWER TO SAMPLE EXAM QUESTION I

All of the assets mentioned in the problem were community property of H and W. The ring was acquired by H during marriage and is presumptively community. Since no source in bequest, inheritance, gift, or property owned before marriage appears, the presumption cannot be overcome. Although H has not proceeded according to law to perfect title to the ring, he certainly obtained, as finder, some rights to possession superior to strangers and some possibility of acquiring title by prescription. These rights are capable of being community owned by analogy to the treatment of "nonvested" pension rights in *Marriage of Brown*. The fact that H has no contract right to an interest in the ring is not controlling. (*Cf.* the military pension cases where a community interest is recognized although the participant has no contract right at all.)

Thus the $20,000 was community and so was the insurance policy purchased with half of this sum. H may name a beneficiary of only his half of the community interest in the proceeds. M takes that half. The right to the other half was owned by W at her death and passed to Sam under the residuary clause of her will. The right to set aside voidable gifts (such as H's beneficiary designation of W's half interest in the policy) passes to W's personal representative, who can exercise it for Sam's benefit (as to one-half).

By California law, W's half interest in the federal bonds purchased with $10,000 of community property would be subject to her testamentary disposition and pass to Sam under her residuary clause. However, federal legislation and regulations have preempted this aspect of California law and require California to permit H to invest community funds in federal bonds held in joint tenancy, thereby depriving W of her testamentary power. This is not a taking of any property right of W, as testamentary power is not classified as a property right. The power of the federal government to raise funds by selling bonds enables it to legislate in this area. Thus, H got the bonds at W's death via a federally created right of survivorship.

W's will seems clearly to put H (and now his estate) to an election. Sam is devisee of the entire community interest in Greenacre, not just W's half interest. If H's estate wishes to keep H's half interest in Greenacre, H's estate must not accept the bequest of W's half interest in the community law practice. If it does so, an election to accept the will would be implied. H's estate must expressly elect against the will.

It probably could be argued successfully that half of H's goodwill cannot pass to Sam under the residuary clause because the asset, although capable of community ownership, is not alienable and thus not subject to testamentary power; *i.e.*, by necessity, H is W's forced heir of her half of the goodwill. However, half of the accounts receivable and such tangible assets as lawbooks, H's building or leasehold, etc., will pass to Sam as residuary legatee if H elects against the will.

The problem suggests that H died before making an election. His personal representative may do so, and since much of the goodwill has died with H, his estate will make the election by comparing the value of the tangible assets and accounts receivable associated with the law business with the value of Greenacre.

Since H died after 1985, intestate and without issue or a second wife surviving, Sam may possibly have a claim as H's heir under the ancestral property statute. If H's estate elects against W's will, H's estate will contain half of Greenacre, former community realty. The ancestral property statute acts only on one-half of the former community property. According to the theory of this statute, that is the half that Sam already got from W; thus, Sam should not inherit anything from H. If H's estate makes no election, Sam has a claim to half the former community assets in H's law practice under the "item theory" even though Sam received Greenacre, which may be equal to the former community personalty.

ANSWER TO SAMPLE EXAM QUESTION II

Trespass Action

The recital in the bill of sale for the diamonds has no legal significance since H did not agree to it. W's 1959 earnings would have been community property even without the antenuptial agreement. Thus, for purposes of characterizing the diamonds, they are community property even if somehow the nonrecordation of the antenuptial agreement made it totally void. Blackacre, being directly traceable to the diamonds, is community property unless the form of title (in W's name alone) requires a different result.

There is a presumption that when W prior to 1975 acquired property by written instrument naming her a grantee, it was her separate property when she conveyed "any interest"; that would include a leasehold. If her transferee gave "valuable consideration," the presumption was *conclusive* in the transferee's favor. F paid rent, and so he is protected by the presumption, unless the presumption is unconstitutional because of sex discrimination.

Even under California's strict-scrutiny approach to determining whether sex discrimination in legislation denies equal protection, the retention of the presumption to benefit third parties who parted with money in reliance on it is reasonable. It carries forward a limited benefit intended to redress in part the unfairness to which married women had formerly been subjected. On these facts, then, use of the sexually discriminatory presumption is not unconstitutional. F had a valid lease, and H trespassed (there being no suggestion that H as co-landlord of the community-owned Blackacre reserved any right to enter the parcel). Therefore, F will be successful in this action.

Gift to Sis; Suit to Quiet Title

The gift to Sis was contrary to statute. By 1983, W had management power over the community property, but she could not without H's **written** consent and joinder in the instrument of conveyance donate the realty at issue to Sis. There is no special short statute of limitations for H's action to set aside the deed of gift. The facts here suggest nothing was done by Sis in reliance on H's oral approval or even that Sis knew of it; hence, H should not be estopped to invoke the written consent and joinder requirement of California Family Code sections 1100(b) and 1102. Some cases involving land transactions have said that the written consent requirement can be "waived," but this is simply to read it out of the statute. It seems improbable that H's oral approval to W's vague suggestion to give "some land" to Sis could forfeit H's right to void the gift deed. However, transfers in violation of sections 1100(b) (anti-gift statute) and 1102 (joinder in realty conveyance statute) are not void from the outset but are merely voidable. Thus, Sis was the owner of the 10 acres when she rented them to F and should be able to keep the rentals she received for periods prior to H's filing the action to void the deed to Sis. (As lessee of Sis, F will lose his rights in west Blackacre when H voids the deed to Sis. As noted above, F will win the quiet title suit concerning his rights as the lessee of east Blackacre.)

W's Support

W, who is now mentally ill, seems to be in need of support, and H seems able to pay it. While the waiver of post-divorce alimony may be valid, no waiver addresses support during marriage, and in any event, such a waiver is likely against public policy. While failure to record may render the antenuptial contract inapplicable to affected real property, lack of recordation does not invalidate the contract. (The presently effective Uniform Act is clear that the failure to record such an agreement has no effect on its validity between the spouses.)

H's Battery

The community's interest as lessor in Blackacre is liable for H's tort. The portion given to Sis is also liable if H recovers it from Sis. The law is not settled as to whether tort victim F can garnish H's cause of action to recover the realty given to Sis.

There is no indication in the problem that H has any separate property. If he did, W's conservator could compel F to initially levy on the separate property of H and exhaust it before levying on the community-owned Blackacre, if the court determined H's battery of F was not a community tort. Since H was trying to recover possession of community land, however, the community-benefit test possibly is satisfied so that community property is primarily liable to F.

ANSWER TO SAMPLE EXAM QUESTION III

A. The doubling of salary at age 50 is not just a pay raise with income to be earned solely by future (separate) labor by H. At least a portion of the large pay increase is a reward for prior services. However, the pay is frozen for 15 more years at double the 1991 pay (or at that pay if H works half time). A fair apportionment of the bonus-type benefit could be made by treating all of the salary increase in 1991 as a return on prior labor. The court would then calculate the raises in salary generally expected by persons in H's job over 1991-2006 and for each year after 1991 reduce the community fraction of the pay received by H on this basis. An additional apportionment must also be made because not all the labor H devoted to acquiring the double-salary bonus was community labor. The facts suggest that H's separation from W was in fact final in January 1989 (they never spoke again) and not tentative. The community was then broken, and the labor in 1989-1991 was, under California Family Code section 771, separate labor. Since the benefit plan is not funded by contributions, no "money" apportionment can be made, only a time apportionment. The community share of the "extra" salary (beyond what H would earn without the benefit plan) is thus 27/30, of which W gets half.

B. The cottage was initially entirely community. The fact that the 1981 deed was in H's name is irrelevant in determining ownership; the source of payment that obtained the conveyance governs. For eight years, all the payments were community earnings. H's use of post-separation earnings, his separate property, to pay off part of the principal on the mortgage on the cottage could under one line of cases "buy in" to a share of title. Under another line of cases a gift could be presumed, although that seems unrealistic in view of the fact the spouses were separated. California Family Code section 2640, if applicable here, makes the remedy clear: The title remains community and H is entitled to reimbursement without interest to the extent his separate funds reduced the principal owing on the mortgage. Since section 2640 applies to division of all community property at divorce, the form of title is irrelevant. However, application of section 2640 to grant reimbursement for pre-1984 separate property contributions has been held unconstitutional where prior law gave the separate contributor no rights based on the contributions. Since there was no co-ownership *title* for the cottage, the foundation for the *Lucas* rule that eliminated all rights arising out of the contribution is absent. Conceivably, a presumed gift could be found on a different theory, but very likely H's contributions were "buying in" to title when made. If the cottage has appreciated in value, denying H his "buy in" remedy by retroactively applying section 2640 to change his remedy to reimbursement would be unconstitutional.

Note that if H is allowed to "buy in" to title, the 1980 *Moore* case limits his "buy in" to the amount of the mortgage payment that reduced principal. *Moore* firmly establishes that interest, tax, and insurance payments on a purchased piece of realty—whether or not included in mortgage payments—do *not* "buy in" to title. Section 2640 also denies reimbursement for such sums.

If section 2640 applies and H's remedy is reimbursement, a problem arises whether the amount of reimbursement can be reduced by the benefit to H of his occupancy of the cottage for almost three years. Case law would have authorized such a reduction. Section 2640, in stating that the amount of reimbursement is the amount of community contributions to reduce principal, should be viewed as merely fixing a maximum and does not address the problem of reducing the claim for reimbursement because of offsetting equities.

C. The money that H sent W after separation was an "accumulation" of hers while living apart from H [Cal. Fam. Code §771] and her separate property. Thus the commingled account had one-third community funds (rents and profits from community property are still community after separation) and two-thirds separate. The issue arises whether the family-expense doctrine—presumption that community funds are withdrawn from commingled mass to pay for food, clothes, etc.—applies when H and W are separated. The reason for the rule seems absent in the case of separated spouses whose current earnings are separate under section 771. If a court had ordered H to pay W support, his current earnings (separate property under section 771) would have been used by him to pay W in order to preserve the community property for division at a divorce. [Cal. Fam. Code §4338] Apparently then, the one-third of the commingled mass consisting of H's earnings is considered the appropriate source of payment for W's food and clothes, etc.

All of that income has been expended. In addition, $300 per month more has been expended by W. If the family-expense doctrine is wholly inapplicable after separation, the pro-community presumption attaching to the bank account possessed during marriage cannot be overcome as to the remaining contents. On the other hand, if the doctrine is applied, the community funds are gone. An equitable solution might be to assume that W drew community and separate funds pro rata from the account, but there is no California authority to support such a presumption.

D. Unless the tax obligation on the house is considered a support obligation H owed W, he is entitled to reimbursement for paying this community debt with funds made separate by California Family Code section 771. No gift is presumed when post-separation earnings are used to pay nonsupport community debts. Since H was sending W enough money to allow her to maintain herself on two-thirds of her monthly income, it seems she did not need the taxes paid for her support and H should be reimbursed. The community should have paid the taxes. Had the community paid, H would have been out of pocket $1,000 rather than $2,000, so $1,000 is the amount of reimbursement he may obtain.

ANSWER TO SAMPLE EXAM QUESTION IV

[This is a typical exam question where the resolution of a preliminary issue is unclear—the characterization of Blackacre after the marriage could go either way. Thus in resolving the ultimate issues you must first consider the result if Blackacre was transmuted from separate property to community by the antenuptial agreement and second consider the result if it was not.]

A. W's separate property and all the community property except H's earnings are liable for W's premarital contract debt. (Under present law, H's earnings are exempt from liability as long as they are retained in a bank account in his name to which no nonexempt community property is added.) If the house is community, it is because of transmutation; the house does not have a source in H's exempt earnings. Thus, C can reach the entire nonexempt interest if the house is community. If it is joint tenancy property, H's half interest is not liable as it is his separate property. If the house is entirely H's separate property, C can reach nothing.

As property owned by H before marriage, Blackacre was H's separate property. The antenuptial agreement sought to transmute it to community. Like the current Uniform Premarital Agreement Act, a statute in effect in 1983 required an antenuptial contract to be in writing. However, such formalities were not required of pre-1985 postnuptial transmutations, and if H and W "treated" Blackacre as community property after marriage, a postnuptial agreement will be implied. Here, however, H did not treat Blackacre as community property, for he alone sold it to Father at a bargain price (suggesting half gift and half sale) for $50,000.

A few cases suggest that H may be estopped to invoke the Statute of Frauds for antenuptial agreements if W married him in reliance on the oral agreement. The facts here do not make clear whether there was any such reliance by W.

Probably, then, Blackacre was H's separate property when, before 1985 and the enactment of California Family Code section 852, it was "sold" to Father. Therefore, the cash received for Blackacre also was H's separate property. On this theory, H then made a gift to W of her half interest when H had the title of the house bought with his separate funds placed in joint tenancy. Therefore, C could reach only W's half interest in the house, plus W's inheritance.

If W did rely on the oral agreement and H is estopped to deny that the agreement transmuted Blackacre to community property, the issue arises whether the proceeds of Blackacre were transmuted to joint tenancy property by the form of the deed of the house. (Note that this question arises not at divorce but when C levies execution so that the special presumption of Family Code section 2580—that an asset acquired during marriage is community property notwithstanding a joint tenancy deed—is not applicable.) California presumes from a recital of a joint tenancy in a deed that H and W transmuted the community funds used to buy the property to joint tenancy. That presumption is readily overcome here, as the facts show that W was unaware of the joint tenancy recital. H could not unilaterally transmute community funds to joint tenancy. A creditor has standing to impeach a joint tenancy deed. Thus, C can reach the full community interest. (Note that Family Code section 852, enacted in 1985, which also would bar a finding of transmutation for lack of an express declaration in the joint tenancy deed does not apply because it is not retroactive.)

B. In the divorce suit, the absence of joint tenancy ownership of the house is even more easily established because of the presumption of community ownership. (Moreover, joint tenancy property is now divisible at divorce in the same manner as community property.) The question arises whether the presumption of community property ownership can be overcome to establish separate ownership by H. It will be overcome if the antenuptial agreement is invalid so that the money used to buy the house was H's separate property. Family Code section 2580 does not apply retroactively to a 1984 acquisition.

If the antenuptial agreement is valid and the house is community property, apparently the court will have to declare H and W tenant-in-common owners of it, as there is not enough community cash to award the house to one spouse and an equal amount of cash to the other. If the party getting the house executed a $30,000 promissory note and gave up all community interest in the $10,000, that would not equalize the division, as the note's market value would probably be less. Thus, although a division making H and W tenants in common is discouraged by the appellate courts, there is not much else to be done here with the house if it is community.

C. All property that W owns after divorce is now her separate property and is liable to C (even if it previously was exempt). Since H was not the obligor on the debt and was not specifically ordered to pay it, it seems that he could not be liable. However, if the debt owed C were a community debt, in order to effectuate a 50-50 division of the community, H would be implicitly required by the divorce decree to pay half of it, and C probably could assert such liability. The point is moot, however, since W's premarital debt could not have benefited the community and must be classified as her separate debt, which was implicitly assigned to her by the divorce decree to effect an equal division of the community.

ANSWER TO SAMPLE EXAM QUESTION V

A. W's separate property is liable on the judgment against her. This includes Blackacre and the painting (its quasi-community nature being irrelevant since it is liable under either classification). H's separate property is not liable. Under present law, H's separate property is liable for W's contract only with respect to obligations for "necessaries" incurred for her benefit during marriage (not the case with X's claim).

H's community earnings are exempt for both tortious and contractual premarital debts of W but only if kept in a bank account in H's name alone. Here, H's earnings are in an account in W's name alone, so the $3,000 is liable. However, H's putting W's name on the bank account is not a transmutation due to lack of an express writing. H can protect the $3,000 in community by invoking California Family Code section 1000(b). W's premarital tort is obviously a separate tort under the "community benefit" test of section 1000(b), enabling H to compel X to levy on W's separate property, which is adequate to pay X off, rather than the cash.

The oil painting is quasi-community property, but sections 901 and 912 direct that such assets be treated as community property for all purposes of debt collection. Thus, H can prevent X from seizing it. Section 1000(b) may not cover all torts, but W's wrong to X seems clearly an "injury to property." Section 1000(b) seems applicable to premarital torts when liability is discharged after marriage.

B. All of the property in which H has an interest is liable on his tort judgment obtained against him by W. Under California Family Code section 782, H is required to first pay W with his separate property, with one exception: Liability proceeds from a community-owned policy may be used even before H's separate property. Thus $100,000 of insurance proceeds first will be paid to W. The statute is unclear as to whether this discharges $100,000 of liability or $50,000. The recovery becomes W's separate property pursuant to section 781, and since W already owns half of the $100,000 of community proceeds, conceivably payment of these should satisfy only $50,000 of the judgment. W can then compel H to resort to Whiteacre to pay the judgment before using the community cash. If community cash were used, such payments logically should discharge the debt of H only to the extent of his half interest.

C. Section 782 makes the same rules discussed in part B above applicable when H pays contribution to a joint tortfeasor. W is entitled to protect the community cash but not the insurance proceeds. H will use the insurance proceeds to pay off D (and, since D has no preexisting ownership interest in them, each dollar D receives pays off a dollar owed him). Should the insurance company not pay D and D were to levy execution on community property, section 781 entitles W to compel D instead to obtain satisfaction out of H's separately owned Whiteacre.

D. All of H's separate property and the community property are liable to N. Recreational activity of H is for the benefit of the community under the test of California Family Code section 1000(b). Thus, as H injured N while driving home from bowling, H can compel N to levy first on the community cash (because the bank account is in W's name only, H cannot simply pay the cash to N) before reaching his other assets. The fact that W has exclusive management of the $3,000 under California Finance Code section 851 does not mean that H's creditor cannot reach it. Apparently W cannot object on a statutory basis if N goes after the oil painting first, but W can assert that treating her quasi-community property as if co-owned by H prior to dissolution of marriage is an unconstitutional taking of her property.

E. W implicitly contracted with Peace Hospital to supply her necessaries. Of course, her separate property and the community property are liable. H's separate property is liable, too, if the "necessaries" doctrine applies. California Family Code section 4301 literally seems to say that H's separate property is not liable because there exists some community property and some quasi-community property (the oil painting). But if Peace levies first on the community cash and the oil painting, the bars to liability of H's separate property for the "necessaries" debt should be removed. In effect, section 4301 then establishes a priority of liability. That statute does not empower H to require exhaustion of W's non-quasi-community separate property (Blackacre) before H's separate property can be seized.

ANSWER TO SAMPLE EXAM QUESTION VI

A. Rights at Annulment

Since Paula and Hal lived together as husband and wife while domiciled in California, this state has sufficient minimal contacts to apply its quasi-community property system and putative marriage system to them in adjusting property rights at annulment. Although the bigamous marriage was void, one party to the "marriage," Paula, believed in good faith in its validity. At least as to her, the marriage is putative. (No facts suggest that Paula's belief was objectively unreasonable.) The statute defining quasi-marital property, California Family Code section 2251, expressly includes quasi-community property, which is the property that would have been community had the parties been domiciled in California at the time of acquisition. At annulment and divorce, quasi-community property includes out-of-state realty [Cal. Fam. Code §125], although a statute directs the court to make, if practicable, a property division that does not disturb the manner in which title to such realty is held [Cal. Fam. Code §2660].

The vacant lot that Hal bought before "marrying" Paula is Hal's purely separate, non-quasi-marital property. Paula has no claim to it (nor does Wanda under California law, if she were to divorce Hal here, as he acquired it after he and Wanda began living separate and apart).

The character of the motel depends on the character of the cash used to buy it under principles of tracing. (If tracing breaks down, the presumption that acquisitions during marriage are community could apply by analogy in favor of a putative spouse to establish that an acquisition is quasi-marital.) At least 50/130 of the purchase price was Hal's purely separate property—being traced to the cash he earned before "marrying" Paula and which he invested in Blackacre. The portion of Blackacre's rise in value due to inflation and market pressures is also purely separate property of Hal and not quasi-community. To the extent labor of Hal or Paula increased Blackacre's value, there is a quasi-community right to reimbursement, assuming the complete community property system is applied by analogy to quasi-community, quasi-marital situations.

The $30,000 earnings from the herb-farming business must be apportioned as partly quasi-community, partly a purely separate return on Blackacre. Since labor is the chief contributing factor and the gain is high compared to value of capital, the applicable test is *Pereira*. This gives Hal one year's legal interest (or other appropriate rate according to proof) as a purely separate return on or from capital. The balance of the $30,000 gain is attributed to labor.

It may be necessary to divide the gain from labor into two parts, that attributable to Hal and that to Paula. The California Supreme Court has held that it is an open question whether the statute creating quasi-marital property rights permits a "guilty" "spouse" (*i.e.*, Hal, who knew that his "marriage" was bigamous) to share in the gains due to labor of the other "spouse." Under the *case law* jurisprudence respecting putative marriages, Hal could not share in Paula's gains, and a portion of the $30,000 should be segregated as Paula's purely separate property.

Thus, the cash paid for the motel was probably owned by a three-part co-tenancy in fractions perhaps like this: primarily Hal's pure separate property; a small fraction quasi-community property; and a small fraction Paula's purely separate property. The motel is owned in the same fractions.

It is next necessary to apportion the savings Paula made managing the motel while living separate and apart from Hal. A reverse *Pereira-Van Camp* approach is used. The court either finds a fair salary for Paula's purely separate labor or a fair return for the capital, most of which benefits Hal, since it is primarily his purely separate property. Capital seems to be the chief contributing factor to the gain, and the gain seems to be relatively small. Therefore reverse *Pereira* is used. Applying even the low legal interest rate to the $130,000 worth of capital, it is clear that the full amount of $6,000 saved is a return of capital. (Paula will be presumed to have treated the funds that she withdrew and spent for herself as her salary.) The return on capital calculated under reverse *Pereira* is owned in the same fractions as the motel itself.

The court will divide the property that is both quasi-community and quasi-marital 50-50 at annulment. Title to purely separate property cannot be disturbed.

B. Rights at Death of Hal

The analysis applicable at annulment also applies in characterizing all of the assets at Hal's death, except the lot in Cleveland. No statute governs the rights of a putative spouse at death of the other, but case law has accorded the good faith survivor at least half of the decedent's earnings during the marriage.

Ohio law will govern the inheritance of the lot in Cleveland. When a lawfully married couple's union is dissolved by death, the definition of quasi-community property excludes foreign realty [Cal. Prob. Code §101], and by analogy, such foreign realty would be excluded when the marriage was only putative.

At death, Paula is owner of half of the quasi-marital property. Hal could have disposed of his half of the quasi-marital property and all assets traceable to his purely separate property (Ohio gains after separating from Wanda and before "marrying" Paula) by will. However, he died intestate. Although it seems unfair, under *Estate of Hafner* it seems that Paula, having taken half as owner, must yield half to Wanda as intestate heir. (The *Hafner* dissent would have Paula share as heir.) As to the purely separate property, neither Paula nor Wanda has a claim as owner and, despite the preference given in *Hafner* for inheritance of separate property by the lawful wife, it is possible that the courts, reading both *Hafner* and *Estate of Leslie*, would make the women co-equal heirs of the purely separate property.

ANSWER TO SAMPLE EXAM QUESTION VII

[This is as difficult and tricky a question as you are likely to encounter in any law school or bar exam.]

1. The Effect of H's Will

H could exercise testamentary power over all of his separate property and his undivided half interest in each item of community property. The language "my property" is construed to mean only H's half interest in items of community. Accordingly, W is not put to an election that would cause her to forfeit Greenacre when she asserts a community interest in Redacre and the $5,000.

a. Characterization of Redacre

The recital in the deed of Redacre to H that it is his separate property has no legal effect, as there is no evidence of any express writing signed or accepted by W that could be treated as transmuting any interest of W to H's separate property. So, the analysis begins with a presumption (since H possessed and acquired Redacre during marriage and cohabitation with W) that it is community. S must demonstrate some source in H's separate estate if she is to get more than a half interest by devise. If W wants to claim Redacre as her separate property, she must show a separate source of her own.

Redacre took on the character of separate or community property when it was deeded to H, and short of a transmutation agreement between H and W, subsequent events would not change that characterization. (The statement of the *Moore* case that a subsequent repayment of a purchase money mortgage can alter the ownership of the encumbered property is probably inapplicable here—Redacre was never mortgaged and the repayment to X did not increase any equity in Redacre.)

Redacre can be traced back to the borrowed money used to buy it. Classification of borrowed money turns on the nature of the credit on which the lender relied. The law asks what lender X was *predominantly* relying on for repayment. [*Comment:* Although one case by the intermediate appellate court holds that loan proceeds obtained during marriage are community unless the lender intended to look solely to separate property for repayment, there is still strong case law support for the "predominant intent" test.] The majority of the cases presume that the lender relies primarily on any security interest he obtained. The cases have yet to divide loan proceeds as part community, part separate, so the significant security interest here is the mortgage on Whiteacre given by W, worth more than twice the other mortgaged parcel. Because of it, the loan proceeds appear to be W's separate property, and so would be Redacre, notwithstanding the "title" in H. (*Note:* The Blackacre mortgage was also completely voidable because W did not sign it.)

However, Whiteacre is worth just over half the amount owed X. Thus, arguably X was relying mainly on the $100,000 value of Greenacre for repayment of H's promissory note, since no deficiency judgment is barred in this type of transaction where the item purchased is not mortgaged. (H's separate property is of course liable on his note.) This would make the loan proceeds H's separate property. If X relied primarily on H and W's earnings, the proceeds were community.

b. Characterization of the $5,000 Cash on Hand

The $5,000 H got by mortgaging Greenacre was H's separate property under the rules of law discussed above. H commingled the $5,000 with $5,000 community property and then withdrew $5,000 to improve Redacre. The latter was probably either community property or H's separate property. The intent of the drawer, H, governs whether community or separate property is taken from a commingled mass. With H dead here, we have no direct evidence of what he intended. Since he apparently thought Redacre was his separate property, it is arguable that he intended to withdraw separate funds to improve it. However, California has held that there is no presumption as to the nature of funds used to improve a piece of property. It is thus impossible for S to overcome the presumption that the $5,000 in the bank account, an asset possessed by H and W during marriage, was community. (Moreover, if the court refuses to apply the pro-community general presumption except on proof of *acquisition* during marriage, it seems clear that the bank account of $5,000 in the names of H and W—an asset consisting of a chose in action against the bank—was *acquired* during marriage.) S gets $2,500 and W gets $2,500, assuming that there are no creditors to pay off.

2. Reimbursement Causes of Action

Dissolution of the community by H's death is one of the occasions when spousal claims to reimbursement may be asserted. H's personal representative may assert H's reimbursement claims. First, H used his tort recovery of $16,000 *in effect* to pay for Redacre. While Redacre is probably H's separate property, it could be W's separate property (based on the security that she gave to generate loan proceeds used for the purchase). If it is, at the very least, W was benefited to the extent of $8,000, for she had mortgaged Whiteacre, and H's payment to X "improved" Whiteacre by causing cancellation of the encumbrance. The tort recovery was community property. H's right not to have his childhood disease publicly disclosed by a magazine may have been one he possessed before marriage, but is not a pre-marriage "property" right he can trace to. Tracing back in time beyond the occurrence of the tort is not done in California, so the presumption that the acquisition (a cause of action) is community cannot be overcome. A presumption of gift by H in "improving" W's estate to the extent of his half of the community funds used to remove the lien on Whiteacre possibly can be overcome. H apparently thought that he was paying off a loan taken out to acquire *his* separate property. So H's estate has a reimbursement claim for half the community property used to benefit W's separate estate—perhaps half of $16,000, at least half of $8,000. (The *Lucas* case requires an agreement between H and W to preserve a right of reimbursement when a spouse uses funds owned by him—H owns half the community—to pay off a mortgage on property owned by the other estate, but *Lucas* should be limited to purchase money mortgages and should not apply to "pure" improvement situations. Also, *Lucas* possibly is limited to cases when title is in the joint names of H and W.)

A presumption of gift to W arising out of H's improving Redacre by having the water well constructed may be overcome here, as it seems that H thought Redacre was his. (At this stage, we are assuming that Redacre was W's separate property.) Additionally, it would seem that if the $5,000 still in the bank account is treated by W as community in resisting S's claim of bequest, W must concede the $5,000 spent on the well was H's separate property, and so reimbursement will be asserted for that amount. (There is no evidence that the value added by the well was less than the amount spent.)

Reimbursement claims in California are not secured by a lien. They seem to be treated as creditor claims, and the separate property of the debtor (W here) as well as her half of the community property would be liable.

This treatment of the $5,000 borrowed on security of Greenacre as H's separate property means that the $5,000 debt owed Z is a separate debt of H (it generated for his estate a separate claim for reimbursement). W can obtain a probate court order that H's separate property be used to pay Z. The separate debt will be assigned to H's separate property for payment.

TABLE OF CITATIONS TO CALIFORNIA FAMILY CODE

U.C.C. Section	Text Reference
125	§455
308	§398
700	§230
721	§166
721(b)	§§261, 262, 265, 338
760	§§1, 5, 11
770	§§2, 33, 446
770(a)(3)	§456
771	§§2, 12, 43, 44, 45, 46, 47, 48, 49, 58, 75, 296, 304, 429, 475, 477
781	§156
781(a)	§138
781(a)(2)	§§136, 141
781(b)	§137
781(c)	§§151, 152, 153
782	§§292, 294
783	§§154, 164
802	§§19, 20, 21
803	§§22, 24, 25, 26, 468
852	§§174, 175, 179, 180, 189
852(c)	§§125, 176
852(d)	§§69, 177
853	§178
910	§§273, 275, 477, 480
911	§§281, 506
912	§273
913(a)	§274
913(b)	§274
914	§276
914(b)	§§280, 341
915(a)	§282
915(b)	§§282, 341
916	§298
916(a)(2)	§300
916(a)(3)	§303
916(b)	§302
920	§§288, 341, 342
1000	§291
1000(b)	§§283, 285, 286, 289, 290, 291, 325
1000(b)(1)	§284
1000(b)(2)	§287
1000(c)	§288
1100	§222
1100(2)	§217
1100(b)	§§248, 249, 250, 252, 253, 254, 255
1100(c)	§§225, 226, 227

U.C.C. Section	Text Reference
1100(d)	§§218, 220, 221, 233
1100(e)	§§261, 262, 338
1101	§268
1101(a)	§266
1101(c)	§233
1101(d)	§266
1101(e)	§240
1101(g)	§266
1102	§§228, 229, 234, 236, 238, 258
1102(c)	§§231, 232
1102(d)	§242
1611	§167
1614	§167
1615	§168
2102	§§263, 265
2200	§406
2210	§406
2251	§§394, 401, 402, 411, 416, 425
2251(a)	§401
2254	§414
2550	§§308, 336, 401
2552(a)	§331
2556	§345
2580	§190
2581	§§124, 126, 192, 307, 478
2601	§317
2602	§§267, 268, 269
2603	§§141, 143, 144, 145, 146, 147, 148, 155, 156, 159, 163, 333
2604	§334
2610	§§198, 199, 503
2621	§325
2622	§325
2622(b)	§§321, 325
2623	§325
2624	§325
2625	§325
2627	§325
2640	§§103, 114, 124, 125, 126, 191, 192, 478
2641	§§200, 326
2650	§§193, 307
2660	§335
4301	§59
4302	§§170, 277
4338	§§304, 305

TABLE OF CASES

Abdale, Estate of - §371
Adams, Estate of - §§14, 371
Addison v. Addison - §§474, 478
Adduddell v. Board of Administration - §420
Allen v. Western Conference of Teamsters - §420
American Olean Title Co. v. Schultze - §297
Anderson, Estate of - §399
Andrade Development Co. v. Martin - §247
Ashodian, Marriage of - §§27, 28
Aubrey v. Folsom - §410
Aufmuth, Marriage of - §§205, 206

Baragry, Marriage of - §46
Barreiro, Estate of - §110
Baxter, Estate of - §371
Beam v. Bank of America - §74
Beebe v. Moormack Gulf Lines - §505
Beemer v. Roher - §362
Behrens, Marriage of - §89
Belmont v. Belmont - §131
Biane, *In re* - §217
Boggs v. Boggs - §§493, 504
Bone v. Dwyer - §8
Bouquet, Marriage of - §§473, 475, 476, 477, 478
Boyd v. Oser - §469
Brennfleck v. Workmen's Compensation Appeals Board - §419
Brigden, Marriage of - §317
Brown, Marriage of - §§208, 310, 312
Bruggemeyer, Estate of - §447
Buol, Marriage of - §§60, 478
Burrows, Estate of - §447
Byrd v. Blanton - §242

Campa, Marriage of - §501
Cardew v. Cardew - §26
Carlson v. Carlson - §§485, 490
Carnall, Marriage of - §199
Cary, Marriage of - §401
Casas v. Thompson - §493
Caswell, Estate of - §10
Centinela Hospital v. Superior Court - §397
Cervantes v. Maco Gas Co. - §162
Chala, Marriage of - §324
Christiana v. Rose - §163
Clark, Estate of - §35
Coats v. Coats - §406

Cohen, Marriage of - §226
Cord v. Neuhoff - §67
Cramer, Marriage of - §199

Dawes v. Rich - §384
Dawley, Marriage of - §169
Dekker, Marriage of - §§71, 74
Denney, Marriage of - §67
Dennis, Marriage of - §329
Dillard v. Dillard - §102
Downer v. Bramet - §38
Drahos v. Rens - §107
Droeger v. Friedman, Sloan & Ross - §241
Duncan v. United States - §62
Dunn v. Mullan - §§26, 122
Durrell v. Bacon - §172
Dynan v. Gallinatti - §226

Eastis, Marriage of - §320
Eldon v. Sheldon - §437
Elfmont, Marriage of - §§158, 161
Ellis v. Ellis - §486
Epstein, Marriage of - §§58, 60, 170
Estate of - *see* name of party

Fabian, Marriage of - §478
Falk v. Falk - §62
Fidelity & Casualty Co. v. Mahoney - §§7, 8
Fields v. Michael - §268
Fincher, Estate of - §433
Fisk, Marriage of - §156
Fithian, Marriage of - §209
Flanagan v. Capital National Bank - §400
Flockhart, Marriage of - §44
Flores v. Brown - §§149, 163
Folb, Marriage of - §§65, 66
Ford v. Ford - §§96, 100, 452
Forrest, Marriage of - §214
Fortier, Marriage of - §204
Foy, Estate of - §396
Free v. Bland - §497
Freese v. Hibernia Savings & Loan Society - §17
Freiberg, Marriage of - §85
Frick, Marriage of - §§112, 113, 128
Frymire v. Brown - §33

George v. Ransom - §464
Giacomazzi v. Rowe - §111
Goff v. Goff - §408

Gonzales, Marriage of (1981) - §40
Gregory v. Gregory - §128
Grinius, Marriage of - §97
Gudelj v. Gudelj - §98

Hafner, Estate of - §429
Hague v. Allstate Insurance Co. - §459
Hanley v. Most - §252
Hansford v. Lassar - §§185, 188
Hardin, Marriage of - §47
Harrington, Marriage of - §329
Harris v. Harris - §§257, 486
Harrod v. Pacific Southwest Airlines - §436
Heikes, Marriage of - §479
Hendricks, *In re* - §324
Hicks v. Hicks - §56
Hilke, Marriage of - §190
Hisquierdo v. Hisquierdo - §§489, 490, 491, 493, 494, 495, 496
Horn, Marriage of - §160
Huber v. Huber - §55
Hug, Marriage of - §§91, 213

Imperato, Marriage of - §75

Jackson v. Swift & Co. - §415
Janes v. LeDeit - §234
Jaschke, Marriage of - §49
Joaquin, Marriage of - §83

Kane v. Huntley Financial - §197
Kelley, Estate of - §359
Kennedy v. Taylor - §194
Kesler v. Pabst - §165
King v. Uhlmann - §238
King, Estate of - §355
Knickerbocker, Marriage of - §309
Krattiger v. Krattiger - §11
Kuzmiak v. Kuzmiak - §§160, 161

Lantis v. Condon - §154
Lawson v. Ridgeway - §128
Lazzarevich v. Lazzarevich - §§413, 415
Leslie, Estate of - §§417, 429
Lionberger, Marriage of - §§313, 502
Logan, Estate of - §95
Long v. Long - §105
Lopez, Marriage of - §74
Lorenz v. Lorenz - §§94, 344
Lucas, Marriage of - §§123, 124, 126, 478
Lucero, Marriage of - §§214, 263

Lusk, Marriage of - §§5, 6, 11
Lynam v. Worwerk - §9

MacDonald, Estate of - §§175, 178, 189
MacGregor v. Unemployment Insurance Appeals Board - §436
McBride v. McBride (1936) - §§92, 345
McCarty v. McCarty - §§491, 493, 494, 496
McCune v. Essig - §486
McKay v. Lauriston - §469
Machado v. Machado - §186
Makeig v. United Security Bank & Trust Co. - §45
Mamula v. McCulloch - §239
Mansell v. Mansell - §493
Mark v. Title Guarantee Trust Co. - §§232, 245
Marriage of - *see* name of party
Marsden, Marriage of - §§54, 112
Marvin v. Marvin - §§393, 401, 413, 415, 430, 431, 433, 434, 435, 436, 437, 438, 439, 441, 442, 443
Melvin v. Carl - §448
Menchaca v. Farmers Insurance Exchange - §409
Milhan, Marriage of - §§484, 494
Mix, Marriage of - §§27, 53, 54
Moore, Estate of - §§351, 353
Moore, Marriage of - §§80, 111, 121, 267
Munguia, Marriage of - §262
Murphy, Estate of - §350

Neilson, Estate of - §173
Nelson, Marriage of - §§91, 213
Nevins v. Nevins - §17
Newell v. Brawner - §222
Nizenkoff, Marriage of - §487
Noe v. Card - §116
Noghrey, Marriage of - §169
Norman v. Unemployment Insurance Appeals Board - §436
Novo v. Hotel del Rio - §§249, 250

Oakley v. Oakley - §409
Olson, Marriage of - §332
Ortega v. Ortega - §77
Owens v. Owens - §71

Paley v. Bank of America - §476
Patillo v. Norris - §422
Peck v. Brummagin - §109
Pendleton, Marriage of - §170

Pereira v. Pereira - §§64, 65, 66, 69, 71, 72, 73, 74, 75, 76, 108, 130, 143, 207, 296, 340
Phillips, Estate of - §470
Poppe, Marriage of - §87
Prince v. Hopson - §428
Provost v. Provost - §336

Raphael, Estate of - §171
Reckart v. Arva Valley Air, Inc. - §286
Recknor, Marriage of - §399
Reilley, Marriage of - §121
Roberts v. Wehmeyer - §469
Robertson v. Willis - §§471, 472, 480
Robinson, Marriage of - §157
Rodriguez v. Bethlehem Steel Corp. - §155
Roebling v. Office of Personnel Management - §502
Roesch, Marriage of - §459
Rozan v. Rozan - §453
Rupley, Estate of - §83
Russell v. Williams - §132

Sail'er Inn v. Kirby - §§31, 467
Sanguinetti v. Sanguinetti - §411
Saslow, Marriage of - §158
Scoville v. Keglor - §129
See v. See - §§57, 58, 59, 60, 61
Seligman v. Seligman - §128
Shattuck, Marriage of - §314
Shaw v. Bernal - §180
Sheldon, Estate of - §167
Sheppard v. Sheppard - §507
Siddall v. Haight - §83
Simonton v. Los Angeles Trust & Savings Bank - §374
Skaden, Marriage of - §212
Slater, Marriage of - §206
Soto v. Vandeventer - §142
Sousa v. Freitas - §§407, 427
Sparks, Marriage of - §§106, 107, 109
Spengler, Marriage of - §93
Springer v. Commissioner - §173
Stenquist, Marriage of - §159
Stitt, Marriage of - §§291, 325

Tammen, Marriage of - §328
Tassi v. Tassi - §71
Thomasset v. Thomasset - §51

Todd v. McColgan - §§73, 74
Tolman v. Smith - §181
Tomaier v. Tomaier - §§185, 452
Tompkins v. Superior Court - §313
Trimble v. Trimble - §243
Turner, Estate of - §108
Tyre v. Aetna Life Insurance Co. - §§356, 360, 361, 363

United States v. Overman - §506

Valle, Marriage of - §264
Van Camp v. Van Camp - §§69, 70, 71, 72, 73, 74, 75, 76, 108, 130, 143, 207, 296, 340
Vargas, Estate of - §§423, 426, 427, 428
Vierra v. Pereira - §236
Vieux v. Vieux - §78
Vryonis, Marriage of - §§396, 397

Wagner v. County of Imperial - §397
Wahlefeld, Estate of - §167
Walrath, Marriage of - §124
Walsh, Estate of - §179
Warren, Marriage of - §§119, 120
Washington v. Washington - §§143, 163
Watts, Marriage of - §340
Wedemeyer v. Elmer - §111
Weinberg v. Weinberg - §339
Welder v. Welder - §62
Wells v. Allen - §28
Westerman, Estate of - §374
Wheeland v. Rodgers - §103
Wikes v. Smith - §196
Wilkinson v. Wilkinson - §405
Williams, Marriage of - §322
Williams v. Williams - §262
Wilson v. Wilson - §11
Winn, Marriage of - §68
Wisnom v. McCarthy - §278
Wissner v. Wissner - §§343, 482, 483, 484, 485
Wolfe, Estate of - §352
Woodall v. Commissioner - §465
Woods v. Security First National Bank - §§167, 172
Wren v. Wren - §172

Yiatchos v. Yiatchos - §§498, 499, 500

INDEX

A

ACQUISITION OF PROPERTY
  See also Classification of property; Descent or bequest; Gifts; Presumptions
  after dissolution, §14
  by labor
    putative marriage, §§403-410
  commingling. *See* Commingling
  credit acquisitions, §§96-102
  descent or bequest, §§33-35. *See also* Descent or bequest
    to both spouses, §34
    tracing, §35
  gifts, §§36-42. *See also* Gifts
    to both spouses, §§40-42
      wedding gifts, §§41-42
    to one spouse, §§36-39
      partial donative intent, §37
      unclear intent, §39
  inception of title doctrine, §§81-84
    California law, §82
    land acquired by labor, §83
    lease renewals, §84
  installment purchases, §§78-84
    transmutation. *See* Gifts
  mixed consideration, §§77-95. *See also* Mixed consideration
  rents and profits, §§2, 63-76. *See also* Rents and profits
  while living apart, §§12-13, 43-49
    intent, §§45-47
    reconciliation, §49
    separation, §48
    tracing, §44
    unilateral intent, §47
ALIENATION OF LAND, §§229-247
ALIMONY, §§304-305
  debt payment as, §324
  premarital debt, §282
  putative marriage, §414
  waiver, §170
ANCESTRAL PROPERTY RULES, §§365-374
ANNULMENT
  lack of good faith, §§395-402
  quasi-marital property, §§402, 411-413
ANTENUPTIAL AGREEMENTS, §§166-170
APPORTIONMENT
  credit acquisitions, §§96-102
    other spouse's signature, §100
    repaying loan, §101
    security, §§98-99
    Texas rule, §102
  "improvement" cases, §§103-128
    and creditors, §§109-110
    fixtures doctrine, §§104-107
    gifts, §§122-126
    lien, §127
    mortgage payments, §§111-115
    reimbursement, §§116-121
      offset, §121
    scope of doctrine, §108
    source of funds unknown, §127
  inception of title doctrine, §§81-84
  life insurance, §§92-95
  mixed consideration, §§77-95. *See also* Acquisition of property
  pension benefits, §§85-91. *See also* Pension benefits
  rents and profits, §§63-76, 113
    community capital and separate labor, §§75-76
    "compromise" formula, §§73-74
    Pereira formula, §§64-76
    pre-marriage appreciation, §113
    reverse apportionment, §§75-76
    Van Camp formula, §§70-76
  tort recoveries. *See* Tort recoveries
ARMED SERVICES INSURANCE, §§483-485
ASSIGNMENT OF DEBTS, §§320-326

B

BANKRUPTCY, §§322-323
BIGAMY
  See Marriage, putative
BONDS
  federal, §§497-500
BURDEN OF PROOF
  general presumption, §§16-18
BUSINESS GOODWILL, §§204-207. *See also* Goodwill
"BUYING IN"
  See "Improvement" cases

C

CHARACTERIZATION
  See Classification of property; Conflict of laws
CHILD SUPPORT
  liability, §282
CHOICE OF LAW
  See Conflict of laws
CLASSIFICATION OF PROPERTY
  See also Acquisition of property; Apportionment; Descent or bequest; Gifts; Separate property
  community property defined, §1
  pension plans. *See* Pension benefits
  presumptions. *See* Presumptions
  rents and profits, §2. *See also* Rents and profits
  separate property defined, §2
COLLEGE DEGREES
  See Educational degrees
COMMINGLING, §§51-62
  and debt liability, §281
  and "pro-wife" presumption, §§27-31
  drawer's intent, §§53-54
  family expense doctrine, §§55-61
  intent unprovable, §62
COMMON LAW MARRIAGES
  See Marriages, putative
"COMPROMISE" FORMULA, §§73-74
CONFIRMATION PROCEEDINGS, §§378-380
CONFLICT OF LAWS, §§444-463

Community Property—155

choice of law problems, §§444-453
    acquisitions by nondomiciliaries, §§445-448
        California approach, §§447-448
    out-of-state acquisitions, §§449-453
        contracts, §450
        land, §§452-453
    torts, §451
    transmutation, §448
quasi-community property, §§454-463
    characterization, §§455-458
    death, §§460-463
    defined, §455
    divorce, §§458-459

CONSORTIUM, LOSS OF, §§155, 437
    See also Tort recoveries

CONSTITUTIONAL LAW, §§464-507
    California Constitution, §§464-468
    due process, §§469-480
    equal protection, §§467-468
    preemption, §§481-507. *See also* Preemption doctrine
    pro-wife presumption, §31

CONSTRUCTIVE TRUST, §441
    See also Marvin relationship

CONTRACTS
    antenuptial, §§166-170
    between spouses, §§166-197. *See also* Transmutation
        effect on creditors, §196
        postnuptial transmutation, §§171-178
        "treatment" of property, §173
    choice of law, §450
    death of spouse and, §361
    disability benefits, §§158-161
    installment, §§78-84
    Marvin relationship, §§430-435. *See also Marvin* relationship
    ownership of, §79
        executory contracts, §79
    rescission of land contracts, §239

CONTRIBUTORY NEGLIGENCE
    See Tort recoveries

CREDIT ACQUISITIONS, §§96-102

CREDITORS' RIGHTS
    See Debt, liability for

D

DEBT, LIABILITY FOR, §§273-305
    after death, §§384-390
    alimony, §§282, 304-305
    community property liable, §273
    "earnings," §281
    effect of divorce, §§298-303. *See also* Divorce
    effect of separation, §§295-297
    general rule, §§273-275
    "improvement" cases, §§103-127
    interspousal contracts, §§193-196
    necessaries, §§276-280
        reimbursement, §280
        third-party contracts, §279
    premarital debts, §§281-282
    separate debts, reimbursement for, §339
    separate property not liable, §274

tort liability, §§283-294
    "combination" torts, §289
    community torts, §§284-286
    interspousal liability, §§292-294
    libel and slander, §291
    reimbursement, §288
    separate torts, §287
    spouses as joint tortfeasors, §290

DEEDS
    See Title

DEGREES
    See Educational degrees

DESCENT OR BEQUEST
    See also Testamentary power
    acquisition by, §§33-35
    tracing, §35

DISSOLUTION OF COMMUNITY
    See Descent or bequest; Divorce; Probate administration; Testamentary power

DIVISION OF PROPERTY
    See Divorce

DIVORCE
    division of community property, §§308-346
        assignment of debts, §§320-326
            as alimony, §324
            separate debts, §§325-326
        bankruptcy, §§322-323
        default divorce, §334
        equal division exceptions, §§333-335
        general rule, §308
        out-of-state land, §335
        pension interests, §§310-315
        promissory note, §§316-319
            impaired value test, §§317-319
        tenant in common divisions, §§307, 309-315
        tort recovery, §§144-148, 333
        valuing assets and debts, §§327-332
            pension plans, §330
            promissory note, §328
            tax liability, §329
    division of separate property, §306
    failure to distribute, §§345-346
    interspousal debts, §§336-342
        benefit test, §§325-326
        separate debt, §§325-326
    nondistributable community assets, §§343-344
    quasi-community property, §§458-459

DOMICILE
    See Conflict of laws

DONATIVE INTENT
    See Gifts

DUAL MANAGEMENT
    See Management and control

DUE PROCESS, §§469-480

"DURING MARRIAGE" TEST, §§5-8

E

EARNED EXPECTANCIES, §§209-214
    merit raises, §211
    tips, §210

"EARNINGS," §§1-2, 281-282
EDUCATIONAL DEGREES, §§199-203, 326
ELECTION BY SURVIVING SPOUSE
    See Testamentary power
EMPLOYEE RETIREMENT INCOME SECURITY ACT
    See ERISA pensions
EQUAL MANAGEMENT
    See Management and control
EQUAL PROTECTION, §§467-468
ERISA PENSIONS, §§501-503
    See also Pension benefits
EVIDENCE
    and pro-community presumption, §§4-10, 15-18
        rebuttal of, §32
    pro-wife presumption, §§22-31
EXPECTANCIES, EARNED
    See Earned expectancies

F

FAMILY EXPENSE DOCTRINE, §§55-61
    See also Commingling
FEDERAL LANDS, §486
FIDUCIARY DUTY OF SPOUSE, §§261-269
    See also Management and control
FIXTURES DOCTRINE, §§104-107

G

GIFTS
    business gifts, §253
    "improvement" cases, §§122-126
    joint tenancies, §126
    power to donate community property, §§248-260
    presumption, §122
    quasi-community property, §269
    remedy against transferor spouse, §§259-260
    to both spouses, §§40-42
        wedding gifts, §§41-42
    to one spouse, §§36-39
        partial donative intent, §37
        tips, §38
        unclear intent, §39
    tracing, §124
    transmutation, §§179-180
    "trifles," §252
GOODWILL, §§204-207
    after remarriage, §207
    partnerships, §206
    professional corporations, §205
GRATUITIES, §§38, 210
    after divorce, §213

H

HOMESTEAD STATUTES, §486

I

IMPAIRED VALUE TEST, §§317-319
"IMPROVEMENT" CASES
    See also Apportionment; Mortgage financing
    and creditors, §§109-110
    apportionment, §§103-128
    transmutation, §180
INCEPTION OF TITLE DOCTRINE, §§81-84
    California law, §82
    land acquired by labor, §83
    lease renewals, §84
INCOMPETENCY OF SPOUSE
    effect on management powers, §§270-272
INHERITANCE
    See Descent or bequest
INJURIES
    See Tort recoveries
IN-LAWS
    See Ancestral property rules
"IN LIEU" TRACING, §161
INSTALLMENT PURCHASES, §§78-84
    See also Acquisition of property
INSURANCE, §294
    See also Life insurance; Workers' compensation; Tort recoveries
INTESTATE SUCCESSION
    ancestral property doctrine, §§365-374
    bigamous marriage, §§426, 429
    due process, §476
    election against will, §355
    putative marriages, §417
ITEM THEORY, §§348-353

JK

JOINT BANK ACCOUNT, §192
JOINT MANAGEMENT
    See Management and control
JOINT TENANCY
    and divorce, §§190-191
    as gift, §126
    rebutting presumption of, §§185-191
    recitals of, §§184-191

L

LEASEHOLD
    as realty, §230
    renewal of, §84
LEGISLATIVE TAKING
    See Due process
LIABILITY OF PROPERTY
    See Debt, liability for
LIBEL AND SLANDER, §291
LICENSES TO PRACTICE, §200
LIEN
    "improvement" cases, §127
    materialman's lien, §235
    mechanic's lien, §235
LIFE INSURANCE
    apportionment, §§92-95
    as will substitute, §356
    federal employees, §485
    voidability of provisions, §363
LIVING EXPENSES

See Family expense doctrine
LONG MARRIAGE, POSSESSION PLUS, §10
LOSS OF CONSORTIUM, §155
  See also Tort recoveries
LOUISIANA LAW
  "improvement" cases, §118
  putative marriages, §394

M

MANAGEMENT AND CONTROL
  See also Gifts
  after death, §§381-383
  bank accounts of business assets, §223
  business managed by one spouse, §§218-223
  commercial dealings, §237
  dual management for alienation, §§229-247
    failure to join, §§241-247
    incompetency, §272
    joinder rule, §§234-235, 240
    oral consent, §236
    purchase money mortgage, §238
    rescission of land contract, §239
    signature of one spouse, §§231-233
      "add-a-name" remedy, §233
  equal management, §§217, 228, 265
    due process, §472
    incompetency, §§270-271
  fiduciary duty, §§261-269
    good faith, §§261, 263
    to account, §§264-265
  gifts. *See* Gifts
  leasehold, §230
  mechanic's lien, §235
  of personal property, §§217-227
  of real property, §§228-247
  of separate property, §§215-216
  remedies for violation, §§266-269
  seizing control, §224
MARRIAGES, PUTATIVE
  bigamous marriages, §§421-429
  "common law" marriage, §397
  defined, §§393-394
  good faith presumption, §395
  lack of good faith by one party, §§396-402
  marriage by estoppel, §399
  out-of-state marriages, §398
  quasi-marital property, §§403-410
    as community, §§404-406
    as tenancy in common, §407
    division at annulment, §§411-415
    partnership, §408
    separate property, §409
    Social Security, §410
  termination by death, §§416-420
    intestacy, §417
    pensions, §420
    workers' compensation, §419
    wrongful death actions, §418
***MARVIN* RELATIONSHIP,** §§430-443
  agreement to live in community, §432
  agreement to share ownership, §433

  and lawful wife, §§442-443
  cohabitants' legal status, §§436-437
  duration of contract, §435
  "meretriciousness," §430
  public policy, §434
  remedies of "nonspouse," §§438-441
    constructive trust, §441
    quantum meruit, §§435, 439-440
  same-sex cohabitants, §430
  separate property, §§431-433
  sexual consideration invalid, §434
MECHANIC'S LIEN, §235
MERETRICIOUS RELATIONSHIP
  See Marvin relationship
MERIT RAISES, §§211-213
MILITARY INSURANCE, §§483-485
MILITARY RETIREMENT PAY, §§491-493
  disability payments, §493
MIXED CONSIDERATION
  disability insurance, §158
  installment contracts, §§78-84
  life insurance, §§92-95
  pension benefits, §§85-91
    incentive stock options, §91
  pro rata separate share, §77
MORTGAGE FINANCING
  "improvement" cases, §§111-115

N

NECESSARIES, §§276-280
  See also Debt, liability for
  standard of life test, §278
NEGLIGENCE
  See Tort recoveries

O

OUT-OF-STATE ACQUISITIONS
  at divorce, §335
  choice of law, §§449-453. *See also* Conflict of laws; Quasi-community property
  gifts of, §269
OUT-OF-STATE MARRIAGES, §398

P

PAIN AND SUFFERING
  See Tort recoveries
PARTNERSHIPS
  goodwill, §206
  Marvin relationship, §433
  quasi-marital property, §408
PENSION BENEFITS
  apportionment, §§85-91
    defined benefit plans, §§86-87
    defined contribution plans, §§88-90
    divorce, §§310-315
    incentive stock options, §91
    "money" apportionments, §89
    "time" apportionments, §90

ERISA, §§501-504
military, §§491-492
putative marriage, §420
terminable interest doctrine, §§198-199
    abrogation of, §198
    post-divorce pre-death benefits, §199
valuation, §330
"vested," §208

PEREIRA FORMULA, §§64-69

PERSONAL INJURIES
See Tort recoveries

POSSESSION PLUS LONG MARRIAGE TEST, §10

POSSESSION TEST, §9

PREEMPTION DOCTRINE, §§481-507
armed services insurance, §§483-485
debtor's exemptions, §506
ERISA pensions, §§501-504
federal bonds, §§497-500
federal land grants, §486
federally created causes of action, §505
Native American law, §507
test, §482
welfare plans, §§487-496
    military disability benefits, §493
    military retirement pay, §§491-492
    Railroad Retirement Act, §§487-490
    reimbursement, §495
    Social Security, §§487-490, 496

PRESUMPTIONS
See also Acquisition of property; Apportionment
acquisition after dissolution, §14
acquisition while living apart, §§12-13. See also Acquisition of property
commingling, §§51-62. See also Commingling
"during" marriage test, §§6-8
family expense doctrine, §§55-61
general pro-community presumption, §§5-10
    burden of proof, §§16-17
    effect of contrary evidence, §§15-18
    exception to, §§19-21
    proof of separate ownership, §32
gifts, §122
"improvement" cases. See Apportionment
joint tenancy, recital of, §§185-192. See also Joint tenancy
    rebutting presumption, §§185-186
possession plus long marriage test, §10
possession test, §9
"pro-wife" presumption, §§22-31
    and additional transferees, §§25-26
    bona fide purchasers, §§30-31
    constitutionality, §31
    exceptions, §27
        commingling, §27
    overcoming, §§28-31
title, §§181-193. See also Title
tracing back, §13
transfers to married women, §§22-31
"unlimited presumption," §11

PROBATE ADMINISTRATION, §§375-392
See also Descent or bequest; Testamentary power
community property, §§375-377
confirmation proceedings, §§378-380
death of survivor, §§391-392
debt liability, §§384-390
    reimbursement, §§389-390
    survivor's defenses, §387
management and control of assets, §§381-383
separate property, §375

PROFESSIONAL CORPORATIONS
goodwill, §205

PROFITS
See Rents and profits

PROMISSORY NOTE, §§316-319

PRO-WIFE PRESUMPTION
See Presumptions

PUTATIVE MARRIAGES
See Marriages, putative; *Marvin* relationship

Q

QUANTUM MERUIT, §§435, 439-440
See also *Marvin* relationship

QUASI-COMMUNITY PROPERTY, §§269, 454-463
characterization, §457
death, §§460-463
defined, §455
divorce, §§458-459
due process, §474
gifts, §269
out-of-state community property, §456

QUASI-MARITAL PROPERTY, §403

R

RAILROAD RETIREMENT ACT, §§489-490

RECONCILIATION, §49

RENTS AND PROFITS, §§2, 63-76
See also Apportionment
apportionment of retained earnings, §§63-76
    "compromise" formula, §73
    Pereira formula, §§64-69
        distributions, §69
        interest rates, §§65-66
        varying profits, §67
    Van Camp formula, §§70-72
        "salary," §71
community capital and separate labor, §§75-76
from separate capital, §§63-76
pre-marriage appreciation, §113
"reverse apportionment," §§75-76

RESULTING TRUST, §441

RETIREMENT PAY
See Pension benefits

"REVERSE APPORTIONMENT," §§75-76

S

SEIZING CONTROL, §224
See also Management and control

SEPARATE DEBT, §§325-326, 339

SEPARATE PROPERTY
California Constitution, §§464-466
death, §347
defined, §2

divorce, §§306-307
"improvement" cases, §§103-128. *See also* Apportionment
liability for necessaries, §§276-280
management and control, §§215-216
Marvin relationship, §§431-433
probate administration, §375
"pro-wife" presumption. *See* Presumptions
quasi-marital property, §409
survivor's election, §354
tort recoveries. *See* Tort recoveries
SEX DISCRIMINATION, §§467-468
SOCIAL SECURITY BENEFITS, §§410, 487-488, 496
STATUTE OF FRAUDS
improvements and mortgage payments, §125
joint tenancies, §189
pre-1985 transmutation, §173
private disability contracts, §161
STATUTE OF LIMITATIONS
reimbursement claims, §§341-342
SUPREMACY CLAUSE, §§481-507. *See also* Preemption doctrine

T

TENANCY IN COMMON
division at divorce, §§309-315
pension interests, §§310-315
Marvin relationship, §§431-433
quasi-marital property, §407
recitals, §193
TERMINABLE INTEREST DOCTRINE, §§198-199
See also Pension benefits
TESTAMENTARY POWER
See also Descent or bequest; Probate administration
ancestral property rules, §§365-374
item theory, §§348-350
restrictions on survivor's interest, §§360-363
business contract, §361
life insurance, §363
long-term investment, §362
survivor's election, §§350-359
method, §§358-359
separate property, §354
will construction, §§351-353
will substitutes, §§356-357
TEXAS LAW
credit acquisitions, §102
"improvement" cases, §118
rents and profits, §456
TIPS, §§38, 210
TITLE
ancestral property, §§371-374
inception of title doctrine, §§81-84
installment contracts, §§78-79
Marvin relationships, §431
mortgage buy-ins, §112
recitals of joint tenancy, §§126, 185-192
recitals of ownership, §§181-184
recording land title, §195
reliance on, §197
TORT LIABILITY
See Debt, liability for
TORT RECOVERIES
cause of action before marriage or during separation, §§134-139
California rule, §§133, 141-143
divorce, §§139, 144-148
expenditures, §147
reimbursement, §§137-138, 145
medical expenses, §§135, 137
tracing back, §§134, 140-143
choice of law, §451
death of nonvictim, §149
death of victim, §§148-149
imputed negligence, §154
wrongful death, §§164-165
interspousal recovery, §§151-154
imputed negligence, §154
insurance, §§152-153
reimbursement, §153
loss of consortium, §155
personal injury damages during marriage, §§133-155
private disability contracts, §§158-161
property damage, §§129-132
business property, §130
insured property, §§131-132
recovery after death, §§149-150
recovery after divorce, §§139, 144-148, 333
pending cause of action, §§139, 144
reimbursement, §145
workers' compensation, §§156-157
wrongful death, §§162-165
divorce, §163
imputed negligence, §§164-165
transmutation, §165
TRACING, §§35, 50
ancestral property, §374
"in lieu" tracing, §161
rents and profits, §§63-76
tort damages, §§129-134, 141-143
TRACING BACK, §13
TRANSMUTATIONS
California Constitution, §466
choice of law, §458
effect on creditors, §196
formalities, §§174-178
improvements, §180
inference of gifts, §§179-180
instruments of title, §§181-193
recitals of joint tenancy, §§185-191
recitals of ownership, §§181-184
recitals of tenancy in common, §193
recording, §195
postnuptial contract, §§171-177
older rule, §§172-173
post-1984 rule, §§174-178
"TRIFLES," §252

U

UNCOMMINGLING
See also Commingling

no withdrawals, §52
rents and profits, §§63-76
UNIVERSITY DEGREES
See Educational degrees
"UNLIMITED" PRESUMPTION, §11

V

VALUATION
See Divorce
***VAN CAMP* FORMULA,** §§70-72
"VESTED" PENSION PLANS
See Pension benefits
VETERANS
See Pension benefits

WXYZ

WASHINGTON LAW
"trifles," §252

WEDDING GIFTS, §§41-42
WELFARE PLANS, §§487-496
See also Preemption doctrine
WIDOW'S ELECTION
See Testamentary power
WILL SUBSTITUTES, §§364-374
See also Ancestral property rules
WILLS
See Descent or bequest; Probate administration; Testamentary power
WORKERS' COMPENSATION, §§156-157
See also Tort recoveries
putative marriages, §419
WRONGFUL DEATH, §§162-165
See also Tort recoveries
putative marriages, §418

Notes

Notes

Notes

Notes

Notes

Notes

Publications Catalog

gilbert LAW SUMMARIES

Gilbert Law Summaries are the best selling outlines in the country, and have set the standard for excellence since they were first introduced more than twenty-five years ago. It's Gilbert's unique combination of features that makes it the one study aid you'll turn to for all your study needs!

Accounting and Finance for Lawyers
TBA
Basic Accounting Principles; Definitions of Accounting Terms; Balance Sheet; Income Statement; Statement of Changes in Financial Position; Consolidated Financial Statements; Accumulation of Financial Data; Financial Statement Analysis.
ISBN: 0-15-900382-2   Pages: 136 $16.95

Administrative Law
By Professor Michael R. Asimow, U.C.L.A.
Separation of Powers and Controls Over Agencies; (including Delegation of Power) Constitutional Right to Hearing (including Liberty and Property Interests Protected by Due Process, and Rulemaking-Adjudication Distinction); Adjudication Under Administrative Procedure Act (APA); Formal Adjudication (including Notice, Discovery, Burden of Proof, Finders of Facts and Reasons); Adjudicatory Decision Makers (including Administrative Law Judges (ALJs), Bias, Improper Influences, Ex Parte Communications, Familiarity with Record, Res Judicata); Rulemaking Procedures (including Notice, Public Participation, Publication, Impartiality of Rulemakers, Rulemaking Record); Obtaining Information (including Subpoena Power, Privilege Against Self-incrimination, Freedom of Information Act, Government in Sunshine Act, Attorneys' Fees); Scope of Judicial Review; Reviewability of Agency Decisions (including Mandamus, Injunction, Sovereign Immunity, Federal Tort Claims Act); Standing to Seek Judicial Review and Timing.
ISBN: 0-15-900000-9   Pages: 300 $19.95

Agency and Partnership
By Professor Richard J. Conviser, Chicago Kent
Agency: Rights and Liabilities Between Principal and Agent (including Agent's Fiduciary Duty, Principal's Right to Indemnification); Contractual Rights Between Principal (or Agent) and Third Persons (including Creation of Agency Relationship, Authority of Agent, Scope of Authority, Termination of Authority, Ratification, Liability on Agents, Contracts); Tort Liability (including Respondeat Superior, Master-Servant Relationship, Scope of Employment). Partnership: Property Rights of Partner; Formation of Partnership; Relations Between Partners (including Fiduciary Duty); Authority of Partner to Bind Partnership; Dissolution and Winding up of Partnership; Limited Partnerships.
ISBN: 0-15-900327-X   Pages: 142 $16.95

Antitrust
By Professor Thomas M. Jorde, U.C. Berkeley, Mark A. Lemley, University of Texas, and Professor Robert H. Mnookin, Harvard University
Common Law Restraints of Trade; Federal Antitrust Laws (including Sherman Act, Clayton Act, Federal Trade Commission Act, Interstate Commerce Requirement, Antitrust Remedies); Monopolization (including Relevant Market, Purposeful Act Requirement, Attempts and Conspiracy to Monopolize); Collaboration Among Competitors (including Horizontal Restraints, Rule of Reason vs. Per Se Violations, Price Fixing, Division of Markets, Group Boycotts); Vertical Restraints (including Tying Arrangements); Mergers and Acquisitions (including Horizontal Mergers, Brown Shoe Analysis, Vertical Mergers, Conglomerate Mergers); Price Discrimination — Robinson-Patman Act; Unfair Methods of Competition; Patent Laws and Their Antitrust Implications; Exemptions From Antitrust Laws (including Motor, Rail, and Interstate Water Carriers, Bank Mergers, Labor Unions, Professional Baseball).
ISBN: 0-15-900328-8   Pages: 193 $16.95

Bankruptcy
By Professor Ned W. Waxman, College of William and Mary
Participants in the Bankruptcy Case; Jurisdiction and Procedure; Commencement and Administration of the Case (including Eligibility, Voluntary Case, Involuntary Case, Meeting of Creditors, Debtor's Duties); Officers of the Estate (including Trustee, Examiner, United States Trustee); Bankruptcy Estate; Creditor's Right of Setoff; Trustee's Avoiding Powers; Claims of Creditors (including Priority Claims and Tax Claims); Debtor's Exemptions; Nondischargeable Debts; Effects of Discharge; Reaffirmation Agreements; Administrative Powers (including Automatic Stay, Use, Sale, or Lease of Property); Chapter 7- Liquidation; Chapter 11- Reorganization; Chapter 13-Individual With Regular Income; Chapter 12- Family Farmer With Regular Annual Income.
ISBN: 0-15-900245-1   Pages: 356 $19.95

Business Law
By Professor Robert D. Upp, Los Angeles City College
Torts and Crimes in Business; Law of Contracts (including Contract Formation, Consideration, Statute of Frauds, Contract Remedies, Third Parties); Sales (including Transfer of Title and Risk of Loss, Performance and Remedies, Products Liability, Personal Property Security Interest); Property (including Personal Property, Bailments, Real Property, Landlord and Tenant); Agency; Business Organizations (including Partnerships, Corporations); Commercial Paper; Government Regulation of Business (including Taxation, Antitrust, Environmental Protection, and Bankruptcy).
ISBN: 0-15-900005-X   Pages: 295 $16.95

California Bar Performance Test Skills
By Professor Peter J. Honigsberg, University of San Francisco
Hints to Improve Writing; How to Approach the Performance Test; Legal Analysis Documents (including Writing a Memorandum of Law, Writing a Client Letter, Writing Briefs); Fact Gathering and Fact Analysis Documents; Tactical and Ethical Considerations; Sample Interrogatories, Performance Tests, and Memoranda.
ISBN: 0-15-900152-8   Pages: 216 $17.95

Civil Procedure
By Professor Thomas D. Rowe, Jr., Duke University, and Professor Richard L. Marcus, U.C. Hastings
Territorial (personal) Jurisdiction, including Venue and Forum Non Conveniens; Subject Matter Jurisdiction, covering Diversity Jurisdiction, Federal Question Jurisdiction; Erie Doctrine and Federal Common Law; Pleadings including Counterclaims, Cross-Claims, Supplemental Pleadings; Parties, including Joinder and Class Actions; Discovery, including Devices, Scope, Sanctions and Discovery Conference; Summary Judgment; Pretrial Conference and Settlements; Trial, including Right to Jury Trial, Motions, Jury Instruction and Arguments, and Post-Verdict Motions; Appeals; Claim Preclusion (Res Judicata) and Issue Preclusion (Collateral Estoppel).
ISBN: 0-15-900272-9   Pages: 447 $19.95

Commercial Paper and Payment Law
By Professor Douglas J. Whaley, Ohio State University
Types of Commercial Paper; Negotiability; Negotiation; Holders in Due Course; Claims and Defenses on Negotiable Instruments (including Real Defenses and Personal Defenses); Liability of the Parties (including Merger Rule, Suits on the Instrument, Warranty Suits, Conversion); Bank Deposits and Collections; Forgery or Alteration of Negotiable Instruments; Electronic Banking.
ISBN: 0-15-900367-9   Pages: 222 $17.95

Community Property
By Professor William A. Reppy, Jr., Duke University
Classifying Property as Community or Separate; Management and Control of Property; Liability for Debts; Division of Property at Divorce; Devolution of Property at Death; Relationships Short of Valid Marriage; Conflict of Laws Problems; Constitutional Law Issues (including Equal Protection Standards, Due Process Issues).
ISBN: 0-15-900235-4   Pages: 188 $17.95

Call 1-800-787-8717 or visit our web site at http://www.gilbertlaw.com for more information.

gilbert LAW SUMMARIES

Conflict of Laws
By Dean Herma Hill Kay, U.C. Berkeley
Domicile; Jurisdiction (including Notice and Opportunity to be Heard, Minimum Contacts, Types of Jurisdiction); Choice of Law (including Vested Rights Approach, Most Significant Relationship Approach, Governmental Interest Analysis); Choice of Law in Specific Substantive Areas; Traditional Defenses Against Application of Foreign Law; Constitutional Limitations and Overriding Federal Law (including Due Process Clause, Full Faith and Credit Clause, Conflict Between State and Federal Law); Recognition and Enforcement of Foreign Judgments.
ISBN: 0-15-900011-4   Pages: 260 $18.95

Constitutional Law
By Professor Jesse H. Choper, U.C. Berkeley
Powers of Federal Government (including Judicial Power, Powers of Congress, Presidential Power, Foreign Affairs Power); Intergovernmental Immunities, Separation of Powers; Regulation of Foreign Commerce; Regulation of Interstate Commerce; Taxation of Interstate and Foreign Commerce; Due Process, Equal Protection; "State Action" Requirements; Freedoms of Speech, Press, and Association; Freedom of Religion.
ISBN: 0-15-900265-6   Pages: 335 $19.95

Contracts
By Professor Melvin A. Eisenberg, U.C. Berkeley
Consideration (including Promissory Estoppel, Moral or Past Consideration); Mutual Assent; Defenses (including Mistake, Fraud, Duress, Unconscionability, Statute of Frauds, Illegality); Third-Party Beneficiaries; Assignment of Rights and Delegation of Duties; Conditions; Substantial Performance; Material vs. Minor Breach; Anticipatory Breach; Impossibility; Discharge; Remedies (including Damages, Specific Performance, Liquidated Damages).
ISBN: 0-15-900014-9   Pages: 326 $19.95

Corporations
By Professor Jesse H. Choper, U.C. Berkeley, and Professor Melvin A. Eisenberg, U.C. Berkeley
Formalities; "De Jure" vs. "De Facto"; Promoters; Corporate Powers; Ultra Vires Transactions; Powers, Duties, and Liabilities of Officers and Directors; Allocation of Power Between Directors and Shareholders; Conflicts of Interest in Corporate Transactions; Close Corporations; Insider Trading; Rule 10b-5 and Section 16(b); Shareholders' Voting Rights; Shareholders' Right to Inspect Records; Shareholders' Suits; Capitalization (including Classes of Shares, Preemptive Rights, Consideration for Shares); Dividends; Redemption of Shares; Fundamental Changes in Corporate Structure; Applicable Conflict of Laws Principles.
ISBN: 0-15-900342-3   Pages: 308 $19.95

Criminal Law
By Professor George E. Dix, University of Texas
Elements of Crimes (including Actus Reus, Mens Rea, Causation); Vicarious Liability; Complicity in Crime; Criminal Liability of Corporations; Defenses (including Insanity, Diminished Capacity, Intoxication, Ignorance, Self-Defense); Inchoate Crimes; Homicide; Other Crimes Against the Person; Crimes Against Habitation (including Burglary, Arson); Crimes Against Property; Offenses Against Government; Offenses Against Administration of Justice.
ISBN: 0-15-900217-6   Pages: 271 $18.95

Criminal Procedure
By Professor Paul Marcus, College of William and Mary, and Professor Charles H. Whitebread, U.S.C.
Exclusionary Rule; Arrests and Other Detentions; Search and Seizure; Privilege Against Self-Incrimination; Confessions; Preliminary Hearing; Bail; Indictment; Speedy Trial; Competency to Stand Trial; Government's Obligation to Disclose Information; Right to Jury Trial; Right to Counsel; Right to Confront Witnesses; Burden of Proof; Insanity; Entrapment; Guilty Pleas; Sentencing; Death Penalty; Ex Post Facto Issues; Appeal; Habeas Corpus; Juvenile Offenders; Prisoners' Rights; Double Jeopardy.
ISBN: 0-15-900347-4   Pages: 271 $18.95

Dictionary of Legal Terms
Gilbert Staff
Contains Over 3,500 Legal Terms and Phrases; Law School Shorthand; Common Abbreviations; Latin and French Legal Terms; Periodical Abbreviations; Governmental Abbreviations.
ISBN: 0-15-900018-1   Pages: 163 $14.95

Estate and Gift Tax
By Professor John H. McCord, University of Illinois
Gross Estate Allowable Deductions Under Estate Tax (including Expenses, Indebtedness, and Taxes, Deductions for Losses, Charitable Deduction, Marital Deduction); Taxable Gifts; Deductions; Valuation; Computation of Tax; Returns and Payment of Tax; Tax on Generation-Skipping Transfers.
ISBN: 0-15-900019-X   Pages: 283 $18.95

Evidence
By Professor Jon R. Waltz, Northwestern University, and Roger C. Park, University of Minnesota
Direct Evidence; Circumstantial Evidence; Rulings on Admissibility; Relevancy; Materiality; Character Evidence; Hearsay and the Hearsay Exceptions; Privileges; Competency to Testify; Opinion Evidence and Expert Witnesses; Direct Examination; Cross-Examination; Impeachment; Real, Demonstrative, and Scientific Evidence; Judicial Notice; Burdens of Proof; Parol Evidence Rule.
ISBN: 0-15-900020-3   Pages: 359 $19.95

Federal Courts
By Professor William A. Fletcher, U.C. Berkeley
Article III Courts; "Case or Controversy" Requirement; Justiciability; Advisory Opinions; Political Questions; Ripeness; Mootness; Standing; Congressional Power Over Federal Court Jurisdiction; Supreme Court Jurisdiction; District Court Subject Matter Jurisdiction (including Federal Question Jurisdiction, Diversity Jurisdiction); Pendent and Ancillary Jurisdiction; Removal Jurisdiction; Venue; Forum Non Conveniens; Law Applied in the Federal Courts (including Erie Doctrine); Federal Law in the State Courts; Abstention; Habeas Corpus for State Prisoners; Federal Injunctions Against State Court Proceedings; Eleventh Amendment.
ISBN: 0-15-900232-X   Pages: 310 $19.95

Future Interests & Perpetuities
By Professor Jesse Dukeminier, U.C.L.A.
Reversions; Possibilities of Reverter; Rights of Entry; Remainders; Executory Interest; Rules Restricting Remainders and Executory Interest; Rights of Owners of Future Interests; Construction of Instruments; Powers of Appointment; Rule Against Perpetuities (including Reforms of the Rule).
ISBN: 0-15-900218-4   Pages: 219 $17.95

Income Tax I - Individual
By Professor Michael R. Asimow, U.C.L.A.
Gross Income; Exclusions; Income Splitting by Gifts, Personal Service Income, Income Earned by Children, Income of Husbands and Wives, Below-Market Interest on Loans, Taxation of Trusts; Business and Investment Deductions; Personal Deductions; Tax Rates; Credits; Computation of Basis, Gain, or Loss; Realization; Nonrecognition of Gain or Loss; Capital Gains and Losses; Alternative Minimum Tax; Tax Accounting Problems.
ISBN: 0-15-900266-4   Pages: 312 $19.95

Income Tax II - Partnerships, Corporations, Trusts
By Professor Michael R. Asimow, U.C.L.A.
Taxation of Partnerships (including Current Partnership Income, Contributions of Property to Partnership, Sale of Partnership Interest, Distributions, Liquidations); Corporate Taxation (including Corporate Distributions, Sales of Stock and Assets, Reorganizations); S Corporations; Federal Income Taxation of Trusts.
ISBN: 0-15-900024-6   Pages: 237 $17.95

Labor Law
By Professor James C. Oldham, Georgetown University, and Robert J. Gelhaus
Statutory Foundations of Present Labor Law (including National Labor Relations Act, Taft-Hartley, Norris-LaGuardia Act, Landrum-Griffin Act); Organizing Campaigns, Selection of the Bargaining Representative; Collective Bargaining (including Negotiating the Agreement, Lockouts, Administering the Agreement, Arbitration); Strikes, Boycotts, and Picketing; Concerted Activity Protected Under the NLRA; Civil Rights Legislation; Grievance; Federal Regulation of Compulsory Union Membership Arrangements; State Regulation of Compulsory Membership Agreements; "Right to Work" Laws; Discipline of Union Members; Election of Union Officers; Corruption.
ISBN: 0-15-900340-7   Pages: 243 $17.95

Legal Ethics
By Professor Thomas D. Morgan, George Washington University
Regulating Admission to Practice Law; Preventing Unauthorized Practice of Law; Contract Between Client and Lawyer (including Lawyer's Duties Regarding Accepting Employment, Spheres of Authority of Lawyer and Client, Obligation of Client to Lawyer, Terminating the Lawyer-Client Relationship); Attorney-Client Privilege; Professional Duty of Confidentiality; Conflicts of Interest; Obligations to Third Persons and the Legal System (including Counseling Illegal or Fraudulent Conduct, Threats of Criminal Prosecution); Special Obligations in Litigation (including Limitations on Advancing Money to Client, Duty to Reject Certain Actions, Lawyer as Witness); Solicitation and Advertising; Specialization; Disciplinary Process; Malpractice; Special Responsibilities of Judges.
ISBN: 0-15-900026-2   Pages: 252 $18.95

Legal Research, Writing and Analysis
By Professor Peter J. Honigsberg, University of San Francisco
Court Systems; Precedent; Case Reporting System (including Regional and State Reporters, Headnotes and the West Key Number System, Citations and Case Finding); Statutes, Constitutions, and Legislative History; Secondary Sources (including Treatises, Law Reviews, Digests, Restatements); Administrative Agencies (including Regulations, Looseleaf Services); Shepard's Citations; Computers in Legal Research; Reading and Understanding a Case (including Briefing a Case); Using Legal Sourcebooks; Basic Guidelines for Legal Writing; Organizing Your Research; Writing a Memorandum of Law; Writing a Brief; Writing an Opinion or Client Letter.
ISBN: 0-15-900305-9   Pages: 162 $16.95

Multistate Bar Examination
By Professor Richard J. Conviser, Chicago Kent
Structure of the Exam; Governing Law; Effective Use of Time; Scoring of the Exam; Jurisdictions Using the Exam; Subject Matter Outlines; Practice Tests, Answers, and Subject Matter Keys; Glossary of Legal Terms and Definitions; State Bar Examination Directory; Listing of Reference Materials for Multistate Subjects.
ISBN: 0-15-900246-X   Pages: 210 $19.95

Personal Property
Gilbert Staff
Acquisitions; Ownership Through Possession (including Wild Animals, Abandoned Chattels); Finders of Lost Property; Bailments; Possessory Liens; Pledges; Trover; Gift; Accession; Confusion (Commingling); Fixtures; Crops (Emblements); Adverse Possession; Prescriptive Rights (Acquiring Ownership of Easements or Profits by Adverse Use).
ISBN: 0-15-900360-1   Pages: 69 $14.95

Professional Responsibility
(see Legal Ethics)

Call 1-800-787-8717 or visit our web site at http://www.gilbertlaw.com for more information.

gilbert
LAW SUMMARIES

Property
By Professor Jesse Dukeminier, U.C.L.A.
Possession (including Wild Animals, Bailments, Adverse Possession); Gifts and Sales of Personal Property; Freehold Possessory Estates; Future Interests (including Reversion, Possibility of Reverter, Right of Entry, Executory Interests, Rule Against Perpetuities); Tenancy in Common; Joint Tenancy; Tenancy by the Entirety; Condominiums; Cooperatives; Marital Property; Landlord and Tenant; Easements and Covenants; Nuisance; Rights in Airspace and Water; Right to Support; Zoning; Eminent Domain; Sale of Land (including Mortgage, Deed, Warranties of Title); Methods of Title Assurance (including Recording System, Title Registration, Title Insurance).
ISBN: 0-15-900032-7   Pages: 496 $21.95

Remedies
By Professor John A. Bauman, U.C.L.A., and Professor Kenneth H. York, Pepperdine University
Damages; Equitable Remedies (including Injunctions and Specific Performance); Restitution; Injuries to Tangible Property Interests; Injuries to Business and Commercial Interests (including Business Torts, Inducing Breach of Contract, Patent Infringement, Unfair Competition, Trade Defamation); Injuries to Personal Dignity and Related Interests (including Defamation, Privacy, Religious Status, Civil and Political Rights); Personal Injury and Death; Fraud; Duress, Undue Influence, and Unconscionable Conduct; Mistake; Breach of Contract; Unenforceable Contracts (including Statute of Frauds, Impossibility, Lack of Contractual Capacity, Illegality).
ISBN: 0-15-900325-3   Pages: 375 $20.95

Sale and Lease of Goods
By Professor Douglas J. Whaley, Ohio State University
UCC Article 2; Sales Contract (including Offer and Acceptance, Parol Evidence Rule, Statute of Frauds, Assignment and Delegation, Revision of Contract Terms); Types of Sales (including Cash Sale Transactions, Auctions, "Sale or Return" and "Sale on Approval" Transactions); Warranties (including Express and Implied Warranties, Privity, Disclaimer, Consumer Protection Statutes); Passage of Title; Performance of the Contract; Anticipatory Breach; Demand for Assurance of Performance; Unforeseen Circumstances; Risk of Loss; Remedies; Documents of Title; Lease of Goods; International Sale of Goods.
ISBN: 0-15-900219-2   Pages: 222 $17.95

Secured Transactions
By Professor Douglas J. Whaley, Ohio State University
Coverage of Article 9; Creation of a Security Interest (including Attachment, Security Agreement, Value, Debtor's Rights in the Collateral); Perfection; Filing; Priorities; Bankruptcy Proceedings and Article 9; Default Proceedings; Bulk Transfers.
ISBN: 0-15-900231-1   Pages: 213 $17.95

Securities Regulation
By Professor David H. Barber, and Professor Niels B. Schaumann, William Mitchell College of Law
Jurisdiction and Interstate Commerce; Securities Act of 1933 (including Registration Requirements and Exemptions); Securities Exchange Act of 1934 (including Rule 10b-5, Tender Offers, Proxy Solicitations Regulation, Insider Transactions); Regulation of the Securities Markets; Multinational Transactions; State Regulation of Securities Transactions.
ISBN: 0-15-9000326-1   Pages: 415 $20.95

Torts
By Professor Marc A. Franklin, Stanford University
Intentional Torts; Negligence; Strict Liability; Products Liability; Nuisance; Survival of Tort Actions; Wrongful Death; Immunity; Release and Contribution; Indemnity; Workers' Compensation; No-Fault Auto Insurance; Defamation; Invasion of Privacy; Misrepresentation; Injurious Falsehood; Interference With Economic Relations; Unjustifiable Litigation.
ISBN: 0-15-900220-6   Pages: 439 $19.95

Trusts
By Professor Edward C. Halbach, Jr., U.C. Berkeley
Elements of a Trust; Trust Creation; Transfer of Beneficiary's Interest (including Spendthrift Trusts); Charitable Trusts (including Cy Pres Doctrine); Trustee's Responsibilities, Power, Duties, and Liabilities; Duties and Liabilities of Beneficiaries; Accounting for Income and Principal; Power of Settlor to Modify or Revoke; Powers of Trustee Beneficiaries or Courts to Modify or Terminate; Termination of Trusts by Operation of Law; Resulting Trusts; Purchase Money Resulting Trusts; Constructive Trusts.
ISBN: 0-15-900039-4   Pages: 268 $18.95

Wills
By Professor Stanley M. Johanson, University of Texas
Intestate Succession; Simultaneous Death; Advancements; Disclaimer; Killer of Decedent; Elective Share Statutes; Pretermitted Child Statutes; Homestead; Formal Requisites of a Will; Revocation of Wills; Incorporation by Reference; Pour-Over Gift in Inter Vivos Trust; Joint Wills; Contracts Relating to Wills; Lapsed Gifts; Ademption; Exoneration of Liens; Will Contests; Probate and Estate Administration.
ISBN: 0-15-900040-8   Pages: 310 $19.95

Gilbert Law Summaries FIRST YEAR PROGRAM

Includes Five Gilbert Outlines:

■ **Civil Procedure**
By Professor Thomas D. Rowe, Jr.
Duke University Law School, and
Professor Richard L. Marcus
U.C. Hastings School Of Law

■ **Contracts**
By Professor Melvin A. Eisenberg
U.C. Berkeley School Of Law

■ **Criminal Law**
By Professor George E. Dix
University Of Texas School Of Law

■ **Property**
By Professor Jesse Dukeminier
U.C.L.A. Law School

■ **Torts**
By Professor Marc A. Franklin
Stanford University Law School

Plus—

■ **Gilbert's Pocket Size Law Dictionary**
Published By Harcourt Brace

■ **The 8 Secrets Of Top Exam Performance In Law School**
By Professor Charles H. Whitebread
USC Law School

All titles are packaged in a convenient carry case with handle. $120 if purchased separately. $95 if purchased as a set. Save $25.
ISBN: 0-15-900254-0   Set $95

Gilbert's Pocket Size Law Dictionary
Gilbert

A dictionary is useless if you don't have it when you need it. If the only law dictionary you own is a thick, bulky one, you'll probably leave it at home most of the time — and if you need to know a definition while you're at school, you're out of luck!

With Gilbert's Pocket Size Law Dictionary, you'll have any definition you need, when you need it. Just pop Gilbert's dictionary into your pocket or purse, and you'll have over 4,000 legal terms and phrases at your fingertips. Gilbert's dictionary also includes a section on law school shorthand, common abbreviations, Latin and French legal terms, periodical abbreviations, and governmental abbreviations.

With Gilbert's Pocket Size Law Dictionary, you'll never be caught at a loss for words!

Available in your choice of 5 colors
■ Brown   ISBN: 0-15-900252-4 $7.95
■ Blue   ISBN: 0-15-900362-8 $7.95
■ Burgundy   ISBN: 0-15-900366-0 $7.95
■ Green   ISBN: 0-15-900365-2 $7.95

Limited Edition: Simulated Alligator Skin Cover
■ Black   ISBN: 0-15-900364-4 $7.95

The Eight Secrets Of Top Exam Performance In Law School
Charles Whitebread

Wouldn't it be great to know exactly what your professor's looking for on your exam? To find out everything that's expected of you, so that you don't waste your time doing anything other than maximizing your grades?

In his easy-to-read, refreshing style, nationally recognized exam expert Professor Charles Whitebread will teach you the eight secrets that will add precious points to every exam answer you write. You'll learn the three keys to handling any essay exam question, and how to add points to your score by making time work for you, not against you. You'll learn flawless issue spotting, and discover how to organize your answer for maximum possible points. You'll find out how the hidden traps in "IRAC" trip up most students... but not you! You'll learn the techniques for digging up the exam questions your professor will ask, before your exam. You'll put your newly-learned skills to the test with sample exam questions, and you can measure your performance against model answers. And there's even a special section that helps you master the skills necessary to crush any exam, not just a typical essay exam — unusual exams like open book, take home, multiple choice, short answer, and policy questions.

"The Eight Secrets of Top Exam Performance in Law School" gives you all the tools you need to maximize your grades — quickly and easily!
ISBN: 0-15-900323-7 $9.95

Call 1-800-787-8717 or visit our web site at http://www.gilbertlaw.com for more information.

LAW SCHOOL LEGENDS SERIES

America's Greatest Law Professors on Audio Cassette

Wouldn't it be great if all of your law professors were law school legends? You know — the kind of professors whose classes everyone fights to get into. The professors whose classes you'd take, no matter what subject they're teaching. The kind of professors who make a subject sing. You may never get an opportunity to take a class with a truly brilliant professor, but with the Law School Legends Series, you can now get all the benefits of the country's greatest law professors…on audio cassette!

Administrative Law
Professor Patrick J. Borchers
Albany Law School of Union University
TOPICS COVERED: Classification Of Agencies; Adjudicative And Investigative Action; Rule Making Power; Delegation Doctrine; Control By Executive; Appointment And Removal; Freedom Of Information Act; Rule Making Procedure; Adjudicative Procedure; Trial Type Hearings; Administrative Law Judge; Power To Stay Proceedings; Subpoena Power; Physical Inspection; Self Incrimination; Judicial Review Issues; Declaratory Judgment; Sovereign Immunity; Eleventh Amendment; Statutory Limitations; Standing; Exhaustion Of Administrative Remedies; Scope Of Judicial Review.
3 Audio Cassettes
ISBN 0-15-900189-7 $45.95

Agency & Partnership
Professor Richard J. Conviser
Chicago Kent College of Law
TOPICS COVERED: Agency: Creation; Rights And Duties Of Principal And Agent; Sub-Agents; Contract Liability–Actual Authority: Express And Implied; Apparent Authority; Ratification; Liabilities Of Parties; Tort Liability–Respondeat Superior, Frolic And Detour; Intentional Torts. *Partnership:* Nature Of Partnership; Formation; Partnership By Estoppel; In Partnership Property; Relations Between Partners To Third Parties; Authority of Partners; Dissolution And Termination; Limited Partnerships.
3 Audio Cassettes
ISBN: 0-15-900351-2 $45.95

Bankruptcy
Professor Elizabeth Warren
Harvard Law School
TOPICS COVERED: The Debtor/Creditor Relationship; The Commencement, Conversion, Dismissal and Reopening Of Bankruptcy Proceedings; Property Included In The Bankruptcy Estate; Secured, Priority And Unsecured Claims; The Automatic Stay; Powers Of Avoidance; The Assumption And Rejection Of Executory Contracts; The Protection Of Exempt Property; The Bankruptcy Discharge; Chapter 13 Proceedings; Chapter 11 Proceedings; Bankruptcy Jurisdiction And Procedure.
4 Audio Cassettes
ISBN: 0-15-900273-7 $45.95

Civil Procedure
By Professor Richard D. Freer
Emory University Law School
TOPICS COVERED: Subject Matter Jurisdiction; Personal Jurisdiction; Long-Arm Statutes; Constitutional Limitations; In Rem And Quasi In Rem Jurisdiction; Service Of Process; Venue; Transfer; Forum Non Conveniens; Removal; Waiver; Governing Law; Pleadings; Joinder Of Claims; Permissive And Compulsory Joinder Of Parties; Counter-Claims And Cross-Claims; Ancillary Jurisdiction; Impleader; Class Actions; Discovery; Pretrial Adjudication; Summary Judgment; Trial; Post Trial Motions; Appeals; Res Judicata; Collateral Estoppel.
5 Audio Cassettes
ISBN: 0-15-900322-9 $59.95

Commercial Paper
By Professor Michael I. Spak
Chicago Kent College Of Law
TOPICS COVERED: Introduction; Types Of Negotiable Instruments; Elements Of Negotiability; Statute Of Limitations; Payment-In-Full Checks; Negotiations Of The Instrument; Becoming A Holder-In-Due Course; Rights Of A Holder In Due Course; Real And Personal Defenses; Jus Teril; Effect Of Instrument On Underlying Obligations; Contracts Of Maker And Indorser; Suretyship; Liability Of Drawer And Drawee; Check Certification; Warranty Liability; Conversion Of Liability; Banks And Their Customers; Properly Payable Rule; Wrongful Dishonor; Stopping Payment; Death Of Customer; Bank Statement; Check Collection; Expedited Funds Availability; Forgery Of Drawer's Name; Alterations; Imposter Rule; Wire Transfers; Electronic Fund Transfers Act.
3 Audio Cassettes
ISBN: 0-15-900275-3 $39.95

Conflict Of Laws
Professor Richard J. Conviser
Chicago Kent College of Law
TOPICS COVERED: Domicile; Jurisdiction; In Personam, In Rem, Quasi In Rem; Court Competence; Forum Non Conveniens; Choice Of Law; Foreign Causes Of Action; Territorial Approach To Choice/Tort And Contract; "Escape Devices"; Most Significant Relationship; Governmental Interest Analysis; Recognition Of Judgments; Foreign Country Judgments; Domestic Judgments/Full Faith And Credit; Review Of Judgments; Modifiable Judgments; Defenses To Recognition And Enforcement; Federal/State (Erie) Problems; Constitutional Limits On Choice Of Law.
3 Audio Cassettes
ISBN: 0-15-900352-0 $39.95

Constitutional Law
By Professor John C. Jeffries, Jr.
University of Virginia School of Law
TOPICS COVERED: Introduction; Exam Tactics; Legislative Power; Supremacy; Commerce; State Regulation; Privileges And Immunities; Federal Court Jurisdiction; Separation Of Powers; Civil Liberties; Due Process; Equal Protection; Privacy; Race; Alienage; Gender; Speech And Association; Prior Restraints; Religion—Free Exercise; Establishment Clause.
5 Audio Cassettes
ISBN: 0-15-900319-9 $45.95

Contracts
By Professor Michael I. Spak
Chicago Kent College of Law
TOPICS COVERED: Offer; Revocation; Acceptance; Consideration; Defenses To Formation; Third Party Beneficiaries; Assignment; Delegation; Conditions; Excuses; Anticipatory Repudiation; Discharge Of Duty; Modifications; Rescission; Accord & Satisfaction; Novation; Breach; Damages; Remedies; UCC Remedies; Parol Evidence Rule.
4 Audio Cassettes
ISBN: 0-15-900318-0 $45.95

Copyright Law
Professor Roger E. Schechter
George Washington University Law School
TOPICS COVERED: Constitution; Patents And Property Ownership Distinguished; Subject Matter Copyright; Duration And Renewal; Ownership And Transfer; Formalities; Introduction; Notice, Registration And Deposit; Infringement; Overview; Reproduction And Derivative Works; Public Distribution; Public Performance And Display; Exemptions; Fair Use; Photocopying; Remedies; Preemption Of State Law.
3 Audio Cassettes
ISBN: 0-15-900295-8 $39.95

Corporations
By Professor Therese H. Maynard
Loyola Marymount School of Law
TOPICS COVERED: Ultra Vires Act; Corporate Formation; Piercing The Corporate Veil; Corporate Financial Structure; Stocks; Bonds; Subscription Agreements; Watered Stock; Stock Transactions; Insider Trading; 16(b) & 10b-5 Violations; Promoters; Fiduciary Duties; Shareholder Rights; Meetings; Cumulative Voting; Voting Trusts; Close Corporations; Dividends; Preemptive Rights; Shareholder Derivative Suits; Directors; Duty Of Loyalty; Corporate Opportunity Doctrine; Officers; Amendments; Mergers; Dissolution.
4 Audio Cassettes
ISBN: 0-15-900320-2 $45.95

Criminal Law
By Professor Charles H. Whitebread
USC School of Law
TOPICS COVERED: Exam Tactics; Volitional Acts; Mental States; Specific Intent; Malice; General Intent; Strict Liability; Accomplice Liability; Inchoate Crimes; Impossibility; Defenses; Insanity; Voluntary And Involuntary Intoxication; Infancy; Self-Defense; Defense Of A Dwelling; Duress; Necessity; Mistake Of Fact Or Law; Entrapment; Battery; Assault; Homicide; Common Law Murder; Voluntary And Involuntary Manslaughter; First Degree Murder; Felony Murder; Rape; Larceny; Embezzlement; False Pretenses; Robbery; Extortion; Burglary; Arson.
4 Audio Cassettes
ISBN: 0-15-900279-6 $39.95

Criminal Procedure
By Professor Charles H. Whitebread
USC School of Law
TOPICS COVERED: Incorporation Of The Bill Of Rights; Exclusionary Rule; Fruit Of The Poisonous Tree; Arrest; Search & Seizure; Exceptions To Warrant Requirement; Wire Tapping & Eavesdropping; Confessions (Miranda); Pretrial Identification; Bail; Preliminary Hearings; Grand Juries; Speedy Trial; Fair Trial; Jury Trials; Right To Counsel; Guilty Pleas; Sentencing; Death Penalty; Habeas Corpus; Double Jeopardy; Privilege Against Compelled Testimony.
3 Audio Cassettes
ISBN: 0-15-900281-8 $39.95

Call 1-800-787-8717 or visit our web site at http://www.gilbertlaw.com for more information.

Evidence
By Professor Faust F. Rossi
Cornell Law School
TOPICS COVERED: Relevance; Insurance; Remedial Measures; Settlement Offers; Causation; State Of Mind; Rebuttal; Habit; Character Evidence; "MIMIC" Rule; Documentary Evidence; Authentication; Best Evidence Rule; Parol Evidence; Competency; Dead Man Statutes; Examination Of Witnesses; Present Recollection Revived; Past Recollection Recorded; Opinion Testimony; Lay And Expert Witness; Learned Treatises; Impeachment; Collateral Matters; Bias, Interest Or Motive; Rehabilitation; Privileges; Hearsay And Exceptions.
5 Audio Cassettes
ISBN: 0-15-900282-6 $45.95

Family Law
Professor Roger E. Schechter
George Washington University Law School
TOPICS COVERED: National Scope Of Family Law; Marital Relationship; Consequences Of Marriage; Formalities And Solemnization; Common Law Marriage; Impediments; Marriage And Conflict Of Laws; Non-Marital Relationship; Law Of Names; Void And Voidable Marriages; Marital Breakdown; Annulment And Defenses; Divorce — Fault And No-Fault; Separation; Jurisdiction For Divorce; Migratory Divorce; Full Faith And Credit; Temporary Orders; Economic Aspects Of Marital Breakdown; Property Division; Community Property Principles; Equitable Distribution; Marital And Separate Property; Types Of Property Interests; Equitable Reimbursement; Alimony; Modification And Termination Of Alimony; Child Support; Health Insurance; Enforcement Of Orders; Antenuptial And Postnuptial Agreements; Separation And Settlement Agreements; Custody Jurisdiction And Awards; Modification Of Custody; Visitation Rights; Termination Of Parental Rights; Adoption; Illegitimacy; Paternity Actions.
3 Audio Cassettes
ISBN: 0-15-900283-4 $39.95

Federal Courts
Professor John C. Jeffries
University of Virginia School of Law
TOPICS COVERED: History Of The Federal Court System; "Court Or Controversy" And Justiciability; Congressional Power Over Federal Court Jurisdiction; Supreme Court Jurisdiction; District Court Subject Matter Jurisdiction— Federal Question Jurisdiction, Diversity Jurisdiction And Admiralty Jurisdiction; Pendent And Ancillary Jurisdiction; Removal Jurisdiction; Venue; Forum Non Conveniens; Law Applied In The Federal Courts; Federal Law In The State Courts; Collateral Relations Between Federal And State Courts; The Eleventh Amendment And State Sovereign Immunity.
3 Audio Cassettes
ISBN: 0-15-900296-6 $39.95

Federal Income Tax
By Professor Cheryl D. Block
George Washington University Law School
TOPICS COVERED: Administrative Reviews; Tax Formula; Gross Income; Exclusions For Gifts; Inheritances; Personal Injuries; Tax Basis Rules; Divorce Tax Rules; Assignment Of Income; Business Deductions; Investment Deductions; Passive Loss And Interest Limitation Rules; Capital Gains & Losses; Section 1031, 1034, and 121 Deferred/Non Taxable Transactions.
4 Audio Cassettes
ISBN: 0-15-900284-2 $45.95

Future Interests
By Dean Catherine L. Carpenter
Southwestern University Law School
TOPICS COVERED: Rule Against Perpetuities; Class Gifts; Estates In Land; Rule In Shelley's Case; Future Interests In Transferor and Transferee; Life Estates; Defeasible Fees; Doctrine Of Worthier Title; Doctrine Of Merger; Fee Simple Estates; Restraints On Alienation; Power Of Appointment; Rules Of Construction.
2 Audio Cassettes
ISBN: 0-15-900285-0 $24.95

Law School ABC's
By Professor Jennifer S. Kamita
Loyola Marymount Law School, and
Professor Rodney O. Fong
Golden Gate University School of Law
TOPICS COVERED: Introduction; Casebooks; Hornbooks; Selecting Commercial Materials; Briefing; Review; ABC's Of A Lecture; Taking Notes; Lectures & Notes Examples; Study Groups; ABC's Of Outlining; Rules; Outlining Hypothetical; Outlining Assignment And Review; Introduction To Essay Writing; "IRAC"; Call Of The Question Exercise; Issue Spotting Exercise; IRAC Defining & Writing Exercise; Form Tips; ABC's Of Exam Writing; Exam Writing Hypothetical; Practice Exam And Review; Preparation Hints; Exam Diagnostics & Writing Problems.
4 Audio Cassettes
ISBN: 0-15-900286-9 $45.95

Law School Exam Writing
By Professor Charles H. Whitebread
USC School of Law
TOPICS COVERED: With "Law School Exam Writing," you'll learn the secrets of law school test taking. In this fascinating lecture, Professor Whitebread leads you step-by-step through his innovative system, so that you know exactly how to tackle your essay exams without making point draining mistakes. You'll learn how to read questions so you don't miss important issues; how to organize your answer; how to use limited exam time to your maximum advantage; and even how to study for exams.
1 Audio Cassette
ISBN: 0-15-900287-7 $19.95

Professional Responsibility
By Professor Erwin Chemerinsky
USC School of Law
TOPICS COVERED: Regulation of Attorneys; Bar Admission; Unauthorized Practice; Competency; Discipline; Judgment; Lawyer-Client Relationship; Representation; Withdrawal; Conflicts; Disqualification; Clients; Client Interests; Successive And Effective Representation; Integrity; Candor; Confidences; Secrets; Past And Future Crimes; Perjury; Communications; Witnesses; Jurors; The Court; The Press; Trial Tactics; Prosecutors; Market; Solicitation; Advertising; Law Firms; Fees; Client Property; Conduct; Political Activity.
3 Audio Cassettes
ISBN: 0-15-900371-7 $39.95

Real Property
By Professor Paula A. Franzese
Seton Hall Law School
TOPICS COVERED: Estates—Fee Simple; Fee Tail; Life Estate; Co-Tenancy—Joint Tenancy; Tenancy In Common; Tenancy By The Entirety; Landlord-Tenant Relationship; Liability For Condition Of Premises; Assignment & Sublease; Easements; Restrictive Covenants; Adverse Possession; Recording Acts; Conveyancing; Personal Property—Finders; Bailments; Gifts; Future Interests.
4 Audio Cassettes
ISBN: 0-15-900289-3 $45.95

Remedies
By Professor William A. Fletcher
University of California at Berkeley, Boalt Hall School of Law
TOPICS COVERED: Damages; Restitution; Equitable Remedies (including Constructive Trust, Equitable Lien, Injunction, and Specific Performance); Tracing; Rescission and Reformation; Specific topics include Injury and Destruction of Personal Property; Conversion; Injury to Real Property; Trespass; Ouster; Nuisance; Defamation; Trade Libel; Inducing Breach of Contract; Contracts to Purchase Personal Property; Contracts to Purchase Real Property (including Equitable Conversion); Construction Contracts; and Personal Service Contracts.
3 Audio Cassettes
ISBN: 0-15-900353-9 $45.95

Sales & Lease of Goods
By Professor Michael I. Spak
Chicago Kent College of Law
TOPICS COVERED: Goods; Contract Formation; Firm Offers; Statute Of Frauds; Modification; Parol Evidence; Code Methodology; Tender; Payment; Identification; Risk Of Loss; Warranties; Merchantability; Fitness; Disclaimers; Consumer Protection; Remedies; Anticipatory Repudiation; Third Party Rights.
3 Audio Cassettes
ISBN: 0-15-900291-5 $39.95

Secured Transactions
By Professor Michael I. Spak
Chicago Kent College of Law
TOPICS COVERED: Collateral; Inventory; Intangibles; Proceeds; Security Agreements; Attachment; After-Acquired Property; Perfection; Filing; Priorities; Purchase Money Security Interests; Fixtures; Rights Upon Default; Self-Help; Sale; Constitutional Issues.
3 Audio Cassettes
ISBN: 0-15-900292-3 $39.95

Torts
By Professor Richard J. Conviser
Chicago Kent College of Law
TOPICS COVERED: Essay Exam Techniques; Intentional Torts—Assault; Battery; False Imprisonment; Intentional Infliction Of Emotional Distress; Trespass To Land; Trespass To Chattels; Conversion; Defenses: Defamation—Libel; Slander; Defenses; First Amendment Concerns; Invasion Of Right Of Privacy; Misrepresentation; Negligence—Duty; Breach; Actual And Proximate Causation; Damages; Defenses; Strict Liability, Products Liability; Nuisance; General Tort Considerations.
4 Audio Cassettes
ISBN: 0-15-900185-4 $45.95

Wills & Trusts
By Professor Stanley M. Johanson
University of Texas School of Law
TOPICS COVERED: Attested Wills; Holographic Wills; Negligence; Revocation; Changes On Face Of Will; Lapsed Gifts; Negative Bequest Rule; Nonprobate Assets; Intestate Succession; Advancements; Elective Share; Will Contests; Capacity; Undue Influence; Creditors' Rights; Creation Of Trust; Revocable Trusts; Pourover Gifts; Charitable Trusts; Resulting Trusts; Constructive Trusts; Spendthrift Trusts; Self-Dealing; Prudent Investments; Trust Accounting; Termination; Powers Of Appointment.
4 Audio Cassettes
ISBN: 0-15-900294-X $45.95

Law School Legends Series
FIRST YEAR PROGRAM

Includes Five Law School Legends Titles:

■ **Civil Procedure**
By Professor Richard D. Freer
Emory University Law School

■ **Contracts**
By Professor Michael I. Spak
Chicago Kent College Of Law

■ **Criminal Law**
By Professor Charles H. Whitebread
USC School of Law

■ **Real Property**
By Professor Paula A. Franzese
Seton Hall Law School

■ **Torts**
By Professor Richard J. Conviser
Chicago Kent College of Law

Plus—

■ **Law School Exam Writing**
By Professor Charles H. Whitebread
USC Law School

All titles are packaged in a convenient carry case. $250 if purchased separately. $195 if purchased as a set. Save $55.
ISBN: 0-15-900306-7 Set $195

NEW!
Call for release dates

Antitrust
ISBN# 0-15-900341-5 $39.95

Estate & Gift Tax
ISBN# 0-15-900354-7 $39.95

Labor Law
ISBN# 0-15-900357-1 $39.95

Product Liability
ISBN# 0-15-900358-X $39.95

Securities Regulation
ISBN# 0-15-900359-8 $39.95

If you accidentally damage a tape within five years from the date of purchase we'll replace it for FREE— No questions asked!

Call 1-800-787-8717 or visit our web site at http://www.gilbertlaw.com for more information.

Legalines

Legalines gives you authoritative, detailed briefs of every major case in your casebook. You get a clear explanation of the facts, the issues, the court's holding and reasoning, and any significant concurrences or dissents. Even more importantly, you get an authoritative explanation of the significance of each case, and how it relates to other cases in your casebook. And with Legalines' detailed table of contents and table of cases, you can quickly find any case or concept you're looking for. But your professor expects you to know more than just the cases. That's why Legalines gives you more than just case briefs. You get summaries of the black letter law, as well. That's crucial, because some of the most important information in your casebooks isn't in the cases at all…it's the black letter principles you're expected to glean from those cases. Legalines is the only series that gives you both case briefs and black letter review. With Legalines, you get everything you need to know—whether it's in a case or not!

Administrative Law
Keyed to the Breyer Casebook
ISBN: 0-15-900169-2   206 pages $17.95

Administrative Law
Keyed to the Gellhorn Casebook
ISBN: 0-15-900170-6   268 pages $19.95

Administrative Law
Keyed to the Schwartz Casebook
ISBN: 0-15-900171-4   155 pages $17.95

Antitrust
Keyed to the Areeda Casebook
ISBN: 0-15-900046-7   209 pages $17.95

Antitrust
Keyed to the Handler Casebook
ISBN: 0-15-900045-9   174 pages $17.95

Civil Procedure
Keyed to the Cound Casebook
ISBN: 0-15-900314-8   316 pages $19.95

Civil Procedure
Keyed to the Field Casebook
ISBN: 0-15-900048-3   388 pages $21.95

Civil Procedure
Keyed to the Hazard Casebook
ISBN: 0-15-900324-5   253 pages $18.95

Civil Procedure
Keyed to the Rosenberg Casebook
ISBN: 0-15-900052-1   312 pages $19.95

Civil Procedure
Keyed to the Yeazell Casebook
ISBN: 0-15-900241-9   240 pages $18.95

Commercial Law
Keyed to the Farnsworth Casebook
ISBN: 0-15-900176-5   170 pages $17.95

Conflict of Laws
Keyed to the Cramton Casebook
ISBN: 0-15-900331-8   144 pages $16.95

Conflict of Laws
Keyed to the Reese (Rosenberg) Casebook
ISBN: 0-15-900057-2   279 pages $19.95

Constitutional Law
Keyed to the Brest Casebook
ISBN: 0-15-900338-5   235 pages $18.95

Constitutional Law
Keyed to the Cohen Casebook
ISBN: 0-15-900261-3   235 pages $20.95

Constitutional Law
Keyed to the Gunther Casebook
ISBN: 0-15-900060-2   395 pages $21.95

Constitutional Law
Keyed to the Lockhart Casebook
ISBN: 0-15-900242-7   348 pages $20.95

Constitutional Law
Keyed to the Rotunda Casebook
ISBN: 0-15-900363-6   281 pages $19.95

Constitutional Law
Keyed to the Stone Casebook
ISBN: 0-15-900236-2   296 pages $19.95

Contracts
Keyed to the Calamari Casebook
ISBN: 0-15-900065-3   256 pages $19.95

Contracts
Keyed to the Dawson Casebook
ISBN: 0-15-900268-0   188 pages $19.95

Contracts
Keyed to the Farnsworth Casebook
ISBN: 0-15-900332-6   219 pages $18.95

Contracts
Keyed to the Fuller Casebook
ISBN: 0-15-900237-0   206 pages $17.95

Contracts
Keyed to the Kessler Casebook
ISBN: 0-15-900070-X   340 pages $20.95

Contracts
Keyed to the Murphy Casebook
ISBN: 0-15-900072-6   272 pages $19.95

Corporations
Keyed to the Cary Casebook
ISBN: 0-15-900172-2   407 pages $21.95

Corporations
Keyed to the Choper Casebook
ISBN: 0-15-900173-0   270 pages $19.95

Corporations
Keyed to the Hamilton Casebook
ISBN: 0-15-900313-X   248 pages $19.95

Corporations
Keyed to the Vagts Casebook
ISBN: 0-15-900078-5   213 pages $17.95

Criminal Law
Keyed to the Boyce Casebook
ISBN: 0-15-900080-7   318 pages $19.95

Criminal Law
Keyed to the Dix Casebook
ISBN: 0-15-900081-5   113 pages $15.95

Criminal Law
Keyed to the Johnson Casebook
ISBN: 0-15-900175-7   169 pages $17.95

Criminal Law
Keyed to the Kadish Casebook
ISBN: 0-15-900333-4   209 pages $17.95

Criminal Law
Keyed to the La Fave Casebook
ISBN: 0-15-900084-X   202 pages $17.95

Criminal Procedure
Keyed to the Kamisar Casebook
ISBN: 0-15-900336-9   310 pages $19.95

Decedents' Estates & Trusts
Keyed to the Ritchie Casebook
ISBN: 0-15-900339-3   277 pages $19.95

Domestic Relations
Keyed to the Clark Casebook
ISBN: 0-15-900168-4   128 pages $16.95

Domestic Relations
Keyed to the Wadlington Casebook
ISBN: 0-15-900167-6   215 pages $18.95

Enterprise Organization
Keyed to the Conard Casebook
ISBN: 0-15-900092-0   316 pages $19.95

Estate & Gift Taxation
Keyed to the Surrey Casebook
ISBN: 0-15-900093-9   100 pages $15.95

Evidence
Keyed to the Sutton Casebook
ISBN: 0-15-900096-3   310 pages $19.95

Evidence
Keyed to the Waltz Casebook
ISBN: 0-15-900334-2   224 pages $17.95

Evidence
Keyed to the Weinstein Casebook
ISBN: 0-15-900097-1   241 pages $18.95

Family Law
Keyed to the Areen Casebook
ISBN: 0-15-900263-X   262 pages $19.95

Federal Courts
Keyed to the McCormick Casebook
ISBN: 0-15-900101-3   213 pages $17.95

Income Tax
Keyed to the Freeland Casebook
ISBN: 0-15-900222-2   154 pages $17.95

Income Tax
Keyed to the Klein Casebook
ISBN: 0-15-900302-4   174 pages $17.95

Labor Law
Keyed to the Cox Casebook
ISBN: 0-15-900107-2   211 pages $17.95

Labor Law
Keyed to the Merrifield Casebook
ISBN: 0-15-900177-3   202 pages $17.95

Partnership & Corporate Taxation
Keyed to the Surrey Casebook
ISBN: 0-15-900109-9   118 pages $15.95

Property
Keyed to the Browder Casebook
ISBN: 0-15-900110-2   315 pages $19.95

Property
Keyed to the Casner Casebook
ISBN: 0-15-900111-0   291 pages $19.95

Property
Keyed to the Cribbet Casebook
ISBN: 0-15-900239-7   328 pages $20.95

Property
Keyed to the Dukeminier Casebook
ISBN: 0-15-900264-8   186 pages $17.95

Property
Keyed to the Nelson Casebook
ISBN: 0-15-900228-1   288 pages $19.95

Real Property
Keyed to the Rabin Casebook
ISBN: 0-15-900262-1   208 pages $17.95

Remedies
Keyed to the Re Casebook
ISBN: 0-15-900116-1   333 pages $20.95

Remedies
Keyed to the York Casebook
ISBN: 0-15-900118-8   289 pages $19.95

Sales & Secured Transactions
Keyed to the Speidel Casebook
ISBN: 0-15-900166-8   320 pages $19.95

Securities Regulation
Keyed to the Jennings Casebook
ISBN: 0-15-900253-2   368 pages $20.95

Torts
Keyed to the Epstein Casebook
ISBN: 0-15-900335-0   245 pages $18.95

Torts
Keyed to the Franklin Casebook
ISBN: 0-15-900240-0   166 pages $17.95

Torts
Keyed to the Henderson Casebook
ISBN: 0-15-900174-9   209 pages $17.95

Torts
Keyed to the Keeton Casebook
ISBN: 0-15-900124-2   278 pages $19.95

Torts
Keyed to the Prosser Casebook
ISBN: 0-15-900301-6   365 pages $20.95

Wills, Trusts & Estates
Keyed to the Dukeminier Casebook
ISBN: 0-15-900337-7   192 pages $17.95

Also Available:

Criminal Law Questions & Answers
ISBN: 0-15-900087-4   179 pages $12.95

Excelling on Exams/How to Study
ISBN: 0-15-900098-X   101 pages $12.95

Torts Questions & Answers
ISBN: 0-15-900126-9   174 pages $12.95

Call 1-800-787-8717 or visit our web site at http://www.gilbertlaw.com for more information.

CASEBRIEFS FOR WINDOWS

Casebriefs Interactive Software For Windows

As a law student you can't afford to waste a minute. That's why you need Casebriefs Software. With Casebriefs you simply click on the name of the case you're looking for, and you instantly have an expert brief of it at your fingertips! The facts. The issue. The holding. The rationale. Expert commentary for each and every case. You'll get everything you need, whether you're preparing for class or studying for your final exam!

When you use Casebriefs, you can focus solely on the cases covered in your casebook, or you can use the Case Library, which includes briefs of all of the major cases from every major casebook. The Case Library is ideal for researching cases for writing assignments, Moot Court briefs, Law Review and other periodicals.

With Casebriefs, searching for cases is a breeze. You can search by topic. You can search alphabetically. You can search the cases in the order in which they appear in your casebook. You can even enter the date you'll cover different cases in class, and sort them by those dates. No matter how you want to look for a case, Casebriefs will help you find it instantly!

For each brief, you can add your own notes, or leave it "as is." Whether you customize the briefs or not, you can print them out and take them to class with you. You can even configure Casebriefs to access Lexis/Nexis and Westlaw directly from the Casebriefs screen (with Lexis/Nexis or Westlaw software and account). Whether you want to compare your own briefs to expert briefs, fill in gaps in your class notes, or research cases for your legal writing class, moot court, law review or other periodicals—Casebriefs is the source you'll turn to, over and over again!

- **Administrative Law**
  Includes briefs of all of the major cases from the Breyer, Gellhorn and Schwartz casebooks, many of the major cases from the Bonfield and Mashaw casebooks, plus a Case Library.
  ISBN# 0-15-900190-0 $27.95

- **Civil Procedure**
  Includes briefs of all of the major cases from the Cound, Field, Hazard, Rosenberg and Yeazell casebooks, many of the major cases from the Marcus and Freer casebooks, plus a Case Library.
  ISBN# 0-15-900191-9 $27.95

- **Conflict Of Laws**
  Includes briefs of all of the major cases from the Cramton and Reese casebooks, many of the major cases from the Brilmayer casebook, plus a Case Library.
  ISBN# 0-15-900192-7 $27.95

- **Constitutional Law**
  Includes briefs of all of the major cases from the Brest, Cohen, Lockhart, Rotunda and Stone casebooks, plus a Case Library.
  ISBN# 0-15-900193-5 $27.95

- **Contracts**
  Includes briefs of all of the major cases from the Calamari, Dawson, Farnsworth, Fuller, Kessler and Murphy casebooks, many of the major cases from the Crandall, Hamilton, Knapp, Murray, Rosett and Vernon casebooks, plus a Case Library.
  ISBN# 0-15-900194-3 $27.95

- **Corporations**
  Includes briefs of all of the major cases from the Cary, Choper, Hamilton and Vagts casebooks, many of the major cases from the O'Kelley and Solomon casebooks, plus a Case Library.
  ISBN# 0-15-900195-1 $27.95

- **Criminal Law**
  Includes briefs of all of the major cases from the Boyce, Dix, Johnson, Kadish and La Fave casebooks, many of the major cases from the Dressler, Foote, Kaplan and Weinreb casebooks, plus a Case Library.
  ISBN# 0-15-900196-X $27.95

- **Criminal Procedure**
  Includes briefs of all of the major cases from the Kamisar casebook, many of the major cases from the Allen, Haddad and Saltzburg casebooks, plus a Case Library.
  ISBN# 0-15-900197-8 $27.95

- **Evidence**
  Includes briefs of all of the major cases from the Waltz, Sutton, and Weinstein casebooks, many of the major cases from the Strong, Green, Lempert and Mueller casebooks, plus a Case Library.
  ISBN# 0-15-900198-6 $27.95

- **Family Law**
  Includes briefs of all of the major cases from the Areen casebook, many of the major cases from the Clark, Ellman, Krause and Wadlington casebooks, plus a Case Library.
  ISBN# 0-15-900199-4 $27.95

- **Income Tax**
  Includes briefs of all of the major cases from the Andrews, Freeland and Klein casebooks, many of the major cases from the Graetz casebook, plus a Case Library.
  ISBN# 0-15-900200-1 $27.95

- **Property**
  Includes briefs of all of the major cases from the Browder, Casner, Cribbet, Dukeminier and Rabin casebooks, many of the major cases from the Donahue, Haar and Kurtz casebooks, plus a Case Library.
  ISBN# 0-15-900201-X $27.95

- **Remedies**
  Includes briefs of all of the major cases from the Re and York casebooks, many of the major cases from the Laycock, Leavell and Shoben casebooks, plus a Case Library.
  ISBN# 0-15-900202-8 $27.95

- **Torts**
  Includes briefs of all of the major cases from the Epstein, Franklin, Henderson, Keeton and Prosser casebooks, many of the major cases from the Dobbs and Shulman casebooks, plus a Case Library.
  ISBN# 0-15-900203-6 $27.95

- **Wills, Trusts & Estates**
  Includes briefs of all of the major cases from the Dukeminier casebook plus a Case Library.
  ISBN# 0-15-900204-4 $27.95

Welcome to gilbertlaw.com

- Pre-Law Center
- Bookstore
- Past Exam Library
- Links to Law Sites
- Welcome Center
- Employment Center
- Wanted! Student Marketing Reps
- 1st Year Survival Manual
- Taking the Bar Exam?

GilbertLaw.com is the site that helps law students study smarter. Shop for study aids in the bookstore or get ready for your first year with the 1st Year Survival Manual.

http://www.gilbertlaw.com

Dictionary of Legal Terms

Gilbert's Dictionary Of Legal Terms Software:
Features over 3,500 legal terms and phrases, law school shorthand, common abbreviations, Latin and French legal terms, periodical abbreviations, and governmental abbreviations.
Includes Free Pocket Size Law Dictionary!

ISBN: 0-15-900250-8   Macintosh $27.95
ISBN: 0-15-900249-4   Windows $27.95

Call 1-800-787-8717 or visit our web site at http://www.gilbertlaw.com for more information.

Employment Guides

A collection of best selling titles that help you identify and reach your career goals.

The National Directory Of Legal Employers
National Association for Law Placement

The National Directory of Legal Employers brings you a universe of vital information about 1,000 of the nation's top legal employers— *in one convenient volume!*

It includes:
- Over 22,000 job openings.
- The names, addresses and phone numbers of hiring partners.
- Listings of firms by state, size, kind and practice area.
- What starting salaries are for full time, part time, and summer associates, plus a detailed description of firm benefits.
- The number of employees by gender and race, as well as the number of employees with disabilities.
- A detailed narrative of each firm, plus much more!

The National Directory Of Legal Employers has been the best kept secret of top legal career search professionals for over a decade. Now, for the first time, it is available in a format specifically designed for law students and new graduates. *Pick up your copy of the Directory today!*
ISBN: 0-15-900248-6 $39.95

Proceed With Caution: A Diary Of The First Year At One Of America's Largest, Most Prestigious Law Firms
William R. Keates

Prestige. Famous clients. High-profile cases. Not to mention a starting salary approaching six figures.

In *Proceed With Caution*, the author takes you behind the scenes, to show you what it's really like to be a junior associate at a huge law firm. After graduating from an Ivy League law school, he took a job as an associate with one of New York's blue-chip law firms.

He also did something not many people do. He kept a diary, where he spilled out his day-to-day life at the firm in graphic detail.

Proceed With Caution excerpts the diary, from his first day at the firm to the day he quit. From the splashy benefits, to the nitty-gritty on the work junior associates do, to the grind of long and unpredictable hours, to the stress that eventually made him leave the firm — he tells story after story that will make you feel as though you're living the life of a new associate.

Whether you're considering a career with a large firm, or you're just curious about what life at the top firms is all about — *Proceed With Caution* is a must read!
ISBN: 0-15-900181-1 $17.95

Guerrilla Tactics for Getting the Legal Job of Your Dreams
Kimm Alayne Walton, J.D.

Whether you're looking for a summer clerkship or your first permanent job after school, this revolutionary book is the key to getting the job of your dreams!

Guerrilla Tactics for Getting the Legal Job of Your Dreams leads you step-by-step through everything you need to do to nail down that perfect job! You'll learn hundreds of simple-to-use strategies that will get you exactly where you want to go. You'll Learn:
- The seven magic opening words in cover letters that ensure you'll get a response.
- The secret to successful interviews every time.
- Killer answers to the toughest interview questions they'll ever ask you.
- Plus Much More!

Guerrilla Tactics features the best strategies from the country's most innovative law school career advisors. The strategies in *Guerrilla Tactics* are so powerful that it even comes with a guarantee: Follow the advice in the book, and within one year of graduation you'll have the job of your dreams… or your money back!

Pick up a copy of *Guerrilla Tactics* today…and you'll be on your way to the job of your dreams!
ISBN: 0-15-900317-2 $24.95

Beyond L.A. Law: Inspiring Stories of People Who've Done Fascinating Things With A Law Degree
National Association for Law Placement

Anyone who watches television knows that being a lawyer means working your way up through a law firm — right?

Wrong!

Beyond L.A. Law gives you a fascinating glimpse into the lives of people who've broken the "lawyer" mold. They come from a variety of backgrounds — some had prior careers, others went straight through college and law school, and yet others have overcome poverty and physical handicaps. They got their degrees from all different kinds of law schools, all over the country. But they have one thing in common: they've all pursued their own, unique vision.

As you read their stories, you'll see how they beat the odds to succeed. You'll learn career tips and strategies that work, from people who've put them to the test. And you'll find fascinating insights that you can apply to your own dream — whether it's a career in law, or anything else!

From Representing Baseball In Australia. To International Finance. To Children's Advocacy. To Directing a Nonprofit Organization. To Entrepreneur.

If You Think Getting A Law Degree Means Joining A Traditional Law Firm — Think Again!.
ISBN: 0-15-900182-X $17.95

America's Greatest Places To Work With A Law Degree
Kimm Alayne Walton, J.D.

"Where do your happiest graduates work?" That's the question that author Kimm Alayne Walton asked of law school administrators around the country. Their responses revealed the hundreds of wonderful employers profiled in *America's Greatest Places To Work With A Law Degree*.

In this remarkable book, you'll get to know an incredible variety of great places to work, including:
- Glamorous sports and entertainment employers – the jobs that sound as though they would be great, and they are!
- The 250 best law firms to work for between 20 and 600 attorneys.
- Companies where law school graduates love to work and not just as in-house counsel.
- Wonderful public interest employers – the "white knight" jobs that are so incredibly satisfying.
- Court-related positions, where lawyers entertain fascinating issues, tremendous variety, and an enjoyable lifestyle.
- Outstanding government jobs, at the federal, state, and local level.

Beyond learning about incredible employers, you'll discover:
- The ten traits that define a wonderful place to work…the sometimes surprising qualities that outstanding employers share.
- How to handle law school debt, when your dream job pays less than you think you need to make.
- How to find – and get! – great jobs at firms with fewer than 20 attorneys.

And no matter where you work, you'll learn expert tips for making the most of your job. You'll learn the specific strategies that distinguish people headed for the top…how to position yourself for the most interesting, high-profile work…how to handle difficult personalities… how to negotiate for more money…and what to do now to help you get your next great job!
ISBN: 0-15-900180-3 $24.95

THE JOB Goddess
Presented by The National Law Journal

The Job Goddess column is a weekly feature of the *National Law Journal's Law Journal Extra*, and is written by Kimm Alayne Walton, author of the national best seller *Guerrilla Tactics For Getting The Legal Job Of Your Dreams*. View recent columns or e-mail the Job Goddess with your job search questions on the Internet at www.gilbertlaw.com

---

Call 1-800-787-8717 or visit our web site at http://www.gilbertlaw.com for more information.